Praise for
K BLOWS TO.
by Peter Carlson

"Fast-paced, delightfully sardonic, and thoroughly enjoyable. . . . It's a revealing portrait of a treacherous decade when the media—especially nascent television, whose news departments seldom questioned the views of the government that controlled their broadcast licenses—were almost as innocent as they were influential."
—*Boston Phoenix*

"Carlson delivers his bizarre travelogue in the most deadpan manner possible, as if to counteract the largely hysterical news reports at the time, which tracked K's every move with the ardor of paparazzi chasing a bare-headed Britney." —*The Onion* A.V. Club

"*K Blows Top* could be the most entertaining book of the year, but it is also, in its blood, a novel, a novel-in-secret, with index and pictures and History as a character." —*London Review of Books*

"For anyone interested in this remarkable moment in the long history of U.S.-Soviet relations, Carlson's book is a treat!"
—*Library Journal*, STARRED review

"The book is consistently informative and funny, but there are episodes that are strangely surreal . . . a fine example of popular history at its most engaging—anecdotal but informative and written with great feeling for the comedic side of current events."
—*Booklist*, STARRED review

"A high-spirited, often hilarious account of a forgotten moment in Cold War history." —*Kirkus*

"Hilarious. . . . In Carlson's hands the cold war is a surprisingly laughing matter." —*Publishers Weekly*

K Blows Top

A Cold War Comic Interlude
Starring Nikita Khrushchev,
America's Most Unlikely Tourist

PETER CARLSON

PUBLICAFFAIRS
New York

Hardcover edition first published in 2009 in the United States by
PublicAffairs™, a member of the Perseus Books Group.
Paperback edition first published in 2010 by PublicAffairs
All rights reserved.

Book Design by Timm Bryson

Library of Congress Cataloging-in-Publication Data
Carlson, Peter, 1952-
    K blows top : a Cold War comic interlude starring Nikita Khrushchev,
America's most unlikely tourist / Peter Carlson. — 1st ed.
        p. cm.
    Includes bibliographical references and index.
ISBN 978-1-58648-497-2 (hardcover)
1. Khrushchev, Nikita Sergeevich, 1894–1971—Travel—United States. 2.
United States—Foreign relations—Soviet Union. 3. Soviet Union—Foreign
relations—United States. 4. Cold War. I. Title.
E183.8.R9C37 2009
947.085'2092—dc22
                                                            2008039090
Paperback ISBN: 978-1-58648-846-8

For my daughters, Emily and Caitlin,
and of course, once again, for Kathy

CONTENTS

Khrushchev fakes a tantrum. . . . Barnstorming to San Francisco. . . .
"Mankind's face is more beautiful than its backside.". . . J. Edgar Hoover gets
caught with his pants down. . . . A riot in the cathedral of capitalism. . . .
A Cossack charge in Coon Rapids, Iowa. . . . Communist dictator in a
home ec class. . . . Camp David. . . . Chasing butterflies. . . . The first to
be shot. . . . Chihuahuas for Khrushchev. . . . Stormy applause.

TRIP THREE

THE BANGING OF THE SHOE   251

Spy in the sky. . . . Obligatory sex scene. . . . "That son-of-a-bitch,
Richard Nixon.". . . Rendezvous with Fidel. . . . The guest who
wouldn't leave. . . . Banging the shoe. . . . "I feel vicious,
malicious, and low!"

PROLOGUE: K BLOWS TOP

Maybe it was Khrushchev throwing a temper tantrum because he wasn't allowed to visit Disneyland.

Or maybe it was Khrushchev debating Nixon about which animal dung smells worst. Or maybe it was Khrushchev's fear that Camp David was really a leper colony. Or maybe it was the American Dental Association's courageous battle to defend the Waldorf-Astoria ballroom from Khrushchev's invasion. Or maybe it was Khrushchev's historic meeting with Marilyn Monroe, who later described the magic moment in her inimitable sexy purr. "Khrushchev looked at me," she said, "the way a man looks on a woman."

I'm not sure which of these delicious anecdotes turned me into the world's most zealous (and perhaps only) Khrushchev-in-America buff, but I'm certain that it happened on a Thursday or a Friday.

This was back in the mid-1980s, when I was a rewrite man at *People* magazine, a job that compelled me to type furiously on Mondays, Tuesdays, and Wednesdays but required almost no work on Thursdays and Fridays. To fill the idle hours, I amused myself by exploring the treasures of the Time-Life library of newspaper clippings. I'd remember some famous person who'd lived since the founding of *Time* magazine in 1923, then call the library and request the clippings on him. A few minutes later, a messenger would drop a folder on my desk. I perused the clips on such great

American characters as John Dillinger, Emma Goldman, and Father Divine. It was fun.

One day, after reading somewhere that Soviet Premier Nikita Khrushchev had been barred from Disneyland during his tour of America in 1959, I called the library and requested the clips on his trip. A few minutes later, a librarian called back. "There are an awful lot of them," she said. "Are you sure you want them all?"

I replied with the phrase that's launched a million misadventures: "Sure, why not?"

Soon a messenger appeared, pushing a cart packed with bulging folders. Lined up against my office wall, they covered more than ten feet of floor space. I turned the first one upside down on my desk and quickly found myself falling through a rabbit hole into a weird wonderland. At first I just glanced at the headlines:

KHRUSHCHEV IS A SHOWMAN ON HIS ARRIVAL

KHRUSHCHEV'S WHISKEY JOKE

KHRUSHCHEV'S U.S. TOUR
LIKE TRAVELING CIRCUS

And this one, which, for some reason, still makes me laugh:

KHRUSHCHEV
TO GET FREE
DRY CLEANING

Actually, most of the headlines did not contain the word "Khrushchev." His name was frequently too long to fit, so the unsung poets who create America's headlines had to conjure up shorter monikers. They nicknamed the visitor Khrush ("Khrush Irked in Hollywood") or Khrushy

("Be Warned! Khrushy Is a Clever TV Performer") or Niki ("Question Sizzles Niki"). Frequently the headline writers referred to the chairman of the Council of Ministers of the Union of Soviet Socialist Republics simply as "K," as if he were a character out of Kafka:

K TAKES FIFTH
BEFORE SENATORS

MR. K ROARS WITH LAUGHTER

DOES MRS. K WEAR THE PANTS?

SEES K ON
TV, SO HE
MURDERS 2

And the classic *New York Daily News* headline that inspired the title of this book:

DENIED TOUR
OF DISNEYLAND,
K BLOWS TOP

Illustrating the adventures of K in America were photos of the pudgy traveler, who mugged shamelessly for the cameras like a mischievous eight-year-old. Khrushchev may have been a dictator responsible for thousands of deaths, but he was also an incurable ham who couldn't bear to disappoint a photographer. Consequently the pictures in the clip folders were wonderfully wacky: Khrushchev grabs a live turkey! Khrushchev pats a fat guy's belly! Khrushchev gawks at chorus girls! Khrushchev pretends to shoplift a napkin holder by stuffing it into his suit jacket while laughing uproariously!

Khrushchev's trip was, as cold war historian John Lewis Gaddis dubbed it, "a surreal extravaganza." Within an hour of reading the first clipping, I was hooked. For months, I spent my Thursdays and Fridays following the adventures of K as he traveled from Washington to New York to Hollywood to San Francisco to Iowa to Pittsburgh to Camp David, creating hilarious havoc all the way.

The trip was a picaresque journey across America, like *Huckleberry Finn, On the Road,* or *National Lampoon's Vacation.* The world's leading Communist traipsed through capitalist America at the height of the 1950s—a land of movie stars, rock and roll, tail fins, suburbs, segregation, missile silos, fallout shelters, and duck and cover drills. He was a not-so-innocent abroad in a landscape populated by posturing pols, hustling PR men, angry protesters, gate-crashers, anti-Communist skywriters, and mobs of frenetic reporters—plus Frank Sinatra, Shirley MacLaine, J. Edgar Hoover, Perle Mesta, Richard Nixon, JFK, LBJ, and a crotchety Iowa corn farmer named Roswell Garst, the only man on earth who could steal a scene from Nikita Khrushchev.

The trip was hilarious but the humor was darkened by the shadow of the atomic bomb, which rendered the cold war the first era in history when rational humans feared an apocalypse that could end civilization. As Khrushchev kept reminding people—by his comic tantrums and his grisly jokes—he was a hot-tempered man who possessed the power to incinerate America.

In time, those folders of yellowed newspaper clippings led me to the memoirs of the people who'd participated in Khrushchev's grand tour: Nixon, Eisenhower, MacLaine, Henry Cabot Lodge, William Safire, Bob Hope and, of course, Khrushchev himself, whose autobiography, secretly dictated and smuggled to the West after his ouster, was as earthy, outrageous, and full of blarney as its author.

The memoirs steered me back two months to Nixon's trip to Moscow—where he jousted with Khrushchev in the now legendary kitchen debate—and then forward to 1960, when Khrushchev returned to

New York for an encore visit now best remembered for the moment when he took off his shoe and banged it on a desk at the United Nations. Soon the story of one trip had expanded into the story of three trips, each one more bizarre than the previous. My boredom-born whim had grown into an eccentric obsession. Fortunately, I kept encountering evidence that other people had shared my delight in this bizarre tale.

"In nearly 40 years of journalism, the Khrushchev visit to America was undoubtedly the most fascinating story that I covered," wrote Chalmers Roberts, who chronicled K for the *Washington Post,* which devoted more space to the story than to any that preceded it. "It had everything: a fabulous personality, conflict, human interest, the unexpected. It was an embarrassment of riches."

"The wildest comic scenes in my life in this comic country have always belonged to Nikita Khrushchev," wrote columnist Murray Kempton. "It is odd that not one of my fellow voyagers has thought to do a book; it has to have been the most profoundly entertaining public experience of our lives. Perhaps no one believes it."

Well, *I* believed it and *I* thought to do a book.

In preparation, I made sneaky forays to the *People* Xerox machine, copying hundreds of clippings and stuffing them into manila envelopes. In 1986, I left *People* to work as a feature writer for the *Washington Post.* Unfortunately, that job required me to work on Thursdays and Fridays, which severely curtailed my Khrushchev scholarship. I stashed my cache of manila envelopes in my basement. And there it sat, unread, for years.

During those years, the Berlin Wall came tumbling down and the Soviet Union withered away. As the fiftieth anniversary of K's trip approached, I dragged the dusty envelopes up from the basement. By then, the old fears of nuclear apocalypse had faded, bathing the cold war in the glow of nostalgia and providing the ironic distance that rendered the story of Khrushchev in America even funnier.

Hooked again, I revived my research. I pored through State Department records, spent hours watching Khrushchev on TV and obtained the

FBI files on the trip, which contained the fruits of the bureau's investigation of a California businessman who dared to give the dictator two Chihuahua puppies. Best of all, I interviewed the people who'd been there, including Khrushchev's son Sergei, who fed me a salami and cheese sandwich and showed me his home movies of the long, strange trip.

Soon I'd gathered enough material to fill a steamer trunk. Boiled down, it was the story of a stranger in a strange land. The stranger was a fat-bellied, thin-skinned, cantankerous, insecure, earthy man who was always eager to show off—a Communist dictator as portrayed by Zero Mostel or Danny DeVito. And the strange land was a big, brash, brawling, sprawling, self-righteous, gloriously democratic, and invigoratingly vulgar country.

"Has anybody on earth ever had as much fun as Nikita Khrushchev has had for the last ten days?" Murray Kempton asked a few days before Khrushchev's departure in 1959. "We can never put mankind back into its sober mold again. Nikita Khrushchev may well go home and be his old self in a few days, but he will miss us as long as he lives. He knows now that no place on earth is as much fun as America."

1. PROVERBS AND BARNYARD AROMAS

Preparing to meet Nikita Khrushchev in the Kremlin, Vice President Richard M. Nixon spent the early summer of 1959 stuffing his head with proverbs.

He got the idea from Bob Considine, the famous columnist. Considine and his boss, William Randolph Hearst Jr., had conducted two long, strange interviews with Nikita Khrushchev, and so Nixon, eager for insights, invited them to lunch in Washington. They informed him that the Soviet premier was tough, smart, and surprisingly funny.

"Bone up on some American proverbs," Considine suggested. "He'll have a Russian proverb for every possible topic and he believes that these proverbs not only sum up all his arguments, but win them for him. You'd better get some proverbs of your own, preferably from Lincoln or Franklin or people like that."

"Well, I'll be damned," said Nixon, and he jotted down a reminder on the back of an envelope.

Just as the United States could not afford to fall behind the Soviet Union in the arms race, Nixon felt he must maintain parity with the premier in the proverb race. He began stockpiling an arsenal of American aphorisms, proverbs, and bits of folk wisdom. Then, being a savvy politician, he let the story of his proverb collection leak out to the press.

"Reckoning with His Host, Nixon Is Packing Proverbs," the New York Times headlined its story. Citing an "informed source," the Times revealed that "the vice president has been recalling old and learning new proverbs" in preparation for his meeting with Khrushchev, who was known to utter such aphorisms as "spit in his eye and he'll say it's dew from heaven."

The *Daily News*—the *Times*'s funkier, feistier crosstown rival—spun the story into a full-page feature that ran beneath a headline that read like a tabloid haiku:

NIXON SHARPENS
OLD SAWS FOR
PROVERB DUEL
WITH KHRUSHY

The *News*, which frequently filled its entire back page with a close-up photo of some luckless pugilist getting hit with a haymaker, couldn't resist an extended boxing metaphor:

> Khrushy is the undisputed Iron Curtain champ at making points with proverbs. Nixon is an unknown at international competition, but he has been in training for this big one ever since Ike decided to send him on a visit to Russia.
>
> Though Nixon's handlers have kept him under wraps, word has leaked out that he will rely on trusty American proverbs when he crosses old saws with Khrushchev. Will Nixon wade right in with Teddy Roosevelt's "Speak softly and carry a big stick"—or will he start off easy with, say, Ben Franklin's "There never was a good war or a bad peace?"

The *News* urged Nixon to pummel the premier with authentic Russian proverbs:

> Can't you just see the look on Nikita's face, for instance, if Nixon said, in Russian, that Soviet promises are "written with a pitchfork on water?" Or that trying to deal with the Reds makes about as

much sense as "pouring an empty bucket into a bucket that has holes in it." While Khrushchev is still reeling, Nixon would follow through with "Make that a notch on your nose."

Back in Washington, Nixon was not spending all of his time memorizing proverbs. With characteristically dogged tenacity, he studied everything he could find on the Soviet premier, poring through reports from the State Department and the Central Intelligence Agency, and even visiting the CIA's secret new office—located above an auto repair shop in a seedy section of town—to inspect photographs taken by the agency's secret U–2 spy plane.

Nixon figured he needed every edge he could get. Although the official purpose of his mission to Moscow was prosaic—he was to cut the ribbon at the American exhibition in Moscow's Sokolniki Park—Nixon was already running for president and he knew that voters would judge him on how well he handled Khrushchev.

At sixty-five, the Soviet dictator was a wily and unpredictable opponent. Son of peasants and grandson of serfs, Khrushchev left school after only a few years to work as a shepherd, a coal miner and a factory hand before joining the Red Army after the Bolshevik revolution. Uneducated but intelligent, ambitious and fiercely loyal to Josef Stalin, he quickly rose in the ranks of the Communist Party. In 1938, Stalin sent him to run the Ukraine, where Khrushchev helped to carry out his boss's paranoid purges. In September 1939, when the Hitler-Stalin pact divided Poland, Khrushchev was dispatched to collectivize the Soviet sector, a brutal process that killed thousands of Poles and sent another half million to labor camps in the Soviet Union. During World War II, General Khrushchev was a commissar in the Red Army, fighting the Nazis in the horrific battles at Stalingrad, Kharkov, and Kiev. After the war, he became part of Stalin's inner circle, and was compelled to spend long nights with the man *Pravda* praised as "leader and teacher of the workers of the world" and "the greatest genius of all times and peoples," while the demented old dictator got drunk, watched cowboy movies, and eyed his underlings for signs of disloyalty.

When Stalin died in 1953, his closest henchmen scrambled for power, and Khrushchev emerged on top, exiling his rivals to obscure posts in far places. At a secret session of the Twentieth Party Congress in 1956, Khrushchev did the unthinkable. He delivered a speech denouncing Stalin's brutality, paranoia, and egomania. Slowly, cautiously, Khrushchev began to liberalize and de-Stalinize the Soviet Union, releasing hundreds of thousands of political prisoners from labor camps and relaxing the state's iron grip on artists and intellectuals. But when Hungarians revolted against their Communist government in 1956, Khrushchev crushed the rebellion with Soviet tanks, killing 20,000 people in the process.

In November 1958, Khrushchev suddenly announced that West Berlin was a "malignant tumor" inside Communist East Germany and demanded that the Western occupying powers—Britain, France, and the United States—leave the city within six months. In May 1959—two months before Nixon's trip to Moscow—that deadline passed without incident. But the threat remained and Khrushchev seemed to enjoy the crisis he'd provoked. "Berlin is the testicles of the West," he later said. "Each time I give them a yank, they holler."

That was typical Khrushchev. During the Suez crisis of 1956, he mocked British prime minister Anthony Eden: "I've just heard a good joke. Eden is sick. Do you know what he's suffering from? *Inflammation of the canal!*" Three years later, he ridiculed West German chancellor Konrad Adenauer: "If Adenauer pulls down his pants and you look at him from behind, you can see Germany is divided. If you look at him from the front, you can see Germany will not stand."

In 1958, Senator Hubert Humphrey visited Moscow and was granted an audience with Khrushchev that he expected would last about an hour. But Humphrey and Khrushchev, two of the world's most notoriously loquacious politicians, ended up yakking for eight solid hours. (It must have been a very tough workday for Khrushchev's translator, Oleg Troyanovsky.) At one point, after bragging about his missiles and his hydrogen bombs, the premier asked the senator to point out his hometown on a map of the United States. Humphrey identified Minneapolis and Khrushchev circled it with a thick blue pencil. "That's so I don't forget to order them to spare the city when the rockets fly," he explained.

To Americans, Khrushchev's most famous statement was an off-the-cuff utterance he made at a diplomatic reception in 1956: "Whether you like it or not, history is on our side. We will bury you." The diplomats at the reception understood that Khrushchev was merely restating, in his own inimitable style, the Marxist belief in the inevitable triumph of Communism. But most Americans who read the quote in newspapers assumed that Khrushchev was planning to slaughter them.

The more Nixon learned about the premier, the more nervous he became about meeting him. On July 22, 1959—the day he was scheduled to fly to Moscow—he stopped at the White House for last-minute advice from President Eisenhower, who revealed some shocking news: Khrushchev was coming to America!

In an exchange of letters over the previous ten days, Eisenhower told his vice president, he had invited Khrushchev to visit and the premier had accepted, saying that he'd like to tour the country for a couple of weeks. The trip was still top secret—it wouldn't be announced until the details were arranged—and Ike ordered Nixon not to mention it to anyone, not even Khrushchev himself. Nixon was flabbergasted. While he'd been cramming for his meeting, studying briefing papers and memorizing proverbs, Ike and the striped-pants boys at the State Department had invited Khrushchev to America—*and nobody even bothered to tell him about it!* It was a karate chop to Nixon's ego.

Eisenhower told his vice president to play it cool in Moscow and maintain "a cordial, almost light atmosphere." But Nixon had other ideas. He told Ike that he wanted to debate the dictator, "to probe and cause some blurting out of Khrushchev's real feelings." Nixon was trapped in a tough spot. As vice president, he was supposed to follow Ike's orders and be diplomatic with Khrushchev. But as a presidential candidate, he had to show his toughness, to prove that he could, in the phrase of the day, "stand up to the Russians."

On the plane to Moscow, Nixon sat up all night worrying. When he arrived at the American embassy, he was still too keyed up to sleep. After churning in his bed for a few hours, he rose before dawn and strolled through Moscow's open-air market. He returned to the embassy for breakfast, then rode to the Kremlin for his historic meeting.

Escorted into Khrushchev's office, he got his first glance at the premier. Bald as an egg, Khrushchev stood only a few inches over five feet but weighed nearly two hundred pounds. He had a round face, bright blue eyes, a mole on his cheek, a gap between his teeth, and a huge pot belly that made him look like a man shoplifting a watermelon.

Something in Khrushchev's chubby hands caught Nixon's eye. After a moment, he realized it was a model of a Soviet satellite. The crafty Russian was rubbing Nixon's nose in the memory of *Sputnik,* the satellite the Soviets had launched into orbit in 1957, scaring the hell out of America. Khrushchev stared at his visitor, eyeing him the way "a tailor might estimate a customer's size for a suit of clothes," Nixon later recalled, "or perhaps more as a undertaker might view a prospective corpse with a coffin in mind."

Khrushchev smiled warmly as the two men posed for pictures. But after he shooed the photographers away, he launched into a tirade about the captive nations resolution. The annual resolution, passed by Congress about a week before, called for Americans to pray for the liberation of the "enslaved peoples" of the "Soviet-dominated nations." Khrushchev pounded the table and denounced the resolution as a provocation to war.

Like a crafty pol confronted by an angry constituent, Nixon promptly passed the buck. The resolution was the work of the Democratic Congress, he said, not the Eisenhower administration.

Khrushchev wasn't convinced. "Any action by an authoritative body like Congress must have a purpose," he insisted, "and I wonder what the purpose of this particular action can be."

The purpose was, of course, to enable the lawmakers to exhibit their anti-Communist zeal while courting the votes of Polish Americans. But how could Nixon explain *that* to Khrushchev?

"The Soviet government thought Congress would never adopt a decision to start a war!" Khrushchev bellowed. "But it appears that, although Senator McCarthy is dead, his spirit still lives. For this reason, the Soviet Union has to keep its powder dry."

Failing to convince Khrushchev that the resolution was meaningless, Nixon dipped into his arsenal of proverbs. "At the White House," he said, "we have a procedure for breaking off long discussions that seem to go nowhere: President Eisenhower says, 'We have beaten this horse to death, let's change to another.' Perhaps that is what we should do now."

Khrushchev, the connoisseur of proverbs, enjoyed that one. "I agree with the president's saying that we should not beat one horse too much," he replied. But he couldn't resist the urge to give this old nag one final whack: "I cannot understand why your Congress would adopt such a resolution on the eve of such an important state visit." He came back with a proverb of his own: "It reminds me of a saying among our Russian peasants that 'People should not shit where they eat.'"

By now, Khrushchev was red-faced and roaring. "This resolution stinks!" he said. "It stinks like fresh horseshit and nothing smells worse than that!"

The interpreter blushed as he translated that little *bon mot*, but Nixon remained poker faced. Having grown up in a small town in southern California, he knew that horse manure was hardly the most pungent of livestock excrement.

"I'm afraid the chairman is mistaken," he said. "There is something that smells worse than horseshit—and that is pigshit!"

For a moment, Khrushchev looked as if he was about to start bellowing again. But then he cracked a smile. "You are right," he said. "So perhaps you are right that we should talk about something else."

The strangest series of diplomatic visits in the twentieth century had begun with two of the most powerful men on Earth arguing about the odor of animal dung.

2. THE ACCIDENTAL INVITATION

Ten days before Nixon arrived in Moscow, Khrushchev was relaxing in his luxurious dacha—his country house—when he received a phone call from his deputy, Frol Kozlov, who had just returned from New York. "I have a special message for you from President Eisenhower," Kozlov said, then he hustled to the dacha to deliver the sealed envelope.

"Dear Mr. Prime Minister," Eisenhower's letter began, "For some time past, it has seemed to me that it would be mutually profitable for us to have an informal exchange of views about problems which interest both of us."

"I couldn't believe my eyes," Khrushchev said later. "We had no reason to expect such an invitation—not then or ever for that matter."

Actually, Eisenhower's letter was not exactly an invitation. It was short and purposely vague, intended to be supplemented by an oral explanation delivered to Kozlov by undersecretary of state Robert Murphy. Murphy had been instructed to tell Kozlov that Ike's invitation came with strings attached: The president would be pleased to host Khrushchev at Camp David, but only if the Soviet, American, British, and French diplomats meeting in Geneva reached an agreement in their deadlocked negotiations to resolve the Berlin crisis that Khrushchev had caused by his sudden 1958 ultimatum. If there was agreement in Geneva, Murphy was supposed to tell Kozlov, then Ike would be "pleased to make the necessary arrangements" for Khrushchev to tour the United States. But somehow Murphy misinterpreted his orders and failed to inform Kozlov about the caveat to the invitation. As Khrushchev heard it, there were no strings attached.

The premier was thrilled. Unlike Stalin, a paranoid who rarely left the Kremlin except to visit his dachas, Khrushchev loved to travel. "Life is short," he once said. "Live it up. See all you can, hear all you can, go all you can." He had traveled extensively—to China, England, Switzerland, Yugoslavia, India, and Burma—but the United States was the place he *really* wanted to visit. After reading about it for decades, he was eager to see it for himself. In fact, he'd been dropping hints for months, shamelessly angling for an invitation. So he would certainly accept Eisenhower's offer. But one thing bothered him: Why had Ike invited him not to the White House but to "Camp David"? Was this an insult? A subtle snub? Just what *is* Camp David? he wondered. Some kind of leper colony?

"One reason I was suspicious was that I remembered in the early years after the revolution, when contacts were first being established with the bourgeois world, a Soviet delegation was invited to a meeting held someplace called the Prince's Islands," he later recalled. "It came out in the newspapers that it was to these islands that stray dogs were sent to die. In other words, the Soviet delegation was being discriminated against by being invited there. In those days, the capitalists never missed a chance to embarrass or offend the Soviet Union. I was afraid maybe this Camp David was the same sort of place, where people who were mistrusted could be kept in quarantine."

Determined to learn about this mysterious place, he asked his foreign ministry but nobody there knew anything about it. He asked his embassy staff in Washington. Nobody there knew either.

"I couldn't for the life of me find out what this Camp David was," he complained.

He controlled the spy apparatus that had stolen the secrets of America's atomic bomb, and yet he couldn't find out anything about a place mentioned in American newspapers almost every weekend.

Finally the crack Soviet intelligence network managed to ferret out the secret that Camp David was a presidential retreat in the Catoctin Mountains outside Washington. In other words, Ike was inviting Khrushchev to his dacha—and the premier was delighted. With that sticky issue resolved, only one problem remained: Khrushchev had already accepted an invitation to tour Sweden, Norway, and Denmark. When he'd planned those trips, they sounded like fun. But now, with the bright lights of Broadway beckoning, the glories of Stockholm and Oslo seemed about as exciting as a bus tour of Uzbekistan. Khrushchev found himself in the position of a schoolgirl who'd agreed to go to the prom with some good-natured dullard only to receive an invitation from the big man on campus. How, he wondered, could he break the date without insulting the Scandinavians? His solution was to claim that *they* had insulted *him*. When a Swedish newspaper printed an attack on his upcoming visit, he abruptly canceled his trip in protest.

"When they spit in my face," he told reporters, "why should I go?"

After taking care of that problem, Khrushchev answered Eisenhower's letter: "I readily accept your suggestion for such a meeting. . . . I also accept with great pleasure your kind suggestion that I make a tour of your country, and I could allocate for that purpose from ten to fifteen days."

When he received Khrushchev's letter of acceptance on July 21, Eisenhower was shocked. What had happened to the qualifications? There had been no progress in Geneva—the Soviets were still refusing to negotiate seriously about Berlin—so there should have been no invitation for Khrushchev to accept.

Ike summoned Murphy and Douglas Dillon, another undersecretary of state, to the White House and demanded an explanation. "Someone has failed," the president said. Murphy admitted that he was the "someone." He simply hadn't understood that progress in Geneva was a precondition for the invitation.

"To say that this news disturbed me is an understatement," Ike wrote in his memoir. Incensed, he delivered a blistering tongue-lashing to the two diplomats. But the damage was done, and the president couldn't very well uninvite Khrushchev. Like it or not—and Ike didn't like it one bit—the premier was coming to the United States. Worse, Khrushchev's letter indicated that he wanted to tour the country for "ten to fifteen days." A Communist dictator rambling around America for two weeks? There was no telling what would happen. Khrushchev was completely unpredictable. After their first meeting in Geneva in 1955, Ike had privately compared him to a "drunken railway hand." In 1956, Khrushchev had visited England, where he got into an angry shouting match with Labour Party leaders who had the audacity to criticize Communism. Later, while Khrushchev toured London, the British spy agency MI6 sent a frogman named Lionel "Buster" Crabb out to inspect the underside of the Soviet naval vessel that had brought Khrushchev to England. Crabb was never seen alive again. Fourteen months later, his body washed ashore minus its head.

Khrushchev's trip to America promised to be, as Ike told Murphy and Dillon, "a most unpleasant experience."

The day after he received Khrushchev's letter, Eisenhower informed Nixon about the premier's visit and the vice president flew to Moscow. The "accidental invitation," as historian Michael Beschloss later called it, transformed Nixon's ceremonial trip to Russia into something considerably more important—the prelude to a major summit. That worried Eisenhower. He had never quite trusted his two-time running mate. In 1956 he'd even toyed with the idea of dropping Nixon from the ticket. Ike had a natural distaste for politicians and Nixon was a particularly unpleasant example of that breed. He was an eye-gouging, elbow-throwing political brawler, and though Ike had frequently used him as the administration's hatchet man, he'd never felt entirely comfortable with his vice president. Ike certainly didn't think he was the right man for what had now become a delicate diplomatic mission.

After all, there was no sense rattling the Russian bear's cage right before letting him loose in the United States.

3. WE DON'T KILL FLIES WITH OUR NOSTRILS

After Nixon and Khrushchev concluded their scholarly colloquy on comparative excrement aromas, they climbed into a limousine and set off for the fair.

Emerging from the limo in Sokolniki Park with their translators, the two leaders were immediately surrounded by a mob of reporters and photographers at the American National Exhibition. They posed for pictures in front of the exhibition's gold-topped geodesic dome, which gleamed in the late morning sun, then strolled off to tour the fair. Their first stop was the RCA exhibit, which contained a state-of-the-art color television camera and a playback monitor designed to let fairgoers see themselves on TV. The two men stood stiffly at the microphone waiting to record statements of official greeting. Khrushchev, sixty-five, wore a shiny gray suit with a row of medals over his heart and a big floppy straw hat. Nixon, a head taller and, at forty-six, a generation younger, wore a somber black suit and a dark tie. Although it was not yet noon, a hint of his famous five o'clock shadow was evident.

Squinting in the harsh glare of the hot lights, Khrushchev shaded his eyes with his hat, then began his statement for the camera. "We want to live in peace and friendship with the Americans because we are the two most powerful countries," he said. "If we live in friendship, then other countries will also live in friendship. But if there is a country that is too war-minded, we could pull its ears a little and say, 'Don't you dare! Fighting is not allowed now.' This is a period of atomic armament, some fool could start a war and even a wise man couldn't finish it."

It was a friendly greeting, but Khrushchev, being Khrushchev, couldn't stop there. "How long has America existed?" he asked Nixon. "Three hundred years?"

"One hundred and fifty years," the vice president replied, underestimating by thirty-three years.

"Well, then, we will say America has been in existence for 150 years and this is the level she has reached," Khrushchev said. "We have existed not quite forty-two years and in another seven years we will be on the same level as America."

He grinned, preparing to deliver his punch line. "When we catch up to you, in passing by, we will wave to you," he said, miming a mocking little wave—something a snotty hot-rodder might flash while roaring past an Amish family in a buggy.

The Russians in the crowd laughed and cheered, which only encouraged Khrushchev. "Then, if you wish, we can stop and say, 'Please follow up!'" he said, beckoning to Nixon with a few contemptuous curls of his chubby index finger, like an aristocrat summoning a particularly dim-witted servant. The crowd laughed again.

"Plainly speaking, if you want Capitalism, you can live that way," Khrushchev continued. "That is your own affair and doesn't concern us. We can still feel sorry for you."

After this string of snide remarks, he started to welcome Nixon to Moscow, "I think you will be satisfied with your visit," and then abruptly raised the subject of the captive nations resolution. "I cannot go on without saying it: If you did not take such a decision—which has not been thought out thoroughly and was approved by Congress—your trip would be excellent. But you have churned the waters yourselves. Why this was necessary, God only knows. What happened? What black cat crossed your path and confused you?"

Finally he ceded the floor to Nixon, who had been standing there, smiling politely throughout his host's bizarre monologue. How could he follow that act? He chose to ignore the insults and launched into a chipper account of his stroll through Moscow's produce market that morning. But Khrushchev, exhibiting the ethics of a shameless vaudevillian, stole the show. He took off his hat and held it in front of his face. Then he stuck it back on his head. He grinned and winked at the crowd, mugging for the camera like Groucho Marx gleefully upstaging Margaret Dumont.

"I can only say that if this competition in which you plan to outstrip us is to do the best for both our peoples, and for peoples everywhere," Nixon droned on, "there must be a free exchange of ideas."

He turned to face Khrushchev. "After all," he said. "you don't know *everything.*" He grinned at the camera, as if he'd just delivered a knockout punch line.

"If I don't know everything," Khrushchev fired back, "you don't know anything about Communism except fear of it."

Nixon ignored the interruption. "There may be some instances where you may be ahead of us," he continued. "For example, in the development of the thrust of your rockets for the investigation of outer space.

And there may be some instances in which we are ahead of you." He pointed to the camera. "In color television, for instance."

"No! No! No!" Khrushchev shook his head and waved his hands in frenzied negation. "We are up with you on this, too. We have bested you in one technique and also in the other." He pointed to his nose. "We, too, as you know, don't kill flies with our nostrils."

The crowd laughed. Khrushchev beamed.

Even Nixon had to smile. "You never concede anything."

"I do not give up," Khrushchev said proudly.

"Wait until you see the picture," said Nixon, sounding like an RCA pitchman. "Let's have more communication and exchange in this very area that we speak of. We should hear you more on our television. You should hear us more on yours."

"That's a good idea," Khrushchev said. "Let's do it like this: You appear before our people. We will appear before your people."

"I can promise you every word you say will be translated into English."

"I doubt it. I want you to give your word that this speech of mine will be heard by the American people."

Unlike the premier, Nixon had no power to program his country's television. But he knew the networks would love this debate, so he agreed. "By the same token," he added, "everything I say will be translated and heard all over the Soviet Union?"

"That's agreed," Khrushchev said. He pulled his right hand way back and then slapped it theatrically into Nixon's palm. He grinned broadly, as if he'd just sold this sucker a bridge in Brooklyn.

Egged on by the crowd's laughter, Khrushchev tried a time-honored trick of populists everywhere—lawyer-bashing. "I know I am dealing with a very good lawyer," he said. "I want to uphold my miner's flag so that the coal miners can say, 'Our man does not concede.'"

"No question about that," Nixon replied. "The way you dominate the conversation, you would make a good lawyer yourself. If you were in the United States Senate, you would be accused of filibustering."

The debate ended, and the RCA technicians replayed it for the protagonists. Watching the instant replay, Nixon concluded that Khrushchev had creamed him. He came out swinging, Nixon thought. He went after me with no holds barred.

It wasn't fair. Khrushchev was a dictator. He could say whatever he pleased and nobody would dare second-guess him. But *he* was just a vice president, a glorified errand boy, duty-bound to execute his president's orders. Ike had instructed him to hold back, to maintain a "cordial atmosphere." But that didn't work with Khrushchev. It was like trying to fight, Nixon thought, with one hand tied behind your back.

"His attack had shaken me right to my toes," Nixon later wrote. "He had been on the offensive and I on the defensive throughout. I knew that he had scored heavily and I felt it was imperative that I find an opportunity to strike back."

And he did find that opportunity. But first he took the premier out for a Pepsi.

4. GET A PEPSI INTO KHRUSHCHEV'S HANDS

The original idea was to bring both Pepsi and Coca-Cola to the fair, pit them against each other and give the Soviets a taste—literally—of good old American competition: Coke versus Pepsi! Freedom of choice! Unfortunately, the Coca-Cola company was mad at the Russians—and with good reason.

For a decade, the Soviets had kept up a barrage of anti-Coke propaganda, portraying it as a toxic swill—the distilled essence of American imperialism. Perhaps the Coke folks could have laughed that off but the powerful Communist parties in Western Europe had parroted the Moscow line on the cola question, which was bad for business. In Italy, the Communist newspaper *L'Unita* ran the headline "Drinks Coca-Cola and Dies" over a story charging that Coke could, among other horrors, "turn a child's hair white overnight." In France, the Communists denounced "Coca-coloniza-tion" and almost succeeded in convincing the xenophobic French to ban the evil American belly wash. All of which irked Coca-Cola executives, who de-cided to protest by boycotting the exhibition in Moscow.

But not Pepsi. The Pepsi-Cola company, a feisty underdog in the fero-cious cola wars, eagerly agreed to go to Moscow, led by the company's flamboyant president, Al Steele, who was the P. T. Barnum of soda pop. A big, gregarious backslapper, Steele was a born salesman who could, as one associate put it, "talk the horns off a brass bull." He coined Pepsi's peppy slogan "more bounce to the ounce" and traveled to twenty coun-tries to promote his product with multimedia extravaganzas that starred his wife, actress Joan Crawford.

In 1959, preparing to take the Pepsi road show to Moscow, Steele and Crawford embarked on a six-week publicity tour of the United States, playing one-night stands, turning on the full showbiz razzmatazz. It turned out to be Al Steele's last hurrah. The day after the grueling tour ended, he dropped dead of a heart attack.

Steele was replaced by a dull gray lawyer who cast a cold eye on Steele's plans for Moscow. Why spend $300,000 giving away free samples in a country where the product isn't even available? But somehow, Don-ald Kendall, the Steele protégé who ran Pepsi's international division, managed to convince his bosses to fund the mission to Moscow.

"My one purpose," Kendall later recalled, "was to get a bottle of Pepsi into the hands of Khrushchev."

"Don't worry," Richard Nixon promised his friend Kendall, "I'll bring him by."

Nixon kept his promise. As the two statesmen toured the American ex-hibition, Nixon brought Khrushchev to the stand where seven perky Pepsi hostesses were handing out free samples in paper cups. Khrushchev took one and the crowd of reporters and photographers watched to see what he'd do with this evil capitalist fizz water. The premier hoisted it to his lips. He drank it. Then he drank a second. And a third. Finally, he ren-dered his verdict: "Very refreshing!"

Very refreshing? To Kremlinologists, this was *very interesting.*

The Kremlinologists, who analyzed and interpreted every cryptic utterance from the Soviet leadership, concluded that Khrushchev's remark was not merely a new party line on the cola question. It also indicated a major ideological shift that might change the course of Soviet-American relations. This was big news and the *New York Times* gave it big play:

COLA CAPTIVATES SOVIET LEADERS

PRAISE OF 'CAPITALIST' REFRESHMENT
HELD TO BE SIGNIFICANT

"Like all Communist leaders, Mr. Khrushchev held the firm conviction that cola is an unholy invention of the capitalist devil," wrote Harrison Salisbury, top Kremlinologist for the *Times.* "But once he tasted this strange brew and found it good, he was quite ready to throw overboard this classic Communist doctrine."

The lesson was obvious: "Not only did this refreshing pause symbolize a reversal in Communist propaganda, it supported a conviction that many observers of the Soviet scene have long held," Salisbury continued. "This conviction is that the way to do business with Mr. Khrushchev is to let him see things and taste things at first hand for himself. These observers believe that the surest and shortest road to the solution of pressing Soviet-American problems lies in giving Mr. Khrushchev a chance to see the United States from the push buttons of the Strategic Air Command at Omaha to a zipper factory in Pennsylvania."

Of course, Donald Kendall was less concerned with Kremlinology than he was with publicity, and he was thrilled with the photo that went out over the news wires. It showed Nixon and Khrushchev sipping Pepsi and smiling, and it was published all over the world, giving Pepsi free advertising worth millions of dollars. That made Kendall look like a genius to Pepsi's board of directors, which later selected him to run the company.

In the early 1970s, when he was president of Pepsi and his friend Richard Nixon was president of the United States, they negotiated a deal with the Kremlin that allowed Pepsi to sell its capitalist cola in the Soviet Union.

"I owe my career," Kendall liked to say, "to Nixon and the Kitchen Debate."

After perking themselves up with Pepsi, Nixon and Khrushchev sauntered across the sun-dappled grass to continue their tour of the American exhibition. As they strolled past a hastily erected, full-scale modern American supermarket, Nixon decided to impress the premier with a story from his childhood.

"You may be interested to know," he said, "that my father owned a small grocery store in California and all the Nixon boys worked there while going to school."

It was, of course, a variation of the log cabin gambit, a staple of American political oratory in which the speaker extols his humble origins and his rise to greatness through hard work and tenacity. The log cabin gambit has been popular in America at least since the "Log Cabin and Hard Cider" campaign of 1840, when a Virginia aristocrat named William Henry Harrison was elected president after touting his fictitious background as a simple backwoods frontiersman.

Khrushchev was not impressed. The former shepherd and coal miner didn't regard a childhood spent tending a grocery store as particularly rough. He snorted contemptuously. "All shopkeepers are thieves," he told Nixon.

5. THE HEAT IN THE KITCHEN

As William Safire watched Nixon and Khrushchev coming toward him, leading a pack of reporters and photographers, he was struck with a brilliant idea.

A savvy young New York PR man, Safire was in Moscow representing All-State Properties, which had erected a typical American tract house at the fair. Safire realized instantly that he must get Nixon and Khrushchev into that house. He hooked one end of a chain to the back bumper of a Jeep and the other end to the fence that stood in front of the house. He hopped into the Jeep, stepped on the gas pedal, and yanked the fence down. It was an act of creative vandalism that made the house much more accessible to the mob that was now approaching.

"This way to the typical American house!" he yelled, figuring that an aimless crowd will obey any authoritative voice. He was right. Nixon led Khrushchev over the fallen fence and into the model home. The press followed, pushing and shoving to get close to the pols in the walkway that had been cut through the center of the house. At that moment, Safire signaled to the house's American guide to let a group of Russian fairgoers in the back door. They too scrambled inside and now Khrushchev and Nixon were, for all practical purposes, trapped inside.

Nixon took the premier by the arm and escorted him to the railing that separated the walkway from the house's kitchen, which had been decorated in a sunny yellow. "I want to show you this kitchen," he said. "It's like those of our houses in California."

Safire was ecstatic. This was a PR man's dream: The vice president of the United States was touting his client's product while dozens of reporters took down every word. Harrison Salisbury of the *New York Times* began climbing over the railing, trying to get into the kitchen, closer to the action. A Soviet guard started to shoo Salisbury away but Safire assured him that Salisbury was the man in charge of demonstrating the kitchen's refrigerator. He was fibbing, of course: Salisbury had covered the Soviet Union for a quarter century. In 1955, his fourteen-point series on Soviet life won the Pulitzer Prize, which prompted the *Worker*, the American Communist newspaper, to publish a fourteen-part series attacking Salisbury's series, which in turn led the FBI to start a file on Salisbury, citing the *Worker*'s "favorable mention" of his work. Salisbury squatted at the feet of Khrushchev and Nixon, scribbling furiously as they debated the ideological implications of kitchen appliances.

Nixon (pointing to the washing machine): "This is the newest model. This is the kind which is built into thousands of units for direct installation in the houses."

Khrushchev: "We have such things."

Nixon: "What we want to do is make more easy the life of our housewives."

Khrushchev: "The Soviets do not share this capitalist attitude toward women."

Nixon: "I think the attitude toward women is universal."

While the statesmen debated and Salisbury transcribed, an Associated Press photographer looking for a better camera angle tried to climb into the kitchen. When the Soviet guard stopped him, the photographer tossed his camera to Safire, who caught it, snapped a picture of Khrushchev and Nixon, and tossed it back.

"You had your hand over the aperture, you idiot," the photographer hissed. He reset the camera and lobbed it back to Safire, who tried again. He aimed the camera, held it steady, pressed the shutter button and tossed it back to the AP man, narrowly missing Khrushchev's bald head.

The next day, that photo appeared in newspapers around the world. It showed a very serious Nixon gesturing emphatically with his right hand while a bored-looking Khrushchev stares at a washing machine topped with a box of SOS. In the background, with his eyes closed, is an obscure Soviet bureaucrat named Leonid Brezhnev, who would become famous five years later, when he led the coup that overthrew Khrushchev.

Nixon continued to tout the wonders of America's new suburban tract houses, which sold for about $14,000, he told Khrushchev, and were easily afforded by the working class. "Our steelworkers are on strike, as you know," Nixon said. "But any steelworker could buy this house. They earn $3 an hour. This house costs about $100 a month to buy on a contract running 25 to 30 years."

"We have steelworkers and peasants who can afford to spend $14,000 on a house," Khrushchev said, not very convincingly. Congenitally incapable of conceding a point, Khrushchev felt compelled to defend his country's kitchen appliances, even if he had to stretch the truth to do it. "You think the Russian people will be dumbfounded to see these things but the fact is that newly-built Russian houses have all this equipment right now. Moreover, all you have to do to get a house is to be born in the Soviet Union. I was born in the Soviet Union so I have the right to a house. In America, if you don't have a dollar, you have the right to choose between sleeping in a house or on the pavement. Yet you say that we are the slaves of Communism."

Nixon dodged that issue with a compliment: "I appreciate that you are very articulate and energetic."

Khrushchev rejected the compliment. "Energetic is not the same as wise."

"If you were in our Senate, we would call you a filibusterer," Nixon said. "You do all the talking and don't let anybody else talk. To us, diversity, the right to choose, the fact that we have a thousand different builders building a thousand different houses, is the most important thing. We don't have one decision made at the top by one government official."

Russians have diversity too, Khrushchev insisted, gesturing to his deputy, Anastas Mikoyan. "For instance, Mikoyan likes very peppery soup. I do not. But this does not mean that we don't get along."

"Would it not be better," Nixon asked, "to compete in the relative merits of washing machines than in the strength of rockets? Is this the kind of competition you want?"

"Yes, that's the kind of competition we want," Khrushchev replied, "but your generals say, 'Let's compete in rockets. We are strong and we can beat you.' But in this respect, we can also show you something."

Listening to the translation of that remark, Nixon decided that it was time to avenge his defeat in the TV studio and show that he could stand up to Khrushchev. He pointed his finger pugnaciously at the premier's chest as a flashbulb popped, yielding just the picture he wanted.

"To me, you are strong and we are strong," he said. "In some ways, you are stronger than we are. In some ways, we are stronger. . . . Neither should use that strength to put the other in a position where he in effect has an ultimatum. In this day and age, that misses the point. With modern weapons, it does not make a difference. If war comes, we both have had it."

Khrushchev smiled. "If all Americans agree with you, then who don't we agree with? This is what we want."

But Nixon persisted. "I hope the Prime Minister understands all the implications of what I have just said. When you place either one of our powerful nations in a position that they have no choice but to accept dictation or fight, then you are playing with the most destructive force in the world." As everyone present understood, Nixon was referring to Khrushchev's threat to cut off West Berlin. "When we sit down at a conference table, it cannot all be one way. One side cannot put an ultimatum to the other."

"Who is raising an ultimatum?"

"We will discuss that later."

"Why not go on now, while people are listening? Let your correspondents compare watches and see who is filibustering. You put great emphasis on dictations. Our country has never been guided by dictation."

"I'm talking about it in the international sense."

"It sounds to me like a threat," Khrushchev said, jabbing *his* forefinger angrily at Nixon. "We, too, are giants. You wanted to threaten—we will answer threats with threats."

"That's not my point. We will never engage in threats."

"You wanted to indirectly threaten me. But we have the means to threaten, too."

Nixon and Khrushchev were behaving like two kids squaring off in a schoolyard. It might have been funny except that these men represented nations armed with enough atomic weapons to incinerate civilization. A few steps away, the American ambassador, Llewellyn "Tommy" Thompson, and the president's brother, Milton Eisenhower, watched in horror, wondering, as the *Times* reported the next day, "why somebody didn't just pull the plug on the whole thing."

Eventually the two pugilists came to the same conclusion and started offering olive branches.

"We want peace and friendship with all nations, especially America," Khrushchev said.

"We want peace, too," Nixon replied. He put his arm on the premier's shoulder. "I'm afraid I haven't been a good host."

Khrushchev smiled and turned toward the model home's American hostess. "Thank the housewife for letting us use her kitchen for our argument."

The soon-to-be-famous kitchen debate was over. The combatants wandered off, taking the press pack with them. Safire was left alone in his kitchen. He grabbed a beer from the refrigerator and sat on the stove to think about what he had witnessed. Earlier that afternoon, he'd watched the debate in the TV studio and concluded that Khrushchev had whipped Nixon. But this time, he thought, Nixon was superb. He saw his opportunity and seized it, winning this second round decisively. Safire decided that he wanted to work for Nixon someday. A decade later, he did, serving as a White House speechwriter.

But that was all in the future. Now, sitting on the stove, Safire lifted his beer in a silent toast to Richard Nixon and took a triumphant sip.

Yuck! It was as warm as spit. He'd forgotten to plug in the damn refrigerator.

6. WHAT IS MEANT BY THE AMERICAN DREAM?

Outside the tract house, Nikita Khrushchev did what politicians everywhere do when they find themselves on a fairground: He waded into the crowd, shaking hands, slapping backs, kissing cheeks.

He was amazingly adept at the art of flesh-pressing, particularly for a politician who rose to power by sucking up to Stalin, not by glad-handing among the hoi polloi. The premier was a natural pol with a Santa Claus grin and a desire to hug everybody in sight. When he saw a buxom Russian laborer cheering him, he enveloped her in a huge bear hug and held it for a long moment, so photographers could get a good shot. Then he grabbed a handsome, red-headed young Russian and, still peeved about the captive nations resolution, asked Nixon, "Does this look like an enslaved person?"

The Russians in the crowd laughed and cheered. Khrushchev was a warm, folksy contrast to Stalin, who was as aloof and vengeful as the Old Testament God. After watching the premier in action, American reporters compared him to the folksiest campaigners they could think of— Harry Truman, Huey Long, Fiorello La Guardia.

For the rest of the afternoon, Nixon and Khrushchev toured the exhibition, which was a full-blown multimedia extravaganza, complete with an art exhibit, two specially made films (one featuring Marilyn Monroe), Edward Steichen's famous *Family of Man* photographic exhibit and IBM's gargantuan RAMAC 305 computer, which was programmed to answer 4,000 questions about the United States. The questions covered everything from the Liberty Bell to the price of cigarettes:

Q: *What is meant by the American Dream?*
A: *That all men shall be free to seek a better life, with free worship, thought, assembly, expression of belief and universal suffrage and education.*
Q: *What is the wardrobe of an average American woman in the middle-income group?*
A: *Winter coat, spring coat, raincoat, five house dresses, four afternoon "dressy" dresses, three suits, three skirts, six blouses, three sweaters, six slips, two petticoats, five nightgowns, eight panties, five brassieres, two corsets, two robes, six pairs of nylon stockings, two pairs of sports socks, three pairs of dress gloves, one bathing suit, three pairs of play shorts, one pair of slacks, one play suit, and accessories.*

That long list of consumer goods dovetailed nicely with the rest of the exhibition, which contained—thanks to the largesse of 795 American corporations—a gigantic collection of the goodies and gadgets that characterized what economist John Kenneth Galbraith had recently termed "the affluent society." There was a display of pots and pans mounted on multicolored plastic panels. There was a fleet of American cars, the 1959 models, many festooned with chrome gee-gaws and swooping tail fins that made them look like aircraft from a low-budget sci-fi flick. And there was a supermarket crammed with canned goods and Q-Tips and Jell-O and frozen food in colorful packages that tempted many Russian visitors to acts of expropriation by shoplifting.

The Soviet press mocked the fair's commercialism: "What is this," asked *Izvestia,* "a national exhibit of a great country or a branch department store?"

There was a reason why the exhibition was awash in stuff: It made for great propaganda in a country where consumer goods were scarce and shoddy. The idea behind the fair had been summed up years earlier by Bruce Barton, the famous advertising man and former congressman who once offered this strategy for combating Communism: "Give every Russian a copy of the latest Sears-Roebuck Catalogue and the address of the nearest Sears-Roebuck outlet." The American exhibition was, in effect, a Sears outlet set down in Moscow in the hope of making Russians salivate over the bounties of capitalism.

Some skeptics scoffed at the idea of equating Americanism with commercialism. Historian Arthur Schlesinger Jr. complained that the United States was combating Communism's "godless materialism" with American "godly materialism." And Adlai Stevenson, the Democrat who had lost two elections to Eisenhower, raised an impertinent question: "With the supermarket as our temple and the singing commercial as our litany, are we likely to fire the world with an irresistible vision of America's exalted purposes and inspiring way of life?"

That afternoon, the premier observed the exhibits with a cold eye and a barbed tongue. When the vice president showed him an American voting booth, Khrushchev replied, "I have no interest in that." When Nixon pointed out the RAMAC computer, Khrushchev was nonplussed. "To shoot off rockets," he said, "we have computers and they are just as complicated as this." Only once did the two men agree on anything. Hearing an American jazz band in the distance, Nixon remarked, "I don't like jazz music," and Khrushchev replied, "I don't like it either."

When the two leaders wandered into a second kitchen, they ended up in a second kitchen debate. This was the RCA Whirlpool Miracle Kitchen, a $250,000 futuristic fantasy that included household robots—a "kitchen of the future" that is, half a century later, still in the future. Unlike Safire's plebian kitchen, this one was an airy, spacious room with a console that enabled the housewife of tomorrow to run her appliances by remote control.

As Nixon and Khrushchev watched, an American model pointed out the kitchen's closed-circuit TV system, which enabled mom to watch the kiddies while they played in other rooms.

Khrushchev was not impressed. "This is probably always out of order," he said.

Nixon laughed and agreed in Russian: "*Da.*"

The model pressed a button that sent a dishwasher zipping out of its cabinet and scurrying across the floor to the kitchen table, where mom could load it up without leaving her after-dinner coffee. When the model pressed another button, an automatic floor-washing machine scooted around the kitchen, cleaning up.

Nixon turned to Khrushchev. "You don't need a wife," he said, smiling.

Khrushchev responded with the kind of clever retort most people wouldn't think of until hours later, if ever: "Don't you have a machine that puts food in your mouth and pushes it down?" he asked.

7. IN THE DECADENT, LIMP-WRISTED WEST

When American reporters sat down that afternoon to bang out their stories, the sheer zaniness of the spectacle they'd witnessed seemed to bring out the tabloid sports reporter that apparently lurks inside even the stodgiest diplomatic correspondent.

"Monday morning quarterbacks of the diplomatic set accorded Vice President Nixon at least a tie today in his battle of wits and words with Soviet Prime Minister Nikita S. Khrushchev," wrote Warren Rogers of the *New York Herald Tribune*.

"Even to correspondents familiar with Mr. Khrushchev's capacity for catch-as-catch-can conversation and Mr. Nixon's ability to field rhetorical line drives," reported Harrison Salisbury in the *Times*, "the day seemed more like an event dreamed up by a Hollywood scriptwriter than a confrontation of two of the world's leading statesmen."

"One of the reasons for the length of the debates is that Khrushchev finds it difficult to believe that he cannot top Nixon, and so he keeps trying," wrote Charles Mohr of *Time* magazine. "Nixon on his own part has not been able to top Khrushchev either."

While reporters had enjoyed the great kitchen debate, there was some doubt as to whether diplomats were quite so enthralled. Some newspapers reported that the State Department was pleased with Nixon's actions; others revealed that State was appalled. And the *Herald Tribune* reported both "facts" simultaneously. "At the State Department, officials were happy that Mr. Nixon had stood up to Mr. Khrushchev," wrote Warren Rogers. A few paragraphs later, Rogers reported that "State Department officials, whose lives are devoted to learning the art of secret diplomacy, were aghast at the delicate issues tumbled about publicly in the off-the-cuff debate."

The sports metaphors and purple prose helped create intense anticipation about the arrival of the videotape shot during the debate at the fair's TV studio. It was the only television footage of Nixon and Khrushchev in combat (there were no TV cameras in Safire's kitchen), and it took more than twenty-four hours to reach the United States. "This historic tape is now being flown across the Atlantic," the *New York Daily News* reported, "scheduled to arrive at Idlewild at 6:55 this morning."

Pressured by the Soviets, the State Department asked NBC, which owned the tape, to withhold it until it could be aired in both countries simultaneously. But NBC refused, claiming that the tape was too important to go unseen any longer. In fact, NBC announced that the tape was too important to air on only one network and therefore it would give copies to its rivals at CBS and ABC. "The completely unexpected outburst by Khrushchev is regarded as being so ominous," reported *Daily News* TV columnist Ben Gross, "that the network believes it should be seen by all Americans."

Stoked by the breathless hype, Americans called TV stations, demanding to know when the already legendary tape would air. The answer was, Almost all the time. The sixteen-minute tape was played and replayed by all the networks at least a half-dozen times over the weekend, giving the country's TV columnists an excuse to join their more exalted op-ed page colleagues in analyzing the episode.

"This observer, along with others, gasped at the spectacle of the Soviet dictator shaking his finger in the face of the vice president of the United States," wrote Gross. "Now, millions of U.S. citizens have had a revealing close-up of the Soviet dictator. They saw him not only as a jovial, laughing fellow but as a tough, rude, excitable, unpredictable antagonist wielding awesome power."

Less frightened and more amused was Harriet Van Horne, TV columnist for the *New York World*. "His remarks to Vice President Nixon may have sounded sinister. But the appearance of the premier is almost uproariously funny. He looks like a delegate to a lodge convention. Loud and jovial, yes. But ready to punch in the nose any slob who doubts the ancient glory of The Brotherhood or questions the badges and ribbons on his lapel."

NBC had given black-and-white copies of the tape to its competitors but kept the color version for itself, Van Horne noted, and the color tape was much more fun. "Here the scene blazed with life and the eye took in countless details not apparent in the black-and-white picture. Mr. Nixon needed a shave, for one thing. And Mr. Khrushchev needs dental repairs."

After the columnists had their say, editors dispatched inquiring reporters to probe the mind of the man in the street.

"I thought they sounded like bickering children," said a housewife in Queens. "It's just like saying, 'My father is stronger than your father.' It didn't sound like adult behavior."

"Nixon looked like a typical American tourist trying to outsmart an old pro," a Bostonian grumbled.

"Khrushchev acted like a clown," said a Chicago restauranteur. "It was a great contrast to see how Nixon handled himself."

"I think this will help Nixon politically—dammit," lamented a Minneapolis Democrat.

"They're both hams," said a salesman in San Francisco. "But it was some show, I'll say that."

Nearly all observers agreed that the kitchen debate had enhanced the vice president's chances in the 1960 presidential election. In Illinois, a disgusted Adlai Stevenson wrote to a friend about the newfound popularity of the man he contemptuously called Curly: "I have no doubt that Curly scored heavily, as you say. Indeed, I have no doubt that he will be a formidable candidate, all of which fills me with a feeling that must be close to nausea and wonder about the new image of the American hero to inspire our little boys."

But *Time* magazine—which was, in those days, an unofficial but reliable organ of the Republican Party—found Nixon perfectly plausible as a manly, red-blooded hero for American lads. The vice president's performance in Moscow was, *Time* pronounced, "the personification of a kind of disciplined vigor that belied tales of the decadent and limp-wristed West."

8. TALKING TO THE BUGS

On Richard Nixon's first night in Moscow, his Secret Service bodyguards discovered disturbing levels of radiation in the vice president's bedroom in Spaso House, the American ambassador's residence.

The Americans had brought radiation detecting devices called dosimeters to Moscow because they'd noticed that when Soviet officials traveled in the United States, their bodyguards carried Geiger counters. If the Soviets were worried about radiation when they traveled in the United States, the Secret Service reasoned, perhaps Americans should worry about radiation when they traveled in the Soviet Union. Consequently the Nixon party came to Moscow with five dosimeter badges—one in Nixon's briefcase, the others carried by aides.

Secret Service agent James Golden, who had arrived in Moscow several weeks before Nixon, had detected no radiation at Spaso House until the night the vice president arrived, when dosimeters began picking up signs of radiation around Nixon's bedroom. The next morning, after Nixon left to meet Khrushchev, Golden and his boss, John T. Sherwood, took several dosimeters into the vice president's bedroom. Again, they detected radiation, and quite a lot of it. The two men wandered around the building, taking dosimeter readings in various places, but they found radiation only in and around Nixon's bedroom. After a few hours of checking and rechecking the instruments, they reached their inevitable conclusion: *The damn Commies were zapping the vice president of the United States!*

Golden and Sherwood decided to protest this invisible attack—but not through cumbersome diplomatic channels.

"We sat down on the beds facing each other and began berating the Russians in loud voices, cursing them for pulling a trick like this," Golden wrote in a report on the incident, "and wondering in loud voices why they were taking us for fools, and asking each other if they thought they were going to get away with this."

The two men were not just letting off steam. They were talking to the bugs—the electronic eavesdropping devices assumed to be hidden in the room. It was a logical assumption. The KGB—the Soviet secret police—was infamous for bugging embassies and it possessed some of the world's most sophisticated eavesdropping devices, thanks to an eccentric electronics genius named Leon Theremin. A physicist by training, Theremin invented the world's first electronic musical instrument, which he named the theremin. In 1927, Theremin took the instrument to America, where Hollywood filmmakers used it to create spooky sound effects for scary movies. He returned to the Soviet Union in 1937 and was promptly arrested, charged with anti-Soviet activities, and shipped to a Siberian prison camp. After being released during World War II, Theremin invented the Soviet Union's first electronic eavesdropping device, prompting Stalin to reward him with a Stalin Prize.

In 1946, in a heart-warming display of international brotherhood, a group of Soviet schoolchildren presented Averell Harriman, the American ambassador, with a two-foot wooden replica of the Great Seal of the United States. Unfortunately, the schoolchildren did not inform Harriman that the seal contained a hollow compartment that held one of Theremin's bugs, which enabled the KGB to listen to the private conversations of four consecutive American ambassadors before it was discovered in 1952.

When Nixon arrived in Moscow in 1959, Theremin was working as a scientist for the KGB, creating new, improved bugs that enabled Soviet spies to continue eavesdropping on conversations in the American embassy complex, including the conversation between Golden and Sherwood in Nixon's bedroom. For nearly a half-hour, the two Americans lambasted the Communists for irradiating Nixon. They hoped that whoever had been assigned the task of eavesdropping on Nixon's room would report their protests to somebody who had the power to shut off the radiation.

Apparently their plan worked. After about four hours, the mysterious radiation disappeared. It did not return for the duration of Nixon's visit.

9. HOW MANY NUKES DOES IT TAKE TO WIPE OUT ENGLAND?

"Mikoyan terrorizes his wife," Khrushchev said, grinning broadly. "He's a real oppressor."

Nixon glanced at Mrs. Mikoyan. She was a short, stout, gray-haired woman in a shapeless gray dress. Her upper lip held a hint of moustache.

"I imagine she can handle him," Nixon replied.

"I was kidding," Khrushchev said.

The premier enjoyed kidding Mikoyan, the old Armenian Bolshevik who had served in the Kremlin for decades. One of the perks of the job of chairman of the Communist Party of the Soviet Union was the power to tease anybody you felt like teasing. Back in the old days, Stalin used to get drunk and order Khrushchev to do the *gopak,* a Ukrainian folk dance. To Stalin, the sight of his chubby aide squatting on his haunches and flinging his feet into the air was hilarious. At least Khrushchev didn't make Mikoyan do *that.*

They were standing on the lawn of Khrushchev's dacha, a forty-room mansion built a few years earlier on the Moscow River about an hour's drive from the Kremlin. Two days after the kitchen debate, the Khrushchevs had invited the Nixons to lunch with the Mikoyans. The host, dressed in a beautiful white-on-white embroidered shirt, was in a jovial mood.

"Do you want to eat outside?" he asked.

"That would be very nice," Nixon replied. "We should decide all the questions like this."

"We should have a summit conference here instead of sitting in Geneva for months eating so many pies," Khrushchev said with a laugh. "First, let's have some pictures taken in front of the house, then take a boat ride on the Moscow River so you can see how the slaves live."

"Yes, the captives," Nixon said with a laugh. The captive nations debate had become a running gag.

The statesmen and their ladies posed for a few pictures, and then the men climbed into a twenty-five-foot motorboat and set off down the river, followed by a press boat full of photographers. Eight times, the boat stopped at river beaches that just happened to be packed with cheerful swimmers. Eight times, Khrushchev asked, "Are you captives? Are you slaves?" Eight times, the swimmers shouted back, *Nyet.*

Photos of the event reveal a comic scene: the swimmers waving and cheering, Khrushchev beaming and gesturing grandly, Nixon smiling wanly, his formal white shirt buttoned at the cuffs, his sober black tie fastened tightly at his collar. He was not a man with a gift for informality.

"You know, Mr. Khrushchev, I admire you," Nixon said at the eighth stop. "You never miss a chance to make propaganda."

"I don't make propaganda," Khrushchev said. "I tell the truth."

Back at the dacha, the statesmen and their wives sat down to a late lunch at a long table set up in the shade of majestic old birches. The table groaned under a load of delicacies and fine wines while Khrushchev played the convivial host.

When Mikoyan leaned across the table to chat with Pat Nixon, who was seated next to the premier, Khrushchev interrupted. "Now, look here, you crafty Armenian, Mrs. Nixon belongs to me," he said with mock anger. "You stay on your side of the table!" With his chubby forefinger, he drew an imaginary line down the center of the table. "This is an Iron Curtain! Don't you step over it!"

Servants arrived bearing platters of raw fish, sliced thin and spiced with salt, pepper and garlic—Soviet sushi. "This was Stalin's favorite dish," Khrushchev informed his guests. "He said it put steel in his backbone."

The premier took a double portion. Nixon, figuring he could use all the steel he could get, did the same.

As they ate, Mikoyan talked about how Stalin, who was a nocturnal animal, would summon his underlings for meetings in the middle of the night. "We sleep much better now that Comrade Khrushchev is our premier," he said. Then, catching his own double-entendre, he smiled and added, "I guess you can take that more ways than one."

The weather was beautiful, the food was delicious, and the wine flowed freely. The meal would have been perfect except for the conversation, which lingered on the grim subject of thermonuclear war. Unfortunately, nobody recorded the discussion verbatim, but aides from the American embassy paraphrased the dialogue in a memo cabled back to the State Department.

Khrushchev opened by bragging about his intercontinental ballistic missiles. In a test a week earlier, he said, his scientists had launched a missile

7,000 kilometers and it had landed only a few kilometers from its target. Of course, there had been a few accidents. He leaned across the table and announced that he would now reveal a secret: A month earlier, a missile had gone astray and overshot its target by 2,000 kilometers. It was heading for Alaska and, although it contained no warhead, he knew the Americans would not be happy to see it coming.

Fortunately, he added, it landed harmlessly in the ocean before it could trigger World War III.

Nixon listened, then lamented the high cost of armaments. For the price of one missile, he said, you could pay for 153,000 TV sets or shoes for several million children.

You Americans are spending too much for your missiles, the premier replied. The Soviets got more bang for their ruble. His experts had informed him, he added, that they could nuke all the targets in the United States, as well as all the American bases in Europe and Asia, at a cost of only 30 million rubles, less than 10 percent of the Soviet defense budget. Presumably the Americans at the table were not so enthusiastic about Khrushchev's bargain basement Armageddon.

Why do you keep building bombers if you have so many missiles? Nixon asked.

Khrushchev didn't answer. Instead, he offered a toast to the health of President Eisenhower. Then he toasted to the health of Nixon, then Mrs. Nixon. Finally he answered the question. The Soviet Union had nearly halted the production of bombers, he said, because he preferred missiles, which are not subject to human emotions. Men frequently balked at dropping bombs on other humans, he noted. It had happened on Soviet bombing missions during World War II. But missiles feel no pity.

When the talk turned from air battles to sea battles, Khrushchev said he felt sorry for navies in the next war because battleships and aircraft carriers would be sitting ducks and their crews would be "fodder for sharks."

What about submarines? Nixon asked. You are building plenty of submarines.

Yes, as many as possible, Khrushchev replied. Then he revealed another secret: His submarines carried missiles with a range of 600 kilometers. Soon they'd have a range of 1,000 kilometers. In the event of war, they would not only destroy the enemy's navy but would also incinerate the enemy's ports and coastal cities.

Hours passed and still the gruesome conversation continued. From 3:30 until nearly 9:00, the distinguished leaders and their ladies sat as course after course of fine cuisine was served and eaten, each accompanied by an appropriate wine. The sun sank, the shadows of the birches grew longer and still they sat, discussing the fine points of nuclear apocalypse.

If the United States put a missile base in Italy, Khrushchev said, he would put one in Albania. If the Americans put one in Greece, he'd put one in Bulgaria. In the event of war, he warned, he would nuke any country that housed an American base. Being a reasonable man, though, he would spare any nation that refused American bases.

Nixon tried to play the peacemaker. Nuclear war is folly, he said. It would destroy both nations. Indeed, it would destroy the entire world.

Khrushchev agreed. Destroying Europe would be easy, he added. In fact, there was really no need for the kind of pinpoint accuracy that his rocket scientists were developing. The nukes were powerful enough to do their job even if they landed 100 kilometers off target.

Then he told a joke that he claimed was currently popular in England, a joke about optimists and pessimists.

What is the difference between an optimist and a pessimist?

There is, alas, no photograph of Khrushchev telling this joke. But it's not hard to picture his lips curled in a cynical grin, his eyes sparkling with mirth as he waited to launch his hilarious punch line.

The pessimist says only six atomic bombs would be needed to wipe out England. The optimist says it would take nine or ten.

Unfortunately, neither the embassy's memo nor Nixon's memoir reveals whether anyone laughed.

10. THE NEW PARTY LINE ON LOVE

The next morning, Richard Nixon took off on a four-day tour of the Soviet Union, accompanied by a planeload of reporters. They flew to
Leningrad, then Novosibirsk ("the Chicago of Siberia"), then Sverdlovsk
("the Pittsburgh of the Urals"), hitting such hotspots as factories, dams,
mines, and collective farms.

Everywhere the walls held signs bearing hortatory slogans: "Let Us
Work for the Victory of Communism!" and "Let Us Develop Socialist
Competition to Complete Our Seven-Year Plan Ahead of Schedule!"
These posters amused American reporters, who were accustomed to
walls that said "Cars Love Shell!" or "Keep Your Tummy Under Tums
Control!"

At every stop, somebody would step out of a crowd, identify himself as
an average worker, and ask a question that sounded like it was written by
the same poet who produced the slogan about the seven-year plan:
"When will the United States cease atomic tests, which imperil the
peoples of the world with fall-outs of strontium 90?" The "workers" were
so obviously planted and their questions so blatantly ghost-written that
the reporters started betting on when the next one would pop up.

This ritual reached its absurd climax while Nixon toured a mine near
Sverdlovsk. Clad in long johns, overalls, knee-high rubber boots, a heavy
miner's coat, and a helmet with a lamp on the brim, the vice president
was hundreds of feet below ground and slogging through thick muck
when suddenly a miner shut off his drill and asked the first question that
popped into his mind: "Mr. Vice President, the Soviet Union has proposed
suspension of atomic tests but the United States refuses. Why?"

Everyone burst out laughing, even the Russians.

Without Khrushchev around, the reporters became bored. The dis-
tances between cities were enormous, the flights seemed endless, and the
only reading material available on Soviet planes was Soviet magazines,
which exhibited the same fondness for tractors that *Playboy* exhibited for

naked coeds. But one magazine article created a brief stir among the jaded gentlemen of the press. It was a debate entitled "Is Romantic Love Possible?"

No, it's not, argued one side. Romantic love is a reactionary bourgeois institution, a relic of capitalistic individualism with no place in the new communist order. This position was illustrated with a picture of a young worker with his clenched fist raised in the air and his face set in grim revolutionary determination. The caption read: "Love must be organized according to plan."

Yes, romantic love *is* possible, argued the other side, which was obviously the correct position because it was articulated by an official party theoretician. In the early days of the revolution, he wrote, the heroic Bolshevik leaders focused so intensely on building socialism that they created the impression that life held no room for romance. But that impression was misleading. What, after all, could be more inspiring than the love between Lenin and his devoted wife, Comrade Krupskaya? Today the Party recognizes that romantic love is indeed possible, even desirable, given the proper circumstances.

It was the new Party line on love—another example of Khrushchev's liberalization. Under normal circumstances, American reporters would have had a ball with this story. But at the moment, the question on every reporter's mind was not, Is romantic love possible? but, Is Nixon going to invite Khrushchev to the United States?

The rumor had been circulating for a week and reporters were desperately hoping it was true. Khrushchev in America promised to be a fabulous story. They chased the rumor but couldn't quite pin it down. Nixon's people were being coy, not confirming anything but hinting that the vice president was urging Ike to invite Khrushchev. A White House reporter asked President Eisenhower if Nixon possessed the authority to invite Khrushchev to America.

"Of course not," Ike snapped back. "But he has every right to listen and converse and discuss it as you and I might."

Reading that, a reporter in Russia asked Nixon if he had recommended that Ike invite Khrushchev to the United States.

"The president in his press conference indicated that I did not issue an invitation to Mr. Khrushchev," Nixon replied, choosing his words very carefully. "As far as any decision as to whether he should come, or when he should come, the president, of course, should and will make that decision."

It was all a charade, of course. The invitation had been secretly issued and secretly accepted two weeks earlier. But Ike was still trying to get Khrushchev to pay a diplomatic price for the visit. The president wanted the premier to meet the condition that Murphy had neglected to attach to the invitation—that the foreign ministers meeting in Geneva would resolve the Berlin crisis before Khrushchev made his visit.

"I can assure you," Eisenhower wrote to Khrushchev while Nixon was touring Russia, "that as far as the American people are concerned, I cannot emphasize too strongly how great an improvement there would be in public opinion if our meeting could take place in an improved environment resulting from progress at Geneva."

But Khrushchev didn't snap at the bait. "It is impossible to overlook the fact that the possibilities of the Ministers of Foreign Affairs are limited, and in view of the complexity of contemporary international conditions, the questions before them can prove too much for them to resolve," the premier wrote back. "But this should not arouse pessimism among us concerning the expediency of convening a meeting at the summit."

In other words, *Berlin is too tough to leave to our underlings. Let's discuss it at Camp David.* He closed his letter with, "Until our approaching meeting, with sincere regards, N. Khrushchev."

Ike realized that he'd been snookered. The wily Communist had gotten exactly what he wanted—a trip to America—without giving anything in Geneva. Eisenhower was irate, but what could he do?

"I couldn't cancel the invitation to Khrushchev," he wrote years later in his memoir, still peeved. "I now had to meet Khrushchev and allow him to tour our country in spite of the fact that he had deliberately engi-neered the breakdown of the foreign ministers meeting."

11. KHRUSHCHEV IN THE COCKPIT WITH THE WHISKEY

The first thing Nikita Khrushchev did upon entering Richard Nixon's plane was to head for the cockpit and plop down in the pilot's seat.

Nixon wasn't there. Back from his Siberian tour, he was holed up in the American embassy, writing the speech that Khrushchev had agreed to let him deliver on Soviet television. His absence left reporters with nothing to cover, so Khrushchev, a man with the media instincts of a Hollywood press agent, announced that he would inspect the Boeing 707 that had carried Nixon to Moscow. He brought along Andrei Nikolaevich Tupolev, the Soviet Union's chief aircraft designer, and he immediately began teas-ing the corpulent Tupolev about his girth, which was even greater than Khrushchev's.

"There's no room for Tupolev in such a cockpit," said the premier, who was wedged tightly into the cramped pilot's seat. "Luckily, we have no pilots like Tupolev."

He climbed out of the cockpit and strolled through the plane. "Very good," he said. "The furnishings are excellent." He liked the plane and wanted one just like it. "Make some notes," he told Tupolev. "Sketch some of these designs."

Tupolev looked confused. Was the boss serious?

Khrushchev turned to his hosts, a group that included Tommy Thompson, the American ambassador. "Andrei Nikolaevich must try to steal something from you," he said, grinning. "All aircraft builders steal from each other. There is nothing unusual about that."

The premier was in a mischievous mood. He was dressed in a casual el-egance, a beige summer suit over an embroidered white linen sports shirt.

Atop his head sat a dapper white straw hat with a powder-blue band. He looked like a prosperous businessman enjoying a night on the town. He meandered back to the galley and inspected the bar. He opened a bottle of American vodka, then theatrically crinkled his nose as if he'd just smelled a very old fish.

"Who makes this vodka?" he asked, skeptically. He put the offending bottle down and picked up one that was filled with a darker liquid. "What's this?"

Kentucky sour mash bourbon, answered one of the Americans. Would you care for a drink?

"Vodka or whiskey?" he asked, but as usual, he didn't wait for an answer. "We are on your territory. We will take whiskey."

Somebody poured him a bourbon on the rocks and he took a sip. "This is very good whiskey," he said. "But you Americans spoil it. You put in more ice than whiskey."

He stuck a couple of pudgy fingers into the drink and dug out some of the ice cubes. He proposed a toast to the United States, then a toast to President Eisenhower, then one to the absent Nixon and one to Thompson.

Thompson smiled graciously. He informed Khrushchev that this 707 was a converted military plane, then offered a toast of his own: "To the time when we convert all military planes to civilian use."

"Very good," Khrushchev said. "Our TU–114 is also a conversion of a military type." As usual, the chairman couldn't resist bragging a bit. "I think we began reequipping our military planes a bit earlier than you."

He picked up a handful of cashews and tossed a couple into his mouth. "I will also tell you a secret: The bomber variant of the TU–114 can fly to the United States and back without refueling."

Why did he say that? Why did he keep conjuring up images of Soviet bombers heading for the United States? He had done it during the lunch with Nixon at his dacha and now he was at it again. Was it a cold, calculated scare tactic? Or was he just a proud man sipping a drink and shooting off his mouth?

"Would you like to fly to America nonstop in this plane?" asked a reporter.

"This one or some other one," he said with a shrug.

"When?"

"When the time is ripe," Khrushchev replied, smiling enigmatically.

12. NIXON IN THE EMBASSY WITH MARTINIS

For two long nights, Richard Nixon huddled in the American embassy, writing his speech for Soviet television. It wasn't easy because the speech had to appeal to two conflicting constituencies—Soviet viewers and American voters.

Nixon the presidential candidate wrote the first draft, "a tough, blasting speech," he called it, a fierce anti-Communist polemic designed to rev up the Republican right wing. Ambassador Thompson told him it was too belligerent. "You're the first American vice president to address the Soviet people," Thompson said. "You've got to make sure you're not the last."

Both Nixon and Thompson knew about the secret plans for an exchange of visits by Khrushchev and Eisenhower and they didn't want to give the Soviets an excuse to prevent Ike from speaking on Russian TV. So Nixon wrote a second draft, this one less pugnacious, more diplomatic. Then, on August 1, he donned a dark suit and a gray tie and traipsed off to a television studio to deliver it.

Khrushchev had promised Nixon a TV appearance but he never promised to advertise it—and he didn't. So Nixon began his speech with an apology for preempting the comedy show viewers had expected to see when they tuned in. He praised the beauty of the Soviet Union and the friendliness of its people and then he began to rebut, point by point, the official Soviet version of the cold war.

"Let us look at the record," he said, swiping Al Smith's trademark line. "We disarmed rapidly after World War II. Then came a series of events which threatened our friends abroad as well as ourselves. The Berlin blockade and the war in Korea are typical of the actions which led the United States and our allies to re-arm. . . . I could cite statement after statement made by previous leaders of the U.S.S.R. which advocated and threatened the use of force against non-Communist countries."

The responsibility for peace, he said, rests with Premier Khrushchev: "If he devotes his immense energies and talents to building a better life for the people of his own country, Mr. Khrushchev can go down in history as one of the greatest leaders the Soviet people have ever produced. But if he diverts the resources and talents of his people to the objective of promoting the Communization of countries outside the Soviet Union, he will only assure that both he and his people will continue to live in an era of fear, suspicion and tension."

It was a good speech. Not only did it play well in America, but many Russians would remember it fondly for decades. It was the first time they'd ever seen anybody appear on Soviet TV to attack the official Party version of reality. Nixon had done a tough job very well but he wasn't satisfied. When he returned to the embassy for a dinner in his honor, he was depressed and angry. He gulped down a martini. Then another. And another. And another. By the time he sat down to dinner, he was bombed, plastered, blotto. His intoxication only exacerbated his bad mood, and he launched into an ugly, expletive-filled monologue on his skill at handling Khrushchev. "He proceeded to review moments of the visit, extolling his own performance: *'Wasn't I clever to. . . . Didn't I handle that one. . . . I sure showed him when I. . . . Wasn't that the best answer you ever . . .* and so on and on, becoming foulmouthed in the process," Vladimir Toumanoff, a senior staffer at the embassy, recalled years later. "These were not just rhetorical questions. He was pleading for reassurance and, as nearly always happens, the confirmations and slightly sycophantic replies from his staff did not help. His insecurity was too deep."

Appalled at Nixon's drunken behavior, Toumanoff left the dinner early. "He was vicious, he was foul-mouthed, he was coarse," Toumanoff recalled. "He was riddled with anger and hostility and self-praise and arrogance. There wasn't an attractive aspect to him that whole evening."

13. KHRUSHCHEV'S COMING! KHRUSHCHEV'S COMING!

Politicians are actors and successful politicians are actors of Oscar caliber. Winning elections requires the ability to feign excitement about spending Saturday night at the sewer workers convention, elation over breakfasting with Presbyterian elders at the crack of dawn, ecstasy over kissing the howling infant with the runny nose.

Dwight D. Eisenhower, America's most successful politician, demonstrated his considerable theatrical talent on the morning of August 3, 1959. Still livid about the "accidental invitation," Ike stepped to a microphone in the White House, flashed his famous grin, and announced Khrushchev's upcoming visit as if there were nothing on Earth he'd rather do.

"I asked this morning for this special press conference on the subject of the impending exchange of visits between Mr. Khrushchev and myself," Eisenhower told the White House correspondents. Then he read a statement that was being released simultaneously in Moscow: "The president of the United States has invited Nikita Khrushchev, Chairman of the Council of Ministers of the Union of Soviet Socialist Republics, to pay an official visit to the United States in September. Mr. Khrushchev has accepted with pleasure. The president has also accepted with pleasure Mr. Khrushchev's invitation to pay an official visit to the U.S.S.R. later this fall."

Khrushchev will spend two or three days in Washington, Ike told the reporters, then he'll travel around the country for ten days or so. Details on exactly where he'll go have not yet been worked out.

Ike's news immediately revived the reporters' memories of Mikoyan's visit the previous winter, when Eastern European immigrants had pelted the old Bolshevik with eggs and tomatoes in Cleveland and Chicago. What would happen if some nut did the same—or *worse*—to Khrushchev? Isn't that the way World War I had started? When Ike opened the floor to questions, the very first one alluded to the Mikoyan debacle: "Have you given some thought to the possibility of incidents, Mr. President?"

"This is always a possibility in this country," Eisenhower admitted. "We do have these uncontrolled individuals and, of course, we talked about that, and they know it. We have not failed to point out this fact to the U.S.S.R. representatives. I am certain, however, that we can control this matter."

"Will you accompany him in the United States?"

"Well, I don't think it would be feasible for me to go all the way through the United States with him. But certainly we—there might be some visiting around. I don't know."

"The impression has somehow been received, Mr. President," said Felix Belair of the *New York Times*, "that before you would issue an invitation to him, there would have to be some evidence of give—I mean in the sense of give-and-take—on the part of Mr. Khrushchev on Western principles. May we take it that there has been some such indication?"

The question was a finger jabbed into Ike's freshest wound, but he didn't let it show. "No," he said laconically, "I don't think you can say that, Mr. Belair."

"Mr. President, could you say, sir, was it just two items of correspondence? You invited him and he accepted?"

Ike flashed that grin again. "Well, I'd say it is a little more complicated than that."

The reporters laughed and the man from the Associated Press said, "Thank you, Mr. President," the signal that the press conference was over. Everybody scurried from the room, hustled to the nearest phones, and called their editors: *Khrushchev's coming! Khrushchev's coming!*

This was, in the parlance of the journalistic trade, a "holy shit! story." The enemy, the anti-Christ, the Boogie Man, the national *bête noir*, was coming to visit! It was unprecedented in American history. George III never dropped by for a chat. Neither did Kaiser Wilhelm or Hitler or Tojo. Truman did not invite Stalin to the White House or ask Mao Zedong if he'd like to go sightseeing. And Khrushchev was not merely coming to meet with Eisenhower—which would be a major story in itself. He would also be gamboling around the country for ten days like a campaigning pol or some kind of Communist Kerouac!

A few people wondered if Khrushchev would be bitten by the same bug that infected King Baudouin. Just a few months earlier, the Belgian king had toured the United States. When he arrived, he was described as a moody, morose young monarch living in the shadow of his embittered father. But somewhere in America Baudouin emerged from his royal shell and became . . . the life of the party. He took cha-cha lessons! He danced until dawn beside a swimming pool in Dallas! In Hollywood, he hobnobbed with Gina Lollobrigida and lunched with Debbie Reynolds! In San Francisco, he scarfed spareribs while ogling a stripper!

"I've never had so much fun in my life!" he announced gleefully. And when he returned home, his subjects marveled at his transformation.

Nobody expected that to happen to Khrushchev, of course, but nobody had expected it to happen to Baudouin either. Maybe there was something in the air in America, some heady, intoxicating vapor that would affect Khrushchev too. Maybe he'd see Broadway or Bourbon Street or the Sunset Strip and fall in love with us. Or maybe he'd have the opposite reaction. Maybe he'd hate America—absolutely *detest* the country—and return home eager to blow us to smithereens. Who knew?

News of Ike's announcement spread quickly, inspiring praise, denunciation, and apocalyptic prophecies. But Ike remained calm. After the press conference, he changed into his golf attire and headed out to the Burning Tree Country Club to play eighteen holes.

"A Surreal Extravaganza"

14. THE WORST HUMAN BEING ON EARTH

At five minutes past noon on Wednesday, June 15, 1955, Washington's air raid sirens howled and President Eisenhower hustled out of the White House and into a Cadillac limousine headed for a secret bomb-proof hideaway in the mountains of Virginia. Along the way, he signed a proclamation placing the United States under martial law.

Three hours later, at 3:25 P.M., a Soviet bomber dropped an atomic weapon that exploded over Washington, killing 96,000 people. At the same time, a missile carrying a five-megaton nuclear warhead exploded in Brooklyn, annihilating 2,991,285 people. All told, the Soviets hit sixty-one American cities, killing 8.2 million people, injuring 5.5 million, and leaving 24 million homeless.

It was all just a drill, of course, a sort of dress rehearsal for the apocalypse. Dubbed Operation Alert, it was designed to prepare Americans for atomic attack. In Washington, 15,000 federal workers were transported to "safe" sites outside the city. In New York, buses stopped at the sound of the sirens and passengers scrambled to the nearest air raid shelter. From his secret bunker, Ike addressed the nation on TV: "We are here to determine whether or not the government is prepared in time of emergency to continue the function of government."

After that, Operation Alert became an annual event, like Halloween or April Fools' Day. In 1956, the drill was expanded to seventy-five cities and the relocated federal bureaucrats practiced postapocalyptic actions, such as issuing proclamations to freeze wages and prices. Unfortunately, there were still a few bugs in the system. On the East Coast, a rainstorm knocked out a "considerable portion" of the civil defense communications network, which seemed ominous. If the network couldn't withstand some wind and water, how would it hold up under a thermonuclear attack?

After the drill, Val Peterson, head of the federal Civil Defense Administration, estimated that a real nuclear attack would kill or injure 50 million Americans and leave the survivors scrounging for food in a scorched, radioactive landscape.

"Life," he said, "is going to be stark, elemental, brutal, filthy, miserable."

Newsreels urged Americans to dig fallout shelters and stock them with canned food and bottled water, plus a gun to fight off intruders and a supply of tranquilizers to soothe frazzled nerves. In Colorado, a suburban developer offered a shelter with every new home. In New York, Governor Nelson Rockefeller proposed a law requiring bomb shelters in all new buildings. In West Virginia, the federal government began constructing a massive secret underground home for Congress under the posh Greenbriar Hotel—a bunker complete with Senate and House chambers, dormitories, a hospital, a crematorium, and a subterranean dining hall with faux windows decorated with bucolic country scenes.

Although the United States in the 1950s was the most prosperous nation in human history, beneath its cheerful affluence lay a palpable sense of impending doom. In schools, millions of children prepared for air-raid drills by watching *Duck and Cover*, a film that taught the correct position to assume during atomic attack—squatting, with nose between knees and arms cradling the cranium. The film, produced by the federal government, featured a cartoon turtle named Bert who survives an attack from a firecracker-throwing monkey by taking cover in his protective shell as a peppy jingle plays.

> *Duck! And cover!*
> *Duck! And cover!*

Singing for adults, satirist Tom Lehrer sounded much less optimistic about surviving an atomic bomb:

We will all bake together when we bake.
There'll be nobody present at the wake
With complete participation
In that grand incineration
Nearly three billion hunks of well-done steak.

The cold war's pervasive paranoia inspired federal prosecutions of domestic Communists, congressional investigations of Reds in Hollywood, and a law requiring all college students receiving federal loans to swear that they weren't members of any organization advocating "the overthrow of the U.S. government by force"—a statute that successfully rid campuses of violent revolutionaries who were too virtuous to lie on a government form.

Amid this culture of dread, Eisenhower realized that his announcement of Khrushchev's impending visit would spark hostile reactions. And it did.

In Gary, Indiana, and Rochester, New York, Eastern European immigrants paraded in protest. In Washington, a retired Army captain filed a lawsuit on behalf of "Fighting Folks of Fighting Men," demanding that Khrushchev be refused admittance to the country under laws barring "criminal aliens." In New York, William F. Buckley's conservative *National Review* sold stickers that read, "Khrushchev Not Welcome Here." In Miami, somebody decorated a graveyard with a sign that read, "Khrushchev Will Be Welcome Here."

Opinion polls reported that nearly three-quarters of Americans supported Ike's invitation, but congressional mail told a different story. Several senators reported that every single letter they received on the issue expressed opposition to the visit. And many of the letters were baroque symphonies of outraged excoriation: "We find ourselves as a nation standing at the brink of a holocaust that defies description and by some weird process of doublethink we are asked to receive (politely if you please) the very scoundrels who put us there," a Lubbock foot doctor wrote to Senate Majority Leader Lyndon Johnson. "Small wonder that we see our leaders in the insane posture of rolling out the appropriately red carpet for Satan's chief warlord and all in the name of peace. May God help us."

Khrushchev's visit was denounced by the Veterans of Foreign Wars, decried by the International Council of Churches, and deplored by Senator Pat McNamara, who called Khrushchev "the worst human being on Earth."

Perhaps the most scathing attack came from the typewriter of Reuben Maury, the legendary editorial writer of the *New York Daily News*. Although Maury was a lawyer from Butte, Montana, his jeremiads in the *News* captured the feisty, cranky voice of blue-collar New York. He called China "a great big slob of a country" and described the United Nations as "a glass cigar box . . . jampacked with pompous do-gooders, nervy deadbeats, moochers, saboteurs, spies and traitors." After banging out his daily rant, Maury would march to the men's room with a bar of soap and a stiff brush, roll up his sleeves and give his hands a full surgical scrubbing.

When Ike announced Khrushchev's visit, Maury fired off a sarcastic masterpiece called "Clasp Hands with Murder, Mr. President?"

"How about a special committee to greet the Kremlin's No. 1 hood at the Washington Airport?" Maury asked. "This committee should include Alger Hiss, several known American Communists and fellow travelers, and a few top-flight gangsters from dope-pushing, prostitution and jewel-theft circles. Al Capone and Lindbergh-baby-killer Bruno Hauptmann would be ideal members of the reception committee, but unhappily they are detained in Hell. We thought of nominating Jimmy Hoffa but concluded that he is too nice a chap to mingle with Khrushchev."

In Massachusetts, anti-Khrushchev sentiment ran so high that Governor Foster Furculo sent a warning to Secretary of State Christian Herter: "I don't know what Mr. Khrushchev's itinerary is, but I strongly recommend that it not include Massachusetts."

FBI director J. Edgar Hoover estimated that at least 25,000 Americans wanted to kill Khrushchev. And a State Department official told reporters that the number of death threats "has us plenty worried."

Just how worried was revealed years later when Wiley T. Buchanan, the State Department's chief of protocol, told a chilling story in his memoir:

> A doctor in a Midwestern state wrote a letter to President Eisenhower, claiming that he had a foolproof way of getting rid of Mr. Khrushchev during the Russian leader's visit to this country. His proposal, which involved the use of radioactive materials, was so ingenious and so potentially lethal that the State Police in his area were requested to keep an eye on him until the Russian premier went home. The police decided that the safest thing to do was to put the worthy doctor in jail—which they proceeded to do. When our security men heard of this, they were appalled and wondered if the doctor might not sue everyone involved for false arrest. The State Police, however, were not concerned. "We have this doctor's letter," they said, "with his signature on it. If he gives us any trouble, we'll simply publicize it. We rather doubt that anyone will want a doctor who is so ingenious when it comes to killing people. So we don't expect to have any trouble." They didn't.

15. YOU ARE CORDIALLY INVITED TO THE DRY PEA CAPITAL OF AMERICA

Not every American wanted to kill Khrushchev. Many Americans wanted Khrushchev to drop by, meet the family, and stay for supper.

"If the premier should wish to visit a typical American family, please let me extend the hospitality of our home," Samuel Sayad of San Francisco wrote to the State Department. "My mother-in-law is famous for her Russian dishes and samovar tea."

Khrushchev was also invited to homes in Seattle and Corpus Christi, a ranch in Nebraska, and a farm in New Jersey, whose owner promised that the dictator could meet a local celebrity—the Brown Swiss cow "which holds the world's milk production record."

In the weeks before Khrushchev's arrival, invitations poured into the White House, Congress, the State Department, and the Soviet embassy. Half the country seemed eager to show the visitor the "real America," which generally corresponded to their own corner of America. Americans seemed to believe that if the Russian Red could just meet us, he would love us.

Those politicians who weren't busy denouncing Khrushchev were demanding that he visit their states. West Virginia governor Cecil Underwood suggested that the premier tour a West Virginia coal mine. New York governor Nelson Rockefeller plugged Niagara Falls. Senator Estes Kefauver of Tennessee touted the Grand Old Opry as "a wonderful place of true Americana for Mr. Khrushchev to see."

Across America, proud city fathers scrambled to issue official invitations. Khrushchev was urged to experience the grandeur of Pittsburgh, Philadelphia, Shreveport, Sioux Falls, and Peoria, as well as the charms of Aberdeen, South Dakota; Blue Earth, Minnesota; Ephrata, Washington ("the Queen City of the Sun Basin"); and Moscow, Idaho ("the largest dry pea shipping center in the United States"). The Houston office of the Federal Housing Administration—an agency whose official policy was to make loans in segregated neighborhoods only—offered to give Khrushchev a guided tour of "some very attractive Negro subdivisions."

To compete with the big cities, America's small towns felt they had to sweeten their invitations with something extra. "We feel sure that from the enclosed literature you will decide to visit our town," officials in Neosho, Missouri, wrote to Khrushchev. Their invitation included a booklet from the Neosho Fish Cultural Station and a postcard of a lovely blonde woman perched on a bridge. Exactly what the blonde might do with or for Khrushchev was not explained.

The mayor of Warsaw, Missouri, volunteered to provide America's foremost enemy with a dangerous weapon. "I could plan for them to visit the largest walnut gunstock factory in the world," he told the State

Department. "I could be prepared to make a presentation of an extra fancy gunstock, appropriately carved, and could probably arrange for almost any kind of gun he wanted in this stock, perhaps a Russian military rifle."

Many Americans felt an urge to give things to Khrushchev. The Jaycees of Levittown, Pennsylvania, offered a Russian translation of the official Jaycee Creed. A Philadelphia shoe store sent President Eisenhower a pair of shoes for Khrushchev and invited the premier to visit so he could learn how "strong and healthy feet make for a strong and healthy America." An Atlantic City hotel offered the dictator free use of its luxurious penthouse suite: "two bedrooms, living room, two baths, kitchen, utility room, sun deck and a Japanese houseboy."

Capitalists competed to woo the famous Communist, inviting him to visit the Chicago Molded Plastics Corporation, the Perfect Carton Corporation, and a Hinky Dinky supermarket. A New York City clothing store bought an advertisement inviting Khrushchev to "observe the American Way in action" at its "Semi-Annual Clearance of Quality Values—35% to 60% Below National Featured Prices."

When Adlai Stevenson suggested that Khrushchev might enjoy strolling the grounds of a state fair, all varieties of fairs and festivals issued invitations—the Kentucky State Fair, the West Texas Fair, the Tri-State Fair and the Four State Fair, as well as the Soybean Festival in Taylorville, Illinois, and the Apple Festival Parade in La Crescent, Minnesota. "The parade consists of about 70 to 100 units and lasts about two hours," the Apple Festival chairman wrote to Khrushchev. "If you would like to enter a float, please let me know."

Jazz trumpeter Louis Armstrong suggested that the premier visit a jazz club to experience "the swingin' feel of freedom." Sitting in his dressing room after a gig in Las Vegas, Armstrong said he'd love to play for Mr. K. "He's a cat, man," Satchmo said. "He's a human being, like anybody else. And if a man don't like music, he wouldn't be in the position he's got."

Terry Lynn Huntingdon, a nineteen-year-old UCLA coed who was crowned Miss USA in the 1959 Miss Universe Pageant, volunteered to entertain Khrushchev: "I really think that maybe I can be of some help—not as a beauty contest winner, but just as an average American girl."

President Eisenhower was amused at the outpouring of suggestions but not too amused to offer a few of his own.

"Sir," a reporter asked at a press conference, "would you tell us what you would particularly like him to see in the United States?"

Ike replied that he wanted Khrushchev to see one of the famous Levittowns—huge suburban developments of inexpensive tract houses in New York and Pennsylvania. He'd also like to take Khrushchev on a helicopter ride over Washington, so the chairman could see the many "modest but decent" homes in the surrounding suburbs. And Ike hoped Khrushchev would visit his hometown, Abilene, Kansas.

"I would like to see him go in the little town where I was born," Ike said, "and let them tell him the story of how hard I worked until I was 21, when I went to West Point. He said in one of his conversations to Mr. Nixon, 'What do you know about work? You never worked.' Well, I can show him evidence that I did, and I want him to see it."

16. SIZE MATTERS

At his dacha on the Black Sea, Nikita Khrushchev worked night and day to prepare for his trip to America. During the long, sunny days, he sat on the beach under linen awnings, conferring with aides and studying briefing papers and drafts of speeches he would deliver in America. At night, he took long, contemplative strolls around the grounds, then summoned a stenographer and began dictating ideas. The invitation itself was a great victory, he believed, and he couldn't stop crowing about it.

"Who would have guessed 20 years ago that the most powerful capitalist country in the world would invite a Communist to visit?" he told aides. "This is incredible. Today, they have to take us into account. It's our strength that led to this—they have to recognize our existence and our power. Who would have thought that the capitalists would invite me, a worker? Look at what we've achieved in these years."

The chairman was proud but he was also nervous, fearing that "capitalists and aristocrats" would try to humiliate him in America. Back in 1919, a Soviet group was invited to meet a Western delegation on an island near Istanbul. It turned out the island was where "stray dogs were sent to die," a deliberate attempt to embarrass the Soviets. That must not that happen again, Khrushchev instructed his aides. They must demand every honor, every silly bit of pompous protocol that was due to the leader of a great nation.

"We will not allow anyone to push us around or to sit on our necks," he insisted.

Khrushchev didn't know much about America and most of what he did know was absurdly archaic. He'd read *The City of the Yellow Devil*, Maxim Gorky's bitter account of his 1906 trip to the United States, and *One-Storied America*, a book of humorous sketches by Soviet reporters Ilya Ilf and Evgeny Petrov about their 1935 trip across America in a Model-T Ford. But much had happened in the United States since 1935—the New Deal, rural electrification, the rise of labor unions, World War II, the GI bill, suburbanization, the first stirrings of the civil rights movement and the longest economic boom in history. Not to mention television, rock and roll, *Playboy* magazine, the Barbie doll, hula hoops, pink plastic flamingos, TV dinners, the paint-by-numbers craze and the perplexing popularity of boomerang-shaped coffee tables.

Khrushchev had traveled extensively since taking power, but America was different. "It's not that I was frightened, but I'll admit that I was worried," he wrote in his memoir. "I felt as though I were about to undergo an important test."

Anastas Mikoyan, who had traveled to the United States earlier in 1959, suggested that Khrushchev bring his wife and children. Privately, Mikoyan hoped that Nina Khrushchev would have a calming influence on her husband. But he told the chairman that his family would make a good impression on the American public.

Khrushchev agreed and decided to bring Nina and the children—their son Sergei, 25, and daughters Yulia, 44, and Rada, 30, as well as Rada's husband, Aleksei Adzubei, who happened to be the editor of the official government newspaper, *Izvestia*. Khrushchev was also to be accompanied by dozens of aides, advisers, underlings, and bodyguards. As Sergei Khrushchev later remembered, one of them managed to work up enough courage to ask the premier if the travelers would be given any American dollars to spend during the trip.

Nyet, Khrushchev replied.

"He said, 'We're bringing you on our plane at governmental expense and you will live there on American expense. For what do you need money?'" Sergei recalled. "And they explained to him that it is a capitalist country and if you want to go to the toilet, you have to pay, you cannot just piss. So he agreed that they would give us some money. I think it was $30 for the whole trip."

With that question settled, only one problem remained: How would they get to America? They'd fly, of course, but aboard what plane?

In 1955, Khrushchev had flown to Geneva for his first summit meeting and he was appalled to see that the Soviet plane was a pathetic, puny little thing, "like an insect," he grumbled, compared to the British and American behemoths. Back home, he ordered his aircraft designer, Andrei Tupolev, to build a plane as big as the capitalist planes—or bigger. Tupolev responded by creating the TU–114, a 177-foot, 220-passenger plane that stood 50 feet off the ground—the world's tallest aircraft. Khrushchev was so pleased that he kept a model of the TU–114 on his desk in the Kremlin.

In June 1959, Deputy Premier Frol Kozlov had flown to Washington in the brand-new TU–114, which stood so tall that the Americans didn't have a staircase high enough to reach the door. Kozlov had to scramble down a ladder like a bridegroom staging a dramatic elopement. Khrushchev was thrilled. "Look at us!" he exulted. "See what we can do!"

He was eager to show off the world's tallest plane by flying it to America, but there was a problem: Mechanics had discovered microscopic cracks in the engines. Khrushchev's pilot, Nikolai Tsybin, warned him the plane wasn't safe and urged him to take another. The Party bosses in the Presidium agreed. After all, the prestige of a big plane is somewhat diminished if it falls out of the sky.

But Khrushchev was determined to fly in the big bird. He summoned Tupolev and asked him if the plane was safe.

"I'm absolutely certain you won't have any trouble," Tupolev said.

Tupolev was so confident about his creation that he proposed a plan to ease Khrushchev's fears. "If you'll allow me," he said, "I'll send my own son, Alyosha, with you."

"I couldn't ask for more than that," Khrushchev replied.

17. NUMBER ONE MAN!

Smiling Mike Menshikov was not smiling. He wasn't happy. All he wanted was the best of everything for his boss, Nikita Khrushchev, but the intransigent Americans at the State Department refused to give it to him.

Mikhail Menshikov was the Soviet ambassador to the United States. Washington reporters nicknamed him "Smiling Mike" because he actually smiled in public, unlike every other Soviet diplomat they'd covered. In private, though, Menshikov was a tough negotiator who seldom smiled. He certainly wasn't smiling during the endless haggles with the State Department about his boss's upcoming trip. Khrushchev had ordered Menshikov to demand the full panoply of diplomatic pomp—all the honors due to the great leader of a great nation—and the Americans kept telling him that Khrushchev didn't deserve them.

The problem, said undersecretary of state Robert Murphy, was that Khrushchev was not the head of the Soviet *state,* he was merely the head of the Soviet *government.* It was the kind of petty hairsplitting that only a diplomat could love, but technically Murphy was right. Kliment Voroshilov, president of the Supreme Soviet, was the head of state. But

Menshikov didn't care. He knew that Khrushchev would be livid if he received anything less than full pomp.

Heads of state arriving in America were greeted by the president and treated to a twenty-one-gun salute, but mere heads of government were met by the vice president and saluted with only nineteen guns. Menshikov knew that his boss wanted all twenty-one guns, if not more. And if Khrushchev stepped off the plane to find himself greeted by the hated Nixon, Menshikov might soon find himself slopping hogs at a collective farm outside Novosibirsk.

In meeting after meeting, Menshikov wrangled over this arcane question with Murphy, the man who'd botched Ike's invitation to Khrushchev. Murphy was not inclined to cut the Soviets much slack.

"Our rules of protocol," Murphy said, "distinguish between head of state and head of government."

"He is *number one man!*" Menshikov insisted. "Everyone knows he is *number one man!*"

When that argument didn't work, Menshikov tried another. Whatever indignities Khrushchev suffered in America, he said, would be visited upon Eisenhower when he made his reciprocal visit to Moscow. That did the trick. The Americans announced that Khrushchev would be treated as a head of government traveling "in the capacity of a head of state." The chairman would get what he wanted—the full-blown, all-out, no-holds-barred pomp.

But there were other arguments. For weeks, Menshikov and Murphy squabbled over the trip itinerary. Their first meetings in early August were amicable enough, as the two men casually tossed out suggestions for a fun road trip. Maybe Khrushchev should see a rodeo, Menshikov said. Or maybe the chairman should visit Oklahoma. After all, he had enjoyed the movie version of the musical *Oklahoma.* (Who would have guessed?)

How about Kentucky? Murphy suggested. It has horse farms and bourbon distilleries and a fine state fair.

But this casual banter ended when the diplomats learned of their leaders' desires. After Ike suggested at his press conference that Khrushchev

PETER CARLSON   63

should see Levittown and visit Abilene and take a helicopter ride over the Washington suburbs, Murphy started pressuring Menshikov to include those activities on the itinerary.

Menshikov balked. A helicopter ride is a "waste of time," he said, and Khrushchev did not want to visit Abilene. The chairman preferred to travel to New York, Pittsburgh, Los Angeles, San Francisco, and the Iowa farm of Roswell Garst, who'd befriended Khrushchev years earlier while selling him a load of hybrid seed corn.

Now it was Murphy's turn to balk. San Francisco was off-limits to Soviet citizens, he reminded Menshikov. Years earlier, protesting the fact that Americans were barred from Vladivostok and other Soviet cities, the State Department had declared that Soviets were barred from San Francisco. Consequently, Murphy said, Khrushchev could tour San Francisco only if Ike could visit Vladivostok.

"But why does the president want to visit Vladivostok?" Menshikov asked, incredulous. "There is nothing there but ice and snow!"

For a while, the two diplomats discussed a Khrushchev family visit to Disneyland. A team of Soviet and American security experts toured the amusement park and reported that security problems would be difficult but "not insurmountable." But Murphy and Menshikov finally decided that the trip would take too much time and, in the words of a State Department memo, "Disneyland was quietly dropped." It would return later, however, in the most flamboyant manner possible.

The thorniest problem was Abilene. Like many visitors to America, Khrushchev had no desire to see Kansas. But Eisenhower had specifically invited him to visit his hometown. How could the premier refuse without insulting the president? After some pondering, Soviet diplomats arrived at a brilliant strategy. In his press conference, Ike had stated that he hoped Khrushchev would talk to people in Abilene who knew "how hard I worked." Therefore, Menshikov told Murphy, traveling to Abilene would be insulting to Ike because it would imply that Khrushchev "did not accept the president's word that as a youth he had worked hard."

Sometimes diplomacy really *is* an art.

After weeks of haggling with Menshikov, Murphy and his colleagues were fed up with the Soviets' intransigence. The problem was "largely psychological," wrote Foy Kohler, the assistant secretary of state, in an internal memo: "It must never be forgotten that the reverse side of Khrushchev's arrogance is the most super-colossal inferiority complex in the world."

Finally, in early September, the two sides agreed on a tentative itinerary. On September 15, Khrushchev would arrive in Washington, where he would be feted at a state dinner at the White House. Then he'd travel to New York to address the United Nations and lay a wreath on FDR's grave. He'd fly to Los Angeles, where he would attend a luncheon at Twentieth Century Fox, then travel to San Francisco to meet with union leaders and tour the headquarters of IBM. He'd fly to Iowa to visit Roswell Garst's farm, then stop off in Pittsburgh to tour a steel mill before heading to Camp David for a few days of talks with Ike.

Eyeballing the itinerary, Bob Considine, the Hearst columnist who had urged Nixon to memorize proverbs, was struck by how much of America Khrushchev was going to miss. He banged out a column headlined "What Mr. K Won't See."

He won't get to meet Toots Shor, Marilyn Monroe, Dizzy Dean, Willie Mays, Miss Rheingold, Gov. Earl Long, or Dracula. He won't see the Yankees the year they lost, hear a college football coach address his captive crew, beat a drum late at night at the Roundtable, get a traffic ticket, pay a tax . . .

The poor square won't ever hear of Steak Row in New York's '40s, or know the heady scents of New Orleans' classic restaurants. He won't be able to slip away from the starch and pomp of his receptions to find a little place in the Village or a night on the town in San Francisco . . .

The poor slob will never see Texas, won't wake up to a desert dawn, will never gasp at the majesty of Niagara Falls. For him, the Mississippi will be a gash in bas-relief, from 30,000 feet, and he'll not know what it has meant. The great and wonderful Southland of the nation will remain a mystery to him, except for use in the future by his propagandists.

Poor misguided fellow. He'll see as little of the U.S. of A. as a Parisian-bound American college boy sees of France.

Considine was wrong on one count. As it turned out, Khrushchev *would* get to meet Marilyn Monroe. And when he did, she would, as instructed, wear a low-cut dress and leave her husband at home.

18. BOOM!

General Nikolai Zakharov and Colonel Vladimir Burdin arrived for the meeting at 3:57 on the afternoon of Wednesday, August 26, accompanied by an aide who took voluminous notes but said nothing. The Russians shook hands with Elmer Hipsley and Keith Lynch, the Americans who were coordinating security for the Khrushchev visit, and then sat down to work.

General Zakharov was the head of the KGB department that protected Soviet leaders. Colonel Burdin was an executive in the American section of the KGB's foreign intelligence directorate. They'd be leading the squad of ten Soviet agents protecting Khrushchev. Determined to leave nothing to chance, the two Soviet security experts demanded to know everything. Was the runway long enough to handle Khrushchev's huge plane? Who would guard the plane when the premier was not in it? When Khrushchev traveled by car, how would he be protected? How many cars would be in the motorcade? How many motorcycles? How many security guards?

Patiently, the Americans answered every question. They even drew a chart to show their procedure for protecting dignitaries in motorcades.

Satisfied with the motorcade procedures, the Soviets announced that they wanted to travel across America to inspect every place Khrushchev would visit. The Americans agreed to arrange their trip and offered to send a State Department security official to accompany them.

General Zakharov asked if there had been any threats on Khrushchev's life.

Yes, Lynch replied, and all of them were being carefully investigated.

For nearly three hours, the general and the colonel asked questions about every conceivable aspect of Khrushchev's security while their aide scribbled notes. When they finished, the general leaned over and whispered something to the colonel in Russian.

"The General wishes to advise you, Mr. Hipsley," Colonel Burdin said, "that any attempt to assassinate Chairman Khrushchev, or the assassination of Chairman Khrushchev, will be viewed as a political crime and will have far-reaching results."

Hipsley assured the colonel that he understood the seriousness of the situation and that every possible precaution would be taken.

The colonel translated this to the general, who again whispered something in Russian.

"The General has said that any such act as this would mean the extermination of us all," the colonel said. "Any act or attempt at assassination would be the end."

To illustrate his point, the colonel raised his hands over his head, then mimed the action of a bomb falling down to the tabletop and exploding in the shape of a mushroom cloud.

"Boom!" he said softly.

19. CONGRESS SOLVES THE PROBLEM

The coming of Khrushchev required the leaders of the House and Senate to decide a very difficult question: Should they invite the Soviet leader to address a joint session of Congress?

Precedent suggested that they should. Since the end of World War II more than thirty foreign leaders had addressed Congress, including the president of Brazil, the king of Belgium, and the queen of the Nether-lands. "Countless presidents and prime ministers have spoken at such ses-sions," wrote Chalmers Roberts in the *Washington Post,* "sometimes to a lot of members who were not even sure what country they came from."

If Khrushchev wasn't invited to address Congress, the Soviets, who were notoriously sensitive about snubs, would no doubt be outraged. Senator Wayne Morse, a Democrat from Oregon, suggested that the premier be invited to address a joint session, and Senator Jacob Javits, a Republican from New York, concurred. Interviewed on *Face the Nation,* J. William Fulbright, chairman of the Senate Foreign Relations Commit-tee, agreed that Khrushchev should be invited—but only if he could be assured of "reasonable courtesy" from Congress.

That was a very big "if." Egged on by the anti-Khrushchev mail, many politicians denounced the very idea of permitting the world leader of godless Communism to sully the sacred halls of Congress. That, said Sen-ator Stephen M. Young of Ohio, would be "abhorrent." House majority leader John W. McCormack announced that he opposed a Khrushchev ad-dress and would not attend if it occurred.

Senator Harry Byrd, the powerful Virginia Democrat, also came out against a Khrushchev speech. "I am one of those Senators who do not be-lieve he should be invited to address a joint session of the Congress," Byrd said as he stood on the back of a truck on his farm, addressing a crowd of 3,500 at his thirty-seventh annual summer picnic. After disposing of the Khrushchev question, Byrd went on to address his usual topics—attacking integration, denouncing miscegenation, and praising the "brave and gal-lant" officials of Virginia's Prince Edward County, who closed their schools rather than integrate them. He also ripped into the Supreme Court for vot-ing to permit Americans to watch the movie *Lady Chatterley's Lover.*

Senator Albert Gore of Tennessee—father of a future vice presi-dent—suggested a compromise: Invite Khrushchev to speak and then hold three days of debate about his speech. But that idea appealed to nei-ther side. The anti-invitation caucus opposed a Khrushchev speech under any circumstances, while pro-invitation politicians feared that three days of vociferous Khrushchev-bashing might incite the premier to launch World War III.

To invite or not to invite? It was a thorny conundrum, but the leaders of Congress were sagacious statesmen. They put their eminent gray heads together, pondered the problem, and arrived at a deceptively simple solution: Congress would simply adjourn and leave Washington before Khrushchev arrived.

It was a stroke of genius. If Congress was not in town, there could be no joint session and the issue was rendered moot. There was only one drawback—the pols would have to work through the Labor Day weekend. But they were willing to make that sacrifice for their country.

In the marathon session that preceded adjournment, Congress passed a foreign aid bill, a public works bill, and—after a filibuster by Senators Strom Thurmond of South Carolina and James O. Eastland of Mississippi—a bill extending the tenure of the Civil Rights Commission.

"Isn't a segregated life the proper life?" Eastland asked Thurmond during their Senate filibuster. "Isn't it the law of nature?"

"That's the way God made the races," replied Thurmond, who had secretly impregnated his teenage black housekeeper decades earlier.

Shortly after 6:00 on the morning of September 15—a few hours before Khrushchev was due to arrive—Congress adjourned amid much celebratory revelry.

"From the House side of the Capitol, calls went out throughout the evening for more ice," noted the *New York Times*, "and an occasional festive whoop came from committee rooms."

20. SHOOT THE MOON

While Congress scrambled to get out of town before Khrushchev's arrival, the Soviet Union fired a shot heard 'round the world.

On the afternoon of September 12, Soviet scientists launched a rocket to the moon. Observatories around the world heard the rocket's radio transmissions and saw the sodium flare it fired as it sped toward the moon at 25,000 miles per hour. About twenty-eight hours after its launch, the final stage of the Lunik II crashed into the moon, 240,000 miles away, depositing a capsule containing a metal pennant bearing an inscription: "The Union of Soviet Socialist Republics. September 1959."

"For the first time in history," the Soviets announced, "a space flight has been achieved from the earth to another celestial body."

The rocket arrived on the moon about forty-one hours before Khrushchev was scheduled to arrive in Washington. A Soviet spokesman said that was a "happy coincidence" but nobody believed him. Everyone understood that the moon shot was a propaganda ploy, a dramatic feat of pyrotechnics, some flash and dazzle to wow the crowds before Khrushchev stepped onstage.

During the cold war, rockets and missiles had become weapons in a never-ending propaganda war. Three months earlier, on June 8, 1959, the United States had scored a propaganda coup by stuffing a mailbox full of letters into the nose of the Regulus I missile and firing the missile from a nuclear submarine submerged off the coast of Florida to an Air Force base near Jacksonville. It was a clever publicity stunt but it didn't compare to shooting the moon, and the Soviets couldn't resist gloating about the powerful fuel that propelled their rocket.

"Apparently, the United States does not yet possess such a fuel," Radio Moscow said, "because this year it abandoned attempts to launch a moon rocket after its four failures between August and December 1958."

That casual insult referred to the American space program's frequent public failures. In 1957, the Vanguard rocket carrying America's first satellite rose about six inches off its launching pad before exploding in flames. In August 1958, America's first attempt to put a satellite around the moon lasted seventy-seven seconds before the lunar vehicle exploded. Two months later, a second rocket soared 71,300 miles into space—and then plummeted back to earth.

Now Vice President Nixon assured Americans that there was no reason to become "hysterical" over the Soviet moon shot. "It's nothing to get excited about," he said. "Scientifically and educationally, we are way ahead of the Soviets." The Russians had failed to hit the moon "three times in the last two weeks" before they finally succeeded, Nixon said, although he did not reveal the source of that information.

"Overall," Nixon told the American people, "we are way ahead."

American scientists didn't agree. "I think we were behind them two years ago and we're farther behind them now," said Dr. Murray Zelikoff, former head of the Air Force's Cambridge Research Center. "I don't honestly see how we're going to catch them."

The Soviet success in hitting the moon left no doubt, rocket scientists said, that the Russians could also hit any target on earth. "This would mean," reported the *New York Journal American*, "that Red rocketeers could pinpoint the borough of their choosing—Manhattan, Brooklyn, Queens, Bronx or Staten Island—and plaster it with ICBMs."

The revelation that the Russians could annihilate any city in the United States caused a massive outbreak of UFO sightings in southern California.

"Whether Lunik II's landing on the moon or Nikita Khrushchev's impending landing on American soil was the cause, hundreds of persons suddenly began hearing and seeing things they hadn't heard or seen before," the *Los Angeles Times* reported. "The typical comment, according to officers, was: *'Something of a frightful nature is going on.'*"

21. A FUNNY LITTLE MAN

The world's tallest airplane left Moscow at seven o'clock on the morning of September 15, 1959, carrying Nikita Khrushchev, his wife and children, and a party of fifty-four, including aides, diplomats, bodyguards and a team of technicians assigned to monitor the "microscopic cracks" in the TU–114's engines.

Khrushchev's son Sergei, an engineer in the Soviet missile program, had warned his father that it wasn't safe to fly on the TU–114, but the dictator was determined to show off his gargantuan plane. His uneasy underlings ordered all Soviet ships in the Atlantic to maintain constant radio contact with the TU–114. And they instructed the plane's pilots that in the event of engine failure, they should dive toward the nearest Soviet ship, although nobody was sure what the ships could actually *do* if the plane plopped into the ocean.

As the plane flew westward, the technicians sat in the cabin, listening to the engine through tubes that resembled stethoscopes and staring at a control panel that bristled with knobs, each knob monitored by a red and green light. Flashing green lights meant the engine was working properly; flashing red lights would indicate trouble.

"The presence of these people and the unusual equipment installed in the passenger salon caused some nervousness," Sergei Khrushchev later recalled. "We were drawn, as if by magnets, to their boxes, checking to make sure that no red lights went on. We couldn't forget those microscopic cracks."

The anxious passengers had apparently forgotten what the Soviet press eagerly reminded the people back home: The plane was propelled by a mystical power, "carried across the ocean not only by its mighty engines . . . but by the solicitous and considerate strength of millions of Soviet toilers, of all progressive people on earth, by their indomitable and passionate desire for peace."

The churning of the plane's four huge turboprops created a loud humming inside the cabin, which prevented many passengers from falling asleep but not Khrushchev. When he awoke, the sun was up and he was nearing his destination.

"All sorts of thoughts went through my head as I looked out the window at the ocean below," he recalled in his memoir. "I was about to meet with the leader of the country which represented the biggest military threat in the world. . . . In a few minutes, we would be face to face with America, the America I'd read about in Ilf and Petrov and Gorky—now

I'd be able to see it with my own eyes, to touch it with my own fingers. All this put me on my guard, and my nerves were strained with excitement."

Shortly after noon on Tuesday, September 15, the plane began its descent over Maryland and Khrushchev caught his first glimpse of the reception awaiting him at Andrews Air Force Base.

Below, on a concrete runway, a crowd of 3,000 waited in the sweltering September sun. President Eisenhower was among them, his face uncharacteristically glum under his gray Stetson. Nearby stood a 56-piece military band, a 120-member military honor guard and the four 75-millimeter howitzers that would fire the 21-gun salute that Menshikov had demanded so relentlessly.

A 125-foot-long red carpet sliced across the white concrete. Gus Bagatelos, an Army private described by his commander as "our best sweeper," stood bearing an official Army broom. A bit of a ham, Bagatelos wielded his broom like a rifle as he marched ceremoniously down the long carpet. When he reached the end, he stopped, swung his broom into position and began to back slowly down the carpet, sweeping with crisp military precision until he reached the other end.

As Khrushchev's plane swooped down toward the runway, everybody looked up to stare at it and Private Bagatelos furtively raised one edge of the red carpet and swept his pile of dirt underneath it.

The TU–114 hit the runway at high speed, its tires emitting puffs of blue smoke as the pilot pumped the brakes. Engines roaring, the plane screamed past the waiting dignitaries to the end of the runway, turned around and lumbered back. The Americans rolled out the huge stairway they'd constructed for the TU–114 and Khrushchev descended. Eisenhower greeted him when he stepped to the bottom.

"Welcome to the United States, Mr. Chairman," the president said with a wan smile. Ike looked, as one reporter noted, "as if he were faced with a visit from unwelcome in-laws."

As the two most powerful men in the world walked down the red carpet, an amazed Army wife standing nearby muttered, "What a funny little man!"

She was right. The dictator of the world's largest country was a short, fat bald guy with a major pot belly. He was decked out in a black suit, a custom-made white shirt with French cuffs, gold cuff links and a white silk tie with a thin blue stripe running down the center. On his right breast two gold medals glimmered in the sun—the Lenin Peace Prize and the Red Banner of Labor.

Khrushchev smiled broadly, his blue eyes twinkling. He introduced Ike to his wife, Nina Petrovna Khrushcheva, a short, stout woman with a grandmotherly face and a warm smile. An orgy of handshaking erupted, as everyone in Khrushchev's party pumped the palms of everybody in Ike's entourage. Smiling Mike Menshikov, ever unctuous, slapped his boss's palm with theatrical exuberance, saying, "Nikita Sergeyevitch, I salute you on American soil."

The howitzers boomed twenty-one times and the military band played the Soviet national anthem, followed by the "Star-Spangled Banner." When the music ended, the president led the premier on a ceremonial inspection of the troops. Khrushchev eyed the enemy soldiers and said something in Russian. An interpreter translated, "These are nice-looking boys."

Eisenhower nodded, took Khrushchev's arm and guided him to the platform for the official speechifying. The president spoke first, reading a dry, formal greeting: "Our common purpose should be a just, universal and enduring peace."

As Ike droned on, Khrushchev began mugging shamelessly, reprising some of the scene-stealing gestures he'd used to upstage Nixon in Moscow two months earlier. He held his homburg over his face like a sunshade. He waved to the crowd and winked at a little girl. He theatrically turned his head to watch a butterfly flutter by. And he did it all, wrote Warren Rogers in the *New York Herald Tribune,* "with the studied nonchalance of an old vaudeville trouper."

When Ike finished, Khrushchev waddled to the lectern to deliver his speech. It began diplomatically enough, with words of thanks and hopes for peace. But it wasn't long before the chairman brought up the moon launch. "On the eve of our meeting with you, Mr. President, Soviet scientists, engineers, technicians and workers gladdened us by launching a rocket to the moon," he said. "We do not doubt that the splendid scientists, engineers and workers of the United States will likewise deliver their emblem to the moon. The Soviet emblem, an old resident of the moon, will welcome your emblem and they will live in peace and friendship."

Khrushchev smiled. He was a man who enjoyed public acknowledgment of his greatness and he reveled in the pomp and splendor of this ceremony. "Everything was shining and glittering," he marveled in his memoir. "Those Americans really know how to lay on a reception."

Eisenhower escorted Mr. and Mrs. Khrushchev to a waiting Lincoln convertible for the ride to Washington. The plan called for Nina Khrushchev to sit in the middle of the backseat with her husband on one side and Ike on the other. But somehow Ike ended up in the middle, squeezed uncomfortably between the two portly Russians. In photos in the next day's newspapers, the president looked grim, "as if the CIA had advised him," journalist I. F. Stone wrote, "to keep his famous smile carefully hidden lest the visiting Old Bolshevik expropriate it."

The limousine set off, following a roaring phalanx of motorcycle cops. On the fifteen-mile ride into Washington, the two leaders passed an estimated 200,000 people, but the crowds were curiously subdued. They didn't cheer. They didn't jeer. They just stood there, silently watching as the leaders passed.

"People were looking at us," Khrushchev noted, "as if we were some kind of oddity."

American reporters struggled to explain the strange silence of the crowds. Columnist David Lawrence called it "the spontaneous expression of people who feared that the man they were watching might someday push a button and start a war." Murray Kempton of the *New York Post* theorized that in the age of the cue card, Americans had lost the ability to act on their own impulses: "No one had held up an idiot card and we are no longer a spontaneous people." George Dixon, the *Washington Post*'s droll local columnist, admitted that he too was confused about how to greet a Communist dictator who'd vowed to bury us: "I didn't know whether to cheer wildly, applaud perfunctorily or just stand there emitting little sounds that could be translated as anything."

The Soviet newspapers had no problem explaining the silence because the crowds in their stories were euphoric.

"Shouts rolled up like waves," reported *Pravda*, the Communist Party's daily paper.

"Washington had never before seen anything like this," reported *Izvestia*, the official Soviet government newspaper, which noted that the huge crowds greeted Khrushchev with "outbursts of applause."

"One had to see the smiles on the faces of the Americans lining the route, hear their joyous cheers and applause . . . to realize with what gladness, warmth and cordiality the inhabitants of the American capital welcomed Khrushchev," gushed *Sovietskaya Rossia*. "Indeed, the expectations of some that the welcome would be reserved—even cold—collapsed like a soap bubble."

22. CHOPPER OVER BURNING TREE

Khrushchev's first meal in America was a sumptuous lunch at Blair House, the official presidential guest residence—fillet of beef with truffles, potatoes, string beans, and a Charlotte Russe praline with raspberry sauce. He was just finishing when he received his first visitor—Henry Cabot Lodge, the American ambassador to the United Nations and the man Ike had selected to be Khrushchev's tour guide on his odyssey across America.

Few men on earth had less in common: Khrushchev was a short, pudgy, uneducated Russian peasant who'd climbed to power by tenacity and brutality; Lodge was a tall, thin, Harvard-educated Boston Brahmin who'd been born into America's aristocracy, scion of one of the families immortalized in an old New England toast:

> *Here's to good old Boston,*
> *Home of the bean and the cod,*
> *Where the Lowells speak only to the Cabots*
> *And the Cabots speak only to God.*

Lodge's ancestors included six U.S. senators, a secretary of state, a Civil War general, and a governor of Massachusetts. His grandfather and namesake, Senator Henry Cabot Lodge, was the dour Republican famous for leading the forces that crushed Woodrow Wilson's hopes that the United States would join the newly formed League of Nations after World War I.

Growing up, Lodge picked mulberries in Henry James's garden, rode horses with George Patton, and visited Edith Wharton's house in France, where he lived with his family for two years, studying French. In the 1920s, he worked as a newsman, writing for the *Boston Transcript* and the *New York Herald-Tribune*. In 1936, after a brief stint in the Massachusetts legislature, he was elected to his grandfather's old seat in the U.S. Senate. Witty, friendly, and popular, Lodge was a liberal Republican who supported many of FDR's New Deal programs. During the war, he resigned from the Senate, to serve in the Army in Europe. After the war, he won reelection to the Senate, but he was defeated in 1952 by a rich, handsome young war hero named John F. Kennedy. In 1953, Eisenhower appointed Lodge ambassador to the United Nations, which was, ironically, the successor to the League of Nations that his grandfather had fought so fiercely.

When Ike picked Lodge instead of Nixon to serve as Khrushchev's guide, pundits speculated that the president was indicating his choice of a successor. Actually, Ike's reasoning was far less Machiavellian. He simply figured that the diplomatic Lodge was less likely than Nixon to get into any eye-gouging, ear-biting brawls with Khrushchev.

When Lodge arrived at Blair House, he introduced himself to his future traveling companion and asked if there was anything he could do.

Khrushchev looked up at Lodge—who at six feet four inches stood a foot higher than the Russian—and smiled. "Before coming over here, I read your speeches," Khrushchev said. "And after I read them, I thought I would be scared of you, but now that I have been with you, talked with you, and seen what a nice man you are, I don't feel scared any more."

That was baloney, of course—any man who'd endured Stalin's murderous whims would hardly be frightened by Lodge's U.N. oratory—but at least it was good-natured, friendly baloney.

"Mr. Lodge, I want you to understand one thing," Khrushchev continued, still smiling playfully. "I have not come to the United States to learn anything about America. We know all we need to know about America and we learn it through our Marxist instruction."

Now it was Lodge's turn to smile "Thank you for telling me, Mr. Chairman," he said. "We will do our utmost to comply with your wishes."

Having spent his entire life around politicians, Lodge quickly sized up Khrushchev as a master of the breed. "His personal magnetism was immediately felt," he later recalled. "Here was a natural politician—a man who, on entering a room full of strangers, would, after a few hours, have persuaded some, charmed and amused others, and frightened still more, so that by the end of the day, he would have over 50 percent of their votes."

The premier informed the ambassador that they had both been generals during the war but Khrushchev had been a higher-ranking general. "Therefore you're my subordinate," he said, smiling, "and I'll expect you to behave as befits a junior officer."

Lodge laughed. "Yes, sir," he said. He stood at attention and saluted crisply. "General Lodge, reporting for duty, sir!"

They'd been bantering for only a few minutes but already the short, fat Russian dictator and the tall, skinny Boston Brahmin had created a comedy team—a cold war version of Laurel & Hardy or Abbott & Costello. Lodge escorted Khrushchev outside, where they climbed into the waiting limousine, accompanied by Menshikov, Soviet foreign minister Andrei

Gromyko, and Khrushchev's translator, Oleg Troyanovsky. After a journey of a few hundred yards, the limo stopped. They'd reached their destination—the White House.

Inside, Eisenhower and Nixon were waiting for them. Grinning, Khrushchev presented the president with a gift. He'd wanted to give it to Ike back at the airport in front of the TV cameras, but his aides talked him out of it. Eisenhower opened the elegant wooden box and found a model of the *Lunik II* space capsule that had recently hit the moon.

The president was astounded. Was this man really rubbing his nose in the moon shot twice on the same afternoon? "This seemed, at first, a strange gift," he later wrote, "but then it occurred to me that quite possibly the man was completely sincere."

Eisenhower led his guests into a room where they could sit comfortably on armchairs and couches. There wasn't enough time for substantive discussions, he said, but at least they could talk about what issues they would discuss at Camp David when Khrushchev returned from his road trip. Obviously, Ike said, Berlin would be one topic.

Khrushchev agreed and suggested another issue—disarmament. "We believe that you do not want war," he said, "and we assume that you also believe this about us."

"I see no profit in mutual suicide," Ike replied.

"The main thing is to establish trust," Khrushchev continued. "Probably we can't take each other's word at this time but we must try to bring about trust. There is no other way."

As the meeting went on, one topic flowed into another. Khrushchev mentioned the speech that he was scheduled to deliver at the United Nations in a few days but refused to reveal any details about it.

"Here is my speech," he said, tapping his jacket pocket, "and no one is going to see it."

But there was one speech that the chairman *did* want to discuss—the speech Nixon had delivered the previous day. Khrushchev had read a translation on the plane.

Sitting across the room, Nixon said he was proud to hear that.

The speech was clearly calculated to arouse anti-Soviet animosity, Khrushchev said, angrily. "After having read that speech, I am surprised to find on arriving here that people in the United States welcomed us with such tolerance and obvious friendliness," he said. "In the Soviet Union, there would have been no welcome whatsoever if I had, in advance, publicly spoken against the visitor."

"That," Ike said, "is the basic difference between our two systems."

It was the perfect comeback. But Nixon, being Nixon, couldn't resist saying more.

You delivered an anti-American speech before my arrival in Moscow, Nixon said.

My speech was not nearly as provocative as yours, Khrushchev replied.

It was just like old times: Nixon and Khrushchev squabbling again. Eisenhower must have felt like a kindergarten teacher trapped with a couple of bickering brats.

"*You* read the speeches," Khrushchev told Ike. "*You* be the judge."

Years later, Eisenhower was still amused at that. "To add to the snowballing comedy of the situation," he wrote, "Mr. Khrushchev suggested that I be the referee as to which speeches were more provocative."

Eisenhower led Khrushchev outside to the South Lawn, where two Marine helicopters squatted like big green dragonflies. Ike loved helicopters and he was eager to take Khrushchev on a ride over Washington at rush hour. It was an ideal way to show off America's economic power by pointing out the long lines of workers driving their private cars to their private homes in the suburbs. Ike had suggested the ride in his press conference a month earlier and Murphy repeated the suggestion to Menshikov countless times. But Smiling Mike always rejected it, claiming that Khrushchev had no desire to waste time on helicopter rides.

But the president persisted. On the ride in from the airport, Ike told Khrushchev that he hoped the premier would join him for a helicopter ride over the city.

"Oh," Khrushchev replied, "if you're going to be in the same helicopter, of course, I will go."

Instantly Ike realized what the problem had been. Khrushchev feared that the helicopter ride might be a trick, that the chopper would suffer some sort of nonaccidental "accident." But of course that wouldn't happen if Eisenhower was aboard. It reminded Ike of another incident, this one back in 1945, shortly after the end of the war. He'd offered his friend Georgi Zhukov, the Soviet general, the use of an American plane. Zhukov hesitated, then asked, "May your son go as my aide?" Ike agreed and Zhukov smiled. "With your plane and your son going with me, I know I shall be quite safe."

Such was the paranoia inspired by working for Josef Stalin.

Once inside one of the choppers, Eisenhower offered Khrushchev a window seat and spread a map of Washington across the premier's lap. The chopper's rotors whirled and it slowly rose into the sky. Khrushchev grinned and waved his homburg for the photographers.

As the helicopter lifted off, Chalmers Roberts, the *Washington Post*'s White House correspondent, called his wife, Lois, at their home overlooking the Potomac River. Roberts figured the chopper would fly over the river as it headed toward the Maryland suburbs. He knew something that he suspected the Secret Service might not realize. For days, workers building a fish ladder in the Potomac had been blasting rock out of the riverbed with dynamite.

"Go out and have a look," he told his wife.

She hustled outside and saw the helicopter carrying the two most powerful men on the planet pass over the river, flying north. A few moments later, as she watched in horror, an explosion in the river blasted large chunks of rock into the sky. Fortunately, none of them hit the chopper, which passed overhead and rumbled safely into Maryland.

Ike pointed out the cars on the roads below—their red brake lights flashing on and off in the stop-and-go traffic. Soon the helicopter flew over a big green meadow, one of Ike's favorite places—the golf course at the Burning Tree Country Club.

The president asked the chairman if he played golf. Khrushchev said he knew nothing about it. Eager to show the premier his favorite sport, Ike told the pilot to drop a little lower. The chopper swooped down over the sixteenth green, where the noise and wind of the rotors caused a golfer to muff an easy four-inch putt.

By sheer coincidence, the golfer was Senator J. William Fulbright, who had invited Khrushchev to tea with the Senate Foreign Relations Committee the next day.

The premier was not as impressed by America's traffic jams as Ike had hoped, nor was he thrilled by the sight of grown men whacking a little white ball around a manicured meadow. But he *loved* the helicopter. If this was the modern statesman's latest status symbol, Khrushchev wanted one. In fact, he wanted more than one.

When he got home, the premier placed an order for three helicopters, specifying that he wanted them to be just like Ike's.

23. WHITE TIE AND TAILS

There comes a moment in every man's life when he must take a stand. Will he stick to his principles or will he blindly follow the crowd?

For Nikita Sergeyevich Khrushchev, such a moment came on his first night in America, and he did not waver, he did not falter, he did not compromise his principles. He resolutely refused to wear white tie and tails to the state dinner held in his honor at the White House.

Instead, he wore a dark business suit with a gray tie.

Fortunately he was not the only male at the dinner who refused to wear white tie and tails. One of the perquisites of being a dictator is that when you stand on principle, you can force your underlings to stand on the same principle. Consequently all the other men in the Soviet delegation also wore dark suits, even Smiling Mike Menshikov, who always wore white tie and tails to these affairs when his boss wasn't around.

Khrushchev's sartorial dissent caused much tongue-clucking and brow-furrowing among the kind of people who worry about what clothes dictators wear to formal dinners, but he really had no choice. A true Communist simply could not, in good conscience, wear white tie and tails. After the Russian revolution, the Bolsheviks discarded the necktie as a symbol of decadent capitalism. Later the revolutionaries mellowed and began to wear ties, but Khrushchev must have figured that if the head of the Communist Party of the Soviet Union donned a white bow tie, a starched white shirt, and a swallow-tailed black coat, the mummified corpse of Lenin would roll over in its see-through mausoleum in Red Square. Khrushchev also believed that the formal gown was another symbol of bourgeois decadence. Accordingly, his daughters, Rada and Yulia, wore informal white dresses to the dinner while his wife wore a simple blue dress.

"Did you know that they're going to wear business suits and street dresses to a full state dinner?" First Lady Mamie Eisenhower asked the White House head usher that night. "My husband would just as soon dress that way, too, if I'd let him."

When the Khrushchevs arrived at the White House, the First Lady greeted them wearing an elegant full-length Scaasi gown. She escorted them upstairs to the family quarters where her husband, dressed in tie and tails, thought the dictator's wife and daughters seemed embarrassed at Khrushchev's sartorial edict: "The women, being feminine even though Communist, were obviously uncomfortable."

After cocktails in the private quarters the group proceeded downstairs to the state dining room, where the drapes were gold, as were the flowers, and candlelight glistened off the antique gold table settings. Amid this splendor, Khrushchev mingled with America's political and financial elite—the Speaker of the House, the secretaries of state, defense, and agriculture, the presidents of the New York Stock Exchange and the U.S. Chamber of Commerce, and heiress Perle Mesta, the famous "hostess with the mostest," who arrived with her "date," FBI director J. Edgar Hoover.

Khrushchev and Hoover may have seemed like two men with nothing in common, but in fact they were the two largest contributors to the Communist Party of the United States. Khrushchev funded the party with secret subsidies—$250,000 in 1959. Hoover funded it with the dues paid by the FBI agents he sent to spy on the party. "He kept it alive: his informants were nearly the only ones that paid the party dues," recalled William Hundley, a Justice Department lawyer who prosecuted Communists in the 1950s. One day, Hundley was poring through yet another dull FBI report on yet another tedious Communist meeting when something interesting caught his eye. "I came across a line where a guy jumped up and said, 'Let's cut out all the bull. When are we going to start the revolution?' I got excited and ran to the FBI supervisor. All the agents had a big huddle, and they came back and said, 'Well, you can't use that. That's one of our informants.'"

Unfortunately, neither Khrushchev nor Hoover mentioned their Communist connection. When Russia's top Communist shook hands with America's top Communist hunter, their brief conversation went like this:

Khrushchev: "I feel like I know you."

Hoover: "I feel like I know you too."

At one point, Nixon introduced the premier to Senator Lyndon Johnson, who was, Nixon pointed out, the leader of the opposition party.

Khrushchev scoffed. "I've never been able to see any difference between your two parties," he said.

Khrushchev was also introduced to Allen Dulles, the director of the Central Intelligence Agency, and the two men discussed the fine points of the espionage trade.

"You, Mr. Chairman, may have seen some of my intelligence reports from time to time," Dulles said, smiling.

"I believe we get the same reports," Khrushchev replied. "And probably from the same people."

"Maybe we should pool our efforts," Dulles said.

"Yes," Khrushchev agreed, "we should buy our intelligence data together and save money. We'd have to pay the people only once."

After the guests were seated, the president rose to toast the premier. Eisenhower was not happy about toasting the man who kept threatening to gobble up West Berlin. In a meeting a week earlier, Ike told Secretary Herter that he wanted to skip the toast altogether. After much discussion, Ike agreed to bow to protocol, but he decided to make his toast as bland as possible.

"Because of our strength, because of our importance in the world, it is vital that we understand each other better," the president said, holding his champagne glass aloft. "In the hope that that effort will be successful, I ask this company to join me in a toast to you, Mr. Chairman."

Unlike Ike, Khrushchev did not strive for blandness in his toast. "Our countries are much too strong and we cannot quarrel with each other," he said. "If we were weak countries, then it would be another matter, because when the weak quarrel, they are just scratching each other's faces and it takes just a couple of days with a cosmetician and everything comes out right again. But if we quarrel, then not only *our* countries can suffer colossal damage but the other countries of the world will also be involved in a world shambles."

The dinner was billed as an "all-American" affair and the menu reflected that theme—roast turkey with cranberry sauce, cornbread stuffing, and a salad slathered with Green Goddess dressing. Guests washed the victuals down with champagne and three varieties of wine.

For the evening's entertainment, Ike had hired his favorite band—a jazzy pop combo called Fred Waring and His Pennsylvanians. Billed as "the man who taught America how to sing," Waring had been a star for three decades, appearing on radio, on television, and in movies. Among his greatest hits was the song "I Scream, You Scream, We all Scream for Ice Cream," a title that probably loses something when translated into Russian. Waring was also the genius behind the famous Waring blender, which he promoted at every gig, selling more than a million of them.

Now, as Khrushchev looked on, Waring launched into a peppy, perky, toe-tapping version of "Zip-A-Dee-Doo-Dah," a song that seemed to embody the can-do spirit of America's postwar optimism, and some of Ike's more inebriated guests began to sing along.

24. IN THE ROILING CAULDRON

In the roiling cauldron of American society, Khrushchev's arrival caused several odd events to occur:

A huge white cross appeared in the sky over Washington, created by a skywriter hired by an anti-Communist group called Christianform.

In New York, a Hungarian refugee climbed to the top of the Statue of Liberty and draped a blindfold over Lady Liberty's eyes so she would not have to gaze upon "this murderer, Khrushchev."

In Mississippi, a woman gave birth to her eighth child and, at the suggestion of her doctor, named the baby Nikita.

A Philadelphia restaurant sent fifty pounds of borscht-flavored ice cream to the Blair House for the dictator's delectation, and the National Institute of Dry Cleaning announced that Khrushchev and his entire party would receive free dry cleaning for the duration of their American trip.

The House Committee on Un-American Activities subpoenaed Arnold S. Johnson, the legislative director of the Communist Party of the United States, to testify about a cross-country trip he had allegedly made to collect unfavorable information on the cities Khrushchev was scheduled to visit.

At a Washington hotel where members of Khrushchev's entourage were staying, FBI agents seized a guest who was overheard speaking into a phone in the lobby, saying, "I'm sending up two storm troopers and some ammunition." The man was released when he explained that he was speaking to his friend upstairs in a code that meant, "I'm sending up two blondes and a bottle of booze."

In the lobby of Washington's Statler-Hilton Hotel, Americans gathered to play a game that the *Washington Star* dubbed "Russian-Spotting." The object was to identify Russians who wandered past. A Boston man claimed he could pick out the Russians because their trouser legs were wider. A Wisconsin man said he could identify the Russians because they held their cigarettes between the thumb and forefinger, unlike Americans, who held their cigarettes between the forefinger and middle finger. Three female workers from the Interior Department said the Russian women were easily identifiable by their size, which was large.

"We're no slim chicks," said an Interior employee, "but after seeing some of the Russian women, we decided we'd do very well in Russia."

Finally, there was the news story that appeared in the *New York Daily Mirror* under this headline:

SEES K ON
TV, SO HE
MURDERS 2

Nevada, Iowa, Sept 16 (UPI)—A university honor student confessed today he got an "urge to kill" a mother and her adopted daughter with his bare hands while watching Nikita S. Khrushchev on television.

Barry Neal McDaniel, rated a brilliant mathematics and physics student at Iowa State University, was charged with the strangulation of Mrs. Monice Irene Larson, 25, and the suffocation of her 4-months-old adopted daughter, Kimery Anne, yesterday.

McDaniel, 20, was brought from the University community of Ames, Iowa, where the killings took place, and locked up in the county jail here.

McDaniel told his lawyer, Frank Lounsberry, that he got the "urge to kill" as he watched the televised accounts of the arrival of Soviet Premier Khrushchev in Washington.

25. ANIMAL HUSBANDRY

Promptly at 9:00 the next morning, Henry Cabot Lodge arrived outside Blair House with a motorcade, ready to take Khrushchev to the U.S. Agricultural Research Center in Beltsville, Maryland, where the chairman could demonstrate his prowess at two skills required of politicians all over the world—enduring hideous boredom and fondling animals.

For innumerable centuries, chiefs, princes and potentates have attempted to impress distinguished visitors by showing off the bounty of their crops and livestock. In the twentieth century, American officials liked to take such visitors to Beltsville, an 11,000-acre government farm with thousands of animals and endless amber waves of grain, plus 950 buildings and 53 miles of roads, as well as a prototype grocery store of the future and several test kitchens, including one devoted entirely to the art of creating a better potato chip. In Beltsville, 2,000 federal employees labored, creating hybrid seeds, cross-breeding livestock, and developing new weed killers, including one called 2,4-D, which was tested for toxicity by Dr. Ezra J. Kraus, a Beltsville scientist who ate a capsule of the stuff every day for three weeks and lived to tell the tale.

Beltsville was a Mecca for newspaper feature writers seeking gee-whiz science stories—sows bred so that they wouldn't sunburn, colonies of "super-cockroaches" created to test new pesticides, and an experimental variety of golf course grass touted as "almost divot-proof." Beltsville was also a pilgrimage site for politicians eager to pose for pictures that proved their zeal for aiding America's farmers. In 1953, President Eisenhower made the pilgrimage to Beltsville, where he was photographed feigning intense interest in a newfangled egg-sorting machine.

At 9:39 on Wednesday, September 16, Nikita Khrushchev—a politician who liked to brag about his agricultural expertise—arrived for his photo-op. He was greeted by agriculture secretary Ezra Taft Benson, who tried to conceal his hatred of the man he had called "this atheistic murderer." A member of the Quorum of the Twelve Apostles, the ruling body of the Mormon Church, sixty-year-old Benson was a supporter of the ultraconservative John Birch Society and a man given to frequent rhetorical denunciations of what he called "creeping socialism and godless Communism." But Benson did share two traits with Khrushchev—both men had worked as shepherds in their youth, and neither missed an opportunity to remind people of that fact.

Benson led Khrushchev into an auditorium and then delivered a welcoming speech expounding the glories of capitalist agriculture. "Capitalism," he said, "has enabled American farmers to develop an agriculture unequaled anywhere in the world in total efficiency, productivity and prosperity."

It was an odd venue for touting capitalist agriculture—a huge government farm employing 2,000 federal bureaucrats. As Benson understood, American agriculture was a hybrid of capitalism and socialism. The farm crisis of the 1930s had spawned countless government agricultural programs—a complex system of subsidies, price supports and direct federal payments to farmers for not planting crops. Consequently, American farmers were no longer the independent yeomen of yore. The only thing farmers hated more than hearing that they were dependent on government subsidies was hearing politicians threaten to cut their government subsidies. Benson learned that lesson in 1957, when he traveled to the National Corn Picking Contest in South Dakota to deliver a speech opposing farm price supports, and angry farmers pelted him with eggs.

At Beltsville, Benson finished his long oratorical ode to American farmers ("free, efficient, creative and hard-working") and then introduced three scientists in white lab coats, who proceeded to lecture on their research. The first discoursed on "plant response to light." The second lectured on "selective post-emergence chemical control of broadleaved weeds." The third explained "the growth of fruits and vegetables by chemical stimulators."

It was dull in the original English and no doubt equally dull in the Russian translation. Together, the ordeal was excruciating. Was Benson trying to bore this "atheistic murderer" into submission?

If so, his effort was futile. Soviet Communism was the world's foremost producer of four-hour speeches and Khrushchev knew how to suffer them in silence. Despite his jetlag, he managed to keep his eyes open and stifle his yawns.

When the lectures were over, Benson invited Khrushchev to go outside into the fresh air and mingle with livestock. The premier perked up. Cows have their faults but lecturing is not among them. Benson asked the chairman if his wife and daughters would prefer to visit the home economics center.

"They can decide," Khrushchev replied, missing no opportunity to make propaganda. "We have freedom in our country."

At that, everybody looked at Nina Khrushchev. "We want to see what he sees," she said, smiling.

So they all headed outside, followed by a frenzied mob of photographers who were sick of shooting pictures of guys shaking hands and eager to shoot pictures of Khrushchev petting animals. The first stop was a field of prize Holsteins. Grinning in his white summer suit, Khrushchev caressed a cow's back. Dozens of cameras clicked.

From the cow pasture, Benson lead the mob to the pigpen, where he showed off a collection of enormous hogs. Khrushchev patted one on the rump and said it was too fat. No, their meat is lean, Benson replied, and he promised to prove it. A scientist appeared, bearing a device that measured a pig's fat content with ultrasound waves. But the pig wiggled and the scientist had trouble attaching the gizmo to its back.

"He wants to keep his fat a secret," the portly dictator said, grinning. "Maybe he is ashamed of it."

After a visit to the sheep pen, Benson led the crowd to inspect the pride of the farm—the Beltsville small white turkey, a diminutive but meaty bird bred for housewives with small families. Khrushchev wasn't impressed. "That's what you get for being so rich and fat," he said, laughing. "You start looking for small turkeys."

"That's what our people want," Benson said, "and we give it to them."

"In Russia," Khrushchev replied, "we try to make our turkeys bigger and bigger."

Benson reached into the cage, pulled out a turkey, and handed it to Khrushchev. Grinning, the dictator grabbed the bird's legs and held it upside down, stroking its belly. Squirming and wiggling, the turkey struggled to break free, but Khrushchev held on tight. It was, come to think of it, a pretty good metaphor for his policy toward Hungary.

"The turkey certainly doesn't like being handled this way," Khrushchev said, laughing.

Cameras fired like machine guns. "One more," the photographers yelled. "One more! One more!"

In the midst of this madness, a reporter shoved a microphone in Nina Khrushchev's face and asked if she had a message for the American people.

"Thank you very much for your good welcome," replied Mrs. Khrushchev, a former teacher of Marxist economics who spoke fairly fluent English. "Thank you for your invitation to the United States."

Immediately, a posse of reporters stampeded toward the Soviet First Lady, hollering questions.

How do you like Washington?

"It is so beautiful and green," she said, smiling.

How do you like Mrs. Eisenhower?

"She is very courteous and kind and a good hostess."

"Do you have a great influence on Mr. Khrushchev?" a wise guy bellowed. "Women rule the world, you know."

She laughed. "That may be true with American women, but it is not so in my case."

Before long, Soviet security guards swarmed in to break up the impromptu press conference and take Mrs. Khrushchev back to her limousine. The reporters followed, yelling more questions. In the confusion, Mrs. Khrushchev headed for the wrong limo, but a tall police sergeant wearing a white helmet and sunglasses came to her rescue.

"I'll take you to the right car," said Sergeant E. E. Skinner. He took her by the hand and together they walked to her limousine, grinning like schoolyard sweethearts. Dozens of cameras clicked, creating photos that would appear in hundreds of newspapers the next day—portraits of a smiling fifty-nine-year-old grandmother with a pleasantly plump face that would, columnist Ralph McGill suggested, cause thousands of Americans to say, "You know, she looks a lot like Mama."

"Wonderful American police," she said, patting Sergeant Skinner's hand as she ducked into her limo.

Her husband slid into another car, sitting next to Lodge. As they headed back to Washington for his speech at the National Press Club, Khrushchev marveled at American journalism.

"If I could have done it," he told Lodge, "I suppose your photographers would have had me lift a cow."

26. QUESTION SIZZLES NIKI

Stalin was a paranoiac, an egomaniac, a coward, Khrushchev said. Stalin was a tyrant, a brute, a mass murderer.

Stalin was a "despotic character" who demanded "absolute submission to his opinion." Stalin crafted a self-glorifying "cult of personality." He denounced loyal Communists as "enemies of the people" and then ordered them tortured until they signed false confessions. "Stalin personally called the investigative judge, gave him instructions, advised him on which investigative methods should be used," Khrushchev said. "These methods were simple—beat, beat, and once again beat."

Khrushchev did not denounce Stalin in 1959 in Washington, where such sentiments inevitably won applause. He denounced Stalin in 1956 in Moscow, where such heresy was a crime against the state.

Khrushchev had only recently ascended to power when he made his speech to the Twentieth Congress of the Soviet Communist Party. On the last day of the congress, as foreign delegates were heading home, the Soviet delegates were summoned to a secret session. For four hours, they listened

in amazement as Khrushchev attacked the man whom he—and they—
had previously praised as "our dear father," "our wise teacher," and "the
greatest genius of all times and nations."

Khrushchev decried Stalin's execution of "tens of thousands of Party
and Soviet workers" (though not the execution of anti-Communists,
which was apparently acceptable). Before World War II, Stalin killed
many of his best military officers, Khrushchev said. During the war, Stalin
issued foolish orders that resulted in the deaths of "hundreds of thousands of our soldiers." After the war, Stalin launched new purges that
killed "tens of thousands." And in his last days, the tyrant was planning to
execute his Kremlin comrades in order to "hide the shameful acts about
which we are now reporting."

The speech was supposed to be secret, but the CIA obtained a copy and
leaked it to the *New York Times*, which published the so-called secret
speech on June 4, 1956. Khrushchev's speech was so shocking that Polish
Communist leader Boleslaw Bierut dropped dead from a heart attack
while reading it.

The secrecy surrounding the speech spawned rumors and legends, one
of which became the topic of the first question Khrushchev was asked at
his news conference at Washington's National Press Club on September
16, 1959.

Before Khrushchev's arrival, the club's officers issued a revolutionary
edict: They would temporarily suspend the rule barring women and allow—for this event only—female reporters into the luncheon press conference. The women were not, however, admitted into the club's bar. "An
innocent woman reporter, hearing gay noises, penetrates the Members'
Bar, unaware of its sanctity," wrote a female *Washington Post* reporter.
"She is immediately ejected."

While Khrushchev rode back from Beltsville, 490 reporters—34 of
them women—gathered outside the club's ballroom. When the doors
opened, they surged forward, elbowing each other to get to the best seats.
In the melee, one of the female reporters fainted.

"Is anyone doing anything for her?" asked one reporter.

"Yes," said another, "trying to get her ticket."

After the lunch, Khrushchev stood in the harsh glare of television lights and delivered a speech that was a plea for peace. In the age of the atomic bomb, he said, war was an unthinkable insanity that would leave the world "covered with ashes and graves."

After the speech and its translation, William Lawrence, the president of the Press Club, stepped to the microphone carrying a stack of questions written by the reporters.

"Written questions are not new to Mr. Khrushchev," Lawrence said. "There is a story—perhaps apocryphal, and if apocryphal, perhaps it should now be denied since it has been published in the West—that at the meeting of the Communist Party Congress during which he delivered his long speech about Mr. Stalin, and about the crimes that Mr. Stalin had committed in the cult of personality, that someone in the audience sent up an unsigned but written question. And Mr. Khrushchev paused in the middle of the speech and read the question to the audience: *'What were you doing while Stalin was committing these crimes?'* Mr. Khrushchev noted that the question was unsigned and suggested that the author arise and identify himself."

The reporters in the Press Club laughed. Khrushchev did not.

"After a brief pause—or a lengthy pause, if you like—no one stood up," Lawrence continued. "'Well, comrades,' Mr. Khrushchev said, 'now you know what I was doing while Stalin was committing these crimes.'"

The reporters laughed again. Listening to the translation, Khrushchev's face reddened.

"Perhaps the Chairman would like to comment on that story," Lawrence said. "If it isn't true, we'd just as soon forget it for all time."

The crowd applauded and Khrushchev strode to the lectern, his red face scowling with unmistakable rage.

"Probably the authors of fables, including the authors of this question, wanted to place me in a difficult position," he said, his voice angry, his chubby hand chopping the air. "And there are laughs. There were laughs even before I replied to the question. But I would say that they laugh best who laugh last. I shall not reply to this question, which I look upon as being provocative, and I would like to take this occasion to deny any such malicious rumors and lies which do not correspond to the truth."

Stunned at the outburst, the reporters sat in hushed silence. "For a moment," wrote columnist Ralph G. Spivack, "the cold war looked as if it might get hot." Thrilled to have witnessed Khrushchev's famous temper only twenty-four hours into his trip, reporters banged out lurid descriptions of Khrushchev's red face, his scowl, his "touchiness," his "boiling anger," his "Ukrainian temper." The next morning, the headline in the New York *Daily Mirror* read, "Question Sizzles Niki."

The question "sizzled" Khrushchev because the incident had never occurred. Nobody passed a note to Khrushchev during the secret speech. The story was a fable—a grim joke that spread because it contained a poetic truth. Like the rest of Stalin's lieutenants, Khrushchev knew about the horrors of the purges and did nothing to stop them. And during the height of Stalin's great terror in the 1930s, Khrushchev signed arrest warrants for thousands of people who were later jailed, tortured, and killed. He also delivered fiery speeches praising Stalin and demanding the death of his enemies. And he did those things for exactly the reason that the joke suggested—pure, naked fear.

In his secret speech, Khrushchev admitted that Stalin terrified him into complicity. "Stalin was a very distrustful man, sickly suspicious; we knew this from our work with him," he told the delegates. "He could look at a man and say: 'Why are your eyes so shifty today?' Or: 'Why are you turning so much today and avoiding looking at me directly in the eyes?'. . . Possessing unlimited power, he indulged in great willfulness and choked a person morally and physically."

While Stalin was alive, Khrushchev kept silent out of fear. But the secret speech, delivered at the first Party Congress after Stalin's death, was an act of courage. "Khrushchev's speech denouncing Stalin," wrote William

Taubman in his Pulitzer Prize–winning biography of Khrushchev, "was the bravest and most reckless thing he ever did." Khrushchev's colleagues in the Kremlin had opposed his plan to reveal Stalin's crimes, but the premier insisted on delivering the speech. He was haunted by guilt over his complicity in the purges, Taubman wrote, and his speech was "an act of repentance, a way of reclaiming his identity as a decent man by telling the truth."

No wonder Khrushchev got angry when a snide question about his act of courage caused a room full of Americans to laugh at him.

The question that sizzled Khrushchev was just the first; there were more to come. The second question referred to the Russian rocket that carried a Soviet emblem to the moon a few days earlier: "Does the sending of the emblem indicate any desire to claim possession of the moon?"

Khrushchev smiled. "I do not want to offend anybody," he said, "but we represent different continents and different psychologies. And I would say that this question reflects capitalist psychology—a person thinking in terms of private ownership."

The reporters laughed.

"But I represent a socialist country, where the word 'mine' has long receded into the past and the word 'our' has taken its place. And therefore, when we launched this rocket and achieved this great thing, we look upon this as *our* victory, meaning not only of our country but of all countries, of all mankind."

That response won a round of applause and Khrushchev grinned.

"In your opening remarks, Mr. Khrushchev, you spoke about avoiding outside interference in the affairs of other nations," Lawrence said, reading the next question. "How then do you justify Russian armed interference in Hungary?"

Khrushchev's grin collapsed into another scowl as he spewed out an angry blast of Russian that his translator struggled to soften: "The question of Hungary has stuck in some people's throats like a dead rat. He feels that it is unpleasant but he cannot spit it out."

Khrushchev said he'd answered that question many times, including once during a visit to Hungary in 1958, two years after the Soviet Army crushed the anti-Communist revolt there, killing 20,000 Hungarians. "And I can assure you that it was a warm and enthusiastic response that we received there on the part of the Hungarian people."

He then announced that he could easily bring up questions "of a similar nature" about American actions in the cold war—perhaps an allusion to the CIA coups in Guatemala and Iran—but he would hold his tongue because "I am here as your guest." It was a deft rhetorical dance that enabled him to sidestep a tough question while pretending to be more polite than his inquisitors.

Lawrence read another question, this one about Khrushchev's most famous utterance: *We will bury you.* "If you did say it, could you explain what you meant?" Lawrence asked.

"Present here is only a very small portion of the American people," Khrushchev said. "But if I were to start to try to bury even this group, one life would not be enough."

He had uttered the sentence, he admitted, but he meant it metaphorically, not literally. "What was meant was not the physical burial of any people," he said, "but the question of the historical force of development." He launched into a brief lecture on the Marxist theory of history, perhaps the first ever heard on American network television. Just as capitalism replaced feudalism, he said, communism would one day replace capitalism. "Looking at the matter from the historical point of view, communism will take the place of capitalism and capitalism will be, so to speak, buried."

With that, the press conference was over. "Mr. Chairman, we want to thank you for coming today to the National Press Club," Lawrence said, and then he presented the premier with the club's official Certificate of Appreciation, suitable for framing.

All three major television networks broadcast the press conference live. Thousands of Americans watched, including many who tuned in expecting to find *Queen for a Day* or *As the World Turns.*

Irate viewers bombarded the press club with phone calls. One man demanded that somebody ask Khrushchev when he was going to pay back the millions of dollars in Lend Lease money that the United States had loaned the Soviets during the war. Another wanted to know what happened to American pilots who'd gone missing over Russia. And an angry woman insisted that Khrushchev be taken off the air *immediately* so she could watch her niece on *Queen for a Day*.

President Eisenhower was not among those Americans who watched the Khrushchev show on TV. Ike had taken the afternoon off to play golf at Burning Tree.

27. KHRUSHCHEV MEETS LINCOLN

Khrushchev had a couple of hours to kill before the tea party at the Senate Foreign Relations Committee, so Lodge took him on a tour of Washington.

They hopped into their limo and headed to the Lincoln Memorial, flanked by police cars and trailed by reporters. Lodge led Khrushchev up the steps of the memorial—where Martin Luther King would deliver his "I have a dream" speech four years later—and the two men gazed at the huge stone Lincoln perched on his giant throne.

"Lincoln was the man who ended slavery and started us on the road to full equality," Lodge told his guest. "He was the man who saved the Union. Otherwise we would be two countries today."

"This is why our people respect Lincoln," Khrushchev replied. "This is why we honor him and bow to him."

With that, he bowed theatrically from the waist toward Lincoln.

He stood staring at Lincoln long enough to enable the photographers to get plenty of shots, then he strolled over to the crowd of reporters and told them about his great love of the Great Emancipator. "We bow to Lincoln and his work," he said. "He was a truly great man, a human man, because he dedicated his life to the struggle for freedom."

It was all a publicity stunt designed to impress Americans, he later admitted in his memoir. "I thought it would be a good idea if journalists wrote that the prime minister of the Soviet Union, who had once been a miner, paid homage to a former American president, who had once been a woodcutter."

On his way back to the limousine, Khrushchev spotted a mother holding a baby. Smiling, the barnstorming pol hustled over to tweak the tyke's cheek and kitchy-koo in soothing Russian.

Driving away, the motorcade passed a school bus, and the young scholars stuck their heads out the windows to shout a message to the chairman of the Council of Ministers of the Union of Soviet Socialist Republics.

"Hey, meatball!" they yelled.

28. COMMUNISM IS LIKE MY WART

The Senate Foreign Relations Committee had invited Khrushchev to drop by for tea. But when he arrived in the committee's ornate room in the Capitol, he announced that he didn't want any.

"It is difficult to drink and talk at the same time," he explained. Then, as if he feared losing the tea-drinker vote, he added, "but in general, I am in favor of tea."

"Well, we might find some vodka," said Senator J. William Fulbright, the committee chairman. "Or some bourbon if you prefer."

That was a historic moment: Khrushchev was hardly the first Communist to be questioned by a congressional committee but he was certainly the only one who was offered a cocktail first.

He declined the honor. "It is a misconception to think that Russians have such a proclivity for vodka," he said. "If they only drank vodka, they would not have time to launch rockets to the moon. Drunkards can't do that."

This casual boast was especially stinging. That morning, the Americans had attempted their first space shot since the Soviet moon flight. A Jupiter rocket containing fourteen pregnant mice—a test of the effect of space flight on the little critters—blasted off the launching pad at Cape Canaveral, soared about 1,000 feet and exploded in a gigantic fireball.

Khrushchev was kind enough not to mention the latest embarrassing failure directly. Instead, he regaled the senators with his famous folksy wisdom. "When a man buys a new pair of shoes," he said, "he often does not feel comfortable in them and sometimes throws them off and takes back the old pair of worn-out shoes to feel more comfortable. Things like that happen in a wider field, too. When something new is born, it takes time for people to get used to it."

What was he getting at? He didn't explain. Instead, he launched into another analogy: "Who among us has not been disappointed sometimes in life when a daughter was born instead of a son, or a granddaughter instead of a grandson? But sometimes nature provides a different result than what a man would want." The same was true with politics, he added: "Now a new kind of society—a socialist society—is being born, first in one country and now in others, 12 or 13."

Then Khrushchev offered a third analogy: Communism is like the wart on my face. "The wart is there," he said, pointing at the growth on the side of his nose, "and I can't do anything about it."

"You are convinced," Fulbright said, "that your system is better than ours—"

"Absolutely convinced," Khrushchev replied.

"But what happens if it suddenly developed that the capitalist system is better and that more and more people prefer capitalism to socialism?" Fulbright asked. "Would you put up with that, or will you use force?"

"If history should show that capitalism proves more able than communism, I would be the first to raise my hand in favor of capitalism," Khrushchev replied. "One cannot favor poverty for the people. However, in that event, I might have to decide whether I should join the Republican

Party or the Democratic Party. That would be a difficult choice because I don't think there is much difference."

The senators laughed, and Fulbright said, "I can tell you which party is better."

"You would advise me," Khrushchev said, "but maybe not correctly."

That got another laugh, and soon Khrushchev demonstrated his prowess at deflecting the tough questions that he didn't want to answer. Asked about the recent Chinese takeover of Tibet, he said, "Address your inquiries to Peking. I represent the USSR, not China." Asked if he would permit free elections in his East German colony, he replied, "If you have questions on that score, send them to the Prime Minister of the German Democratic Republic. The address is well-known."

Everett Dirksen, the frog-voiced Senate minority leader, asked about press censorship in the Soviet Union.

"We have no censorship," the premier said. "There is only control to prevent abuse of freedom of the press."

"Then you say censorship will continue?" Dirksen asked.

"I would not call it censorship."

"What would you call it?"

"Name it yourself," Khrushchev said.

The senators were impressed. Seasoned political pros, they recognized Khrushchev's talent at the timeless political arts that they too had mastered—obfuscation, question-dodging, homespun storytelling and shameless mendacity.

"Our guest would be a most formidable antagonist in any parliamentary forum anywhere in the world," said Senator Richard Russell.

"Not an antagonist—a defender," Khrushchev replied.

Russell asked Khrushchev about the Soviet space program: "We have had setbacks in launching rockets. What about you?"

"Why do you ask *me*?" Khrushchev replied. "Your vice president already answered that question. Evidently, he knows more about it than I do."

The premier was still steamed at Nixon's comment that the Soviets had launched three unsuccessful attempts to hit the moon before they finally succeeded. "I will tell you a secret," Khrushchev said. "Our scientists wanted to launch that rocket about a week ago. The rocket was prepared and put on the launching site. But when they began testing the equipment, they found that it wasn't working properly. Then they decided to take that rocket away and put a new one in its place. . . . The first rocket was not launched. It will be tested and, if needed, we might launch it later on."

Having not quite denied Nixon's statement, Khrushchev issued a challenge to the vice president: "I can swear on the Bible that this is a fact. If the vice president can, he can swear on the Bible that he was right, too."

Now *that* was the kind of diplomatic proposal that quickened the blood of American reporters. A Nixon-Khrushchev Bible-swearing contest promised to be even more fun than the great kitchen debate in Moscow.

Alas, it wasn't to be. When reporters buttonholed Nixon to ask him about Khrushchev's challenge, he just smiled and shook his head.

"No comment," he said.

The *New York Post* covered the story beneath a headline that could hardly have pleased a man who was running for president in a religious nation:

NIXON SILENT
ON MR. K'S
BIBLE CHALLENGE

29. DISMAL, RUMP-SPRUNG, AND WRINKLED

From the backseat of a chauffeur-driven Rolls Royce, columnist Dorothy Kilgallen informed her millions of readers that Mrs. Khrushchev's *couture* was simply appalling.

"The grisliness of her attire amounts almost to a demonstration of piety," Kilgallen wrote. "Her blue and blue-gray suit could be charitably described as dismal. It was rump-sprung, wrinkled, at least four inches longer at the hem than is currently correct, and it had no point of view, right or wrong. It was just there, covering her like a home-made slip cover on a sofa."

The *New York Journal-American* printed Kilgallen's catty dispatch on the front page, beneath a banner headline: "Our Miss K Says Mrs. K's Clothes Fit Like Slip Cover."

At forty-six, Kilgallen was the most famous female reporter of the era, as well as a star of radio and television. Her career began in 1931 when she dropped out of college to write for Hearst's *New York Journal*, specializing in sensational murders, trials and executions. In 1936, in a stunt typical of the tabloid age, she raced two male reporters around the world, filing stories all the way. She lost the race, but the adventures of the "spunky globe-circling girl reporter" were immortalized in the movie *Fly Away Baby*, which made Kilgallen famous enough to appear in a Camel cigarette ad, touting Camel's amazing properties as a laxative for harried travelers: "I snatched meals anywhere, ate all kinds of food. But Camels helped me keep my digestion tuned up."

In 1938, she began writing a gossip column called the "Voice of Broadway," trolling for trivia at the Stork Club and 21 and the Copacabana, competing with the other great gossip mongers of the age—Walter Winchell, Hedda Hopper, and Louella Parsons. In 1940, she married actor Richard Kollmar and soon the happy couple began an eighteen-year run as costars of a radio show called *Breakfast with Dorothy and Dick,* broadcasting from their swanky Park Avenue townhouse, chatting about showbiz, politics, and the wonderfulness of their sponsors' products. In 1950, Kilgallen began her thirteen-year stint on TV's most popular game show, *What's My Line?*

They were rich and famous and their lives were glamorous, except that Dick was an alcoholic and chronic philanderer, and Dorothy, also an alcoholic, was having an affair with singer Johnnie Ray, who was also enjoying flings with countless young men.

When Queen Elizabeth visited New York in 1957, Kilgallen's boss, William Randolph Hearst Jr., enthroned his star columnist in a chauffeur-driven Rolls Royce and she slipped into the royal motorcade, right behind Governor Averell Harriman.

She loved traveling by chauffeured Rolls so much that Hearst rented one to carry her to Washington to cover Khrushchev's arrival. Kilgallen, who loved minks and diamonds and never left home without her little white gloves, took one look at Mrs. Khrushchev's clothes and saw her angle.

"It would be difficult to find clothes comparable to hers in the waiting room of a New York employment agency for domestic help," she wrote. "In this decadent capitalistic republic, applicants for jobs as laundresses, chambermaids, and cooks usually are far more a la mode than Russia's first lady."

When Mrs. Khrushchev appeared at the Beltsville farm wearing the same dress she'd worn on her arrival—the dress Kilgallen had compared to a slipcover—the columnist unloaded again. "Any woman who would come thousands of miles to wear the same old dress two days in a row is not here to pick up pointers on fashion," she wrote. "Nina Khrushchev is on U.S. soil to backstop her man, to listen to him and smile proudly at his global jokes. He is the important one, he looks scrubbed and freshly shirted and well-pressed. His wife gives the impression of not caring whether she has her hair washed today, tomorrow or two weeks from Friday."

But perhaps there was hope, Kilgallen suggested. When the Russians reached New York, maybe Mrs. Khrushchev would succumb to the seductive allures of Manhattan's beauty salons and department stores:

> Admittedly, Russia's version of Mamie Eisenhower has shown, so far, no chinks in the armor of blatant Communist dowdiness. But she is female.
>
> It is hard to believe that somewhere, deep inside that façade, there is not a female yearning that would respond to a couple of hours in a sumptuous Gotham beauty salon.

And Lord knows how hairdressers and makeup experts in town
must be yearning to get their hands on her. Her figure is hopeless
but she has a sweet, sympathetic face with an attractive if not aristocratic turned-up nose when viewed in profile.

Wonders might be achieved if she would attempt to experiment
with eyebrow pencil, some powder to contradict the impression
that she has just turned away from a session over a hot stove, and
the modern miracle known as lipstick.

If she could be talked into a pair of white gloves, hooray for our
side.

No doubt some readers found Kilgallen's pieces amusing, but many
others were appalled. After all, she was insulting the wife of an easily insulted dictator who possessed hydrogen bombs and a hot temper.

For perhaps the first time in history, Hearst and his editors admitted
publicly that they'd published something that crossed the bounds of good
taste. As a penance, they ran a generous selection of the many angry letters they'd received.

"Revolting," said one.

"A new low," said another.

"We are ashamed of Miss Kilgallen," said a third.

But Miss Kilgallen was not ashamed of herself. Incensed that her
bosses declined to defend her, she quit in a huff, and "The Voice of Broadway" went silent.

But not for long. Her bosses telephoned, sweet-talked her into lunch at
the 21 club, and assured her that she was wonderful, irreplaceable,
beloved. Her feathers smoothed, the diva relented and returned to work.
In her next column, she ignored Nina Khrushchev and opted for a different angle: There was one bit of glamour in the stodgy Khrushchev entourage—Henry Cabot Lodge.

"The Ambassador is tall, smooth and handsome," Kilgallen wrote,
"and he gives the impression of breeding and equanimity under the most

trying of circumstances. He is in wild contrast to Khrushchev—the Russian shouts and pokes and reddens and uses a knife and fork as if they were extremely recent discoveries. Lodge has a pleasant, cultivated, reasonable voice and perfect manners—yet the two seem to get along well together."

30. TWO JEWISH SALESMEN WERE TRAVELING ON A TRAIN . . .

Before he left for New York, there was one last sight Nikita Khrushchev wanted to see in Washington—the luggage lockers at Union Station.

Two days earlier, the Soviet embassy had called H. M. Lingenfelter, the station manager, to ask if Khrushchev could get a demonstration of the station's coin-operated baggage lockers. A few minutes before eight o'clock on Thursday morning, September 17, Khrushchev stood in a brown suit and maroon tie and watched as Lingenfelter opened the locker, put his briefcase into it, closed the door, inserted a quarter, and—voilà!—removed the key.

Khrushchev was impressed. "Very sensible idea," he said.

Do the Soviets have lockers like these? a reporter asked.

The answer was no. In Soviet stations, passengers waited in long lines to check and retrieve their luggage, which is precisely why Khrushchev wanted to see these American contraptions.

After his locker inspection, Khrushchev climbed aboard the K Train—the shiny silver fifteen-car, twin-engine train that would carry him to Manhattan, together with Lodge and their entourages and the media horde. Railroad workers had spent the previous day spiffing up the K Train, while an army of nearly 1,000 federal, state, and local police carefully inspected the two hundred miles of track between Washington and New York, plus every bridge and tunnel along the way. Guards wearing white armbands were stationed at every mile of track, keeping watch for snipers, saboteurs, bombers, and freelance lunatics.

The K Train pulled out of Union Station at 8:21, following at a safe distance behind a train that was sent out ahead, presumably to detonate any
bombs that might be hidden beneath the tracks.

It was a bright, warm late-summer morning and Khrushchev sat in the
sun-dappled club car, sharing a table with Lodge, Gromyko, and Lodge's
translator, Alex Akalovsky, who was, as always, taking notes. The chairman had been given a pamphlet that explained, in Russian, the sites he
would see on the way—steel mills, auto factories, a chemical plant, and
lots of small family farms. But Khrushchev got bored looking out the
window and began talking about one of his favorite subjects—nuclear
war. The premier spoke of nuclear war so often that Akalovsky created
his own shorthand symbol for the phrase, drawing a little mushroom
cloud in his notebook.

When it comes to nuclear war, missiles are much better than bombers,
Khrushchev told Lodge. Bombers can easily be shot down, he said, but
missiles fly higher and faster and they're almost impossible to hit from the
ground.

As the train rumbled through Delaware at eighty miles per hour,
Khrushchev continued his grim monologue. We have missiles that can
carry nuclear warheads to the other side of the world, and you Americans
do not, he said. Therefore, the Soviet Union is stronger than the United
States.

Such things go in cycles, Lodge replied. "We were ahead with the
atomic bomb. You are ahead in rockets at the moment. And I am sure that
you can be in no doubt of our retaliatory power. It is quite impossible—if
you were to use these missiles—not to expect suicidal results for you. You
can hit our cities but not our retaliatory military installations."

Khrushchev nodded.

"Our bombers and our Navy and our other things would devastate the
Soviet Union," Lodge said.

Khrushchev nodded again. War, he said, would be mutual suicide.

By now, the train was chugging toward Philadelphia, the City of Broth-
erly Love, and Lodge decided to change the subject. He pointed out the

window at rundown wooden houses on one side of the train tracks and a new housing development on the other. "We have a lot more bad housing than you have," Khrushchev admitted, "and I have not come here to look at bad things."

Smiling, the chairman revealed that his advisers had warned him to beware of Lodge, who would try to show him only good things while hiding the bad. Then he mentioned Lodge's reputation for arguing vigorously with Soviet diplomats at the United Nations.

"Go in and give the Russian diplomats hell," Khrushchev told Lodge. "Beat them up. It's good for them. They will get wiser that way."

"I disagree," said Gromyko, who was among the Russian diplomats most likely to get beaten up if Lodge took Khrushchev's advice.

"You see!" the chairman said, laughing. "The man speaks up for himself."

Khrushchev loved needling his underlings. It put him in a good mood. Grinning, he announced that riding the train reminded him of an old joke. Two Jewish salesmen were traveling on a train, Khrushchev said. They were competitors and each wanted to find out where the other was going.

"Where are you going?" the first salesman asked.

The second salesman was headed for Cherkasky but he didn't want his competitor to know that. He thought to himself, I'll say I'm going to Byeletzekoff so he won't know I'm really going to Cherkasky. But then he thought, He knows that I don't want him to know where I'm going, so if I tell him I'm going to Byeletzekoff, he'll know I'm going to Cherkasky. It would be better to tell him I'm going to Cherkasky even though I really *am* going there.

So he said, "I'm going to Cherkasky."

The first salesman was equally shrewd. He thought, He doesn't want me to know where he is going. If he had told me he was going to Byeletzekoff, he would know that I would know that he was going to Cherkasky. So he has told me he is going to Cherkasky thinking that I will think he's going to Byeletzekoff.

So the first salesman turned to the second salesman and said, "How long will you be in Cherkasky?"

Khrushchev cracked up. He was always his own best audience.

That's the way you diplomats talk to each other, he told Lodge and Gromyko. I try to speak more directly.

He paused a moment, trying to look serious but not quite succeeding. "So, which one of you is going to Cherkasky?" he asked.

31. ON THE SIDEWALKS OF NEW YORK

Their curiosity stoked by media-induced Khrushchev mania, more than 100,000 New Yorkers packed sidewalks all over midtown Manhattan, hoping to catch a glimpse of the famous visitor.

They gathered outside Penn Station, where Khrushchev's train would arrive. They stood outside the Waldorf-Astoria, where the dictator was booked into a luxury suite, and around the Commodore Hotel, where he was scheduled to address a luncheon of high-powered New York politicians and businessmen. And they waited near the subway stop at 72nd Street, where, according to rumor, Khrushchev would board an IND train—the biggest crowd seen in the neighborhood, one resident said, since the night in 1957 when Mafia hitman Vincent "Chin" Gigante shot Frank Costello, the "prime minister of the underworld," in the head. (Costello lived to tell the tale, although he refused to tell the tale in court—he was no rat—and Gigante was acquitted.)

"Keep moving, keep moving," the cops kept chanting to the crowds clogging the sidewalks, but nobody moved.

At 11:00 A.M., the crowds swelled when an air raid siren started wailing, causing nervous workers to flee their offices and bleary-eyed drinkers to shuffle out of bars, wondering if the end of the world was nigh.

"When's he arriving?" a woman asked a cop outside Penn Station. Around noon, the cop said.

"It will be too soon whenever he does," she grumbled.

"What are *you* complaining about?" the cop replied. "*I* have to guard him."

So did an army of other cops—more than 3,000 of the men the newspapers loved to call "New York's Finest," including a much ballyhooed squad of sixteen beefy bodyguards, all of them said to be sharpshooters or judo experts. The previous day, cops had sealed manhole covers (lest somebody plant a bomb in one) and removed trash baskets (lest somebody throw one at the premier's limo). Now they cleared all traffic from the thoroughfares that the chairman's motorcade would traverse, causing traffic jams in nearby streets, which in turn caused cranky New York drivers to lean on their horns and holler at each other.

"Watch out for Khrushchev," a cabbie yelled at the truck driver who cut him off. "He'll send you to Siberia."

When a grocery delivery boy wearing a red uniform pedaled his three-wheeled cart right down the center of the newly emptied 34th Street, the crowds cheered. When a cop chased him away, they booed.

Protesters, many of them Hungarian refugees, carried signs: "Big Brother Is Watching You" and "Don't Have a Crush on Khrush" and "Nikie, Go To The Moon—Leave New York For Us." A woman wearing an American Indian outfit—headband, moccasins, and a fringed buckskin jacket—held a sign reading "Manhattan Is Not For Sale Any More!"

"It's a shame what he did," a man standing outside the Waldorf bellowed in a thick accent. "It's a shame that he did not permit free elections in Russia. Dear Americans, why do you permit him to come?"

"Oh, shut up," a dear American replied.

On 81st Street, a blonde in the crowd on the sidewalk yelled flirtatiously to a gentleman watching from the window of his comfortable brownstone, "Might I join you?"

"No," he replied, and the eavesdropping bystanders giggled.

Street corner wisenheimers cracked grim jokes about what might happen if somebody shot Khrushchev, and countless reporters trolled the crowds for colorful quotes that captured the folksy wisdom of New York's fabled man in the street:

"I just want to see what he looks like."

"I'm interested in seeing how the crowd reacts to him."

"I want to be here if anything happens."

"I came just to see that murderer. But it would be better if *nobody* came to see him."

"I hate Khrushchev."

"I believe he is a good man. He's not like Stalin anyway."

"I don't like *him* but I like *her*. She represents womanhood."

"I won't wave at him. I won't be that cordial. But I *will* smile."

Outside Penn Station at 12:27 somebody yelled, "Here he comes!"

A moment later, Khrushchev's thirty-four-car motorcade roared down 34th Street, surrounded by nearly one hundred motorcycle cops. Hardly anybody in the crowd caught even a fleeting glimpse of the famous visitor.

After the motorcade sped past, one grumpy New Yorker spoke for the disappointed multitudes: "We waited all this time for *that?*"

32. THE DENTISTS FIGHT BACK

A blood-red tide floods the face of the Earth.

In the filmstrips of the 1950s, it's the standard method of illustrating the ominous spread of Communism. The lesson begins with a map of the Earth in 1917, every nation a pure white. As the narrator tells the story of the Bolshevik revolution, Russia goes red. As he recounts the grim history of the twentieth century, the red tide spreads—flooding Latvia, Estonia, Lithuania, then Poland, Hungary, Czechoslovakia, Yugoslavia, Romania, Bulgaria, Albania, East Germany, Mongolia, North Korea, China, North Vietnam, Tibet.

In less than fifty years, the blood-red tide had swamped a huge swath of the world. Americans wondered: Where will it stop? Who will fight back? Who will hold their ground against the relentless march of the Communists?

In September 1959, America received an unexpected answer: the American Dental Association. The dentists would hold their ground against the Reds—and that ground was the Grand Ballroom of the Waldorf-Astoria Hotel.

They were gathered at the Waldorf for their one-hundredth annual convention, the largest assemblage of dentists in history, more than 30,000 of them, including visiting delegations of dental dignitaries from sixty-four nations. Four years earlier, the American Dental Association had booked the hotel's Grand Ballroom for September 17, in order to convene the official legislative session of the ADA's House of Delegates. But on September 10, as the convention began, Percy T. Phillips, D.D.S., the association's president, received two letters. One came from Robert F. Wagner, the mayor of New York, the other from Wiley T. Buchanan, the State Department's chief of protocol. Both letters communicated the same message: The dentists would have to give up the Grand Ballroom so that Wagner could host an official luncheon there for Nikita Khrushchev.

"The City of New York is responsible for the security measures surrounding the visit of this distinguished guest," Wagner wrote, "and it therefore becomes imperative to the city that the luncheon to be held in honor of Mr. Khrushchev be held in the Grand Ballroom of the same hotel where he is being housed."

"We regret exceedingly at all times to interfere in the private plans of distinguished organizations such as yours," wrote Buchanan. "However, because of the national interest and great importance of a completely safe state visit, we must insist upon compliance."

Clearly Wagner and Buchanan believed that the dentists would surrender meekly and move their meeting to a smaller room in the Waldorf. But the dentists were made of sterner stuff. Like the fabled defenders of the Alamo, the American Dental Association drew a line in the sand and refused to budge. On September 11, Dr. Phillips fired back a letter that resounded like American history's classic statements of defiance—"Give me liberty or give me death!" and "Damn the torpedoes, full speed ahead!"—although not quite so pithy.

"The Grand Ballroom of the Waldorf-Astoria Hotel is under contract to the Association," Phillips wrote. "Any change in the announced program will seriously inconvenience the members and guests of the Association and, as well, will damage the reputation of the officers and committees who carry the serious responsibility of planning such an historic event for the dental profession."

After a few more paragraphs of this incendiary rhetoric, Phillips unleashed the battle cry that sent the dentists to the barricades: "The association, therefore, must inform you that it respectfully declines your request, and that it will use all possible means to enforce its contract with the Waldorf-Astoria."

As Phillips hinted in his letter, one of the possible means was picking up the phone and calling newspapers. And sure enough, word of the Battle of the Grand Ballroom quickly leaked out.

"Stubborn Dentists Won't Be Yanked," reported the *Chicago Sun-Times*.

In the *New York Daily News*, the lead paragraph of the story was a classic of tabloid prose: "Like a stubbornly embedded wisdom tooth, the American Dental Association refused yesterday to be extracted from its scheduled convention session in the grand ballroom of the Waldorf-Astoria on Thursday so that Russia's No. 1 comrade, Nikita Khrushchev, can lunch in plush, capitalistic style."

These stories thrilled the conservatives who opposed Khrushchev's visit, and they bombarded Dr. Phillips with telegrams of solidarity:

STAND FAST IN THE BALLROOM

DO NOT LET THEM PRESSURE YOU
INTO GIVING UP THE WALDORF BALLROOM
FOR THAT BLOODY HANDED MURDERER

KEEP ON EXTRACTING THE POISONOUS FANGS OF COMMUNISM

On September 13, two days before Khrushchev arrived in Washington, reporters flocked to the Waldorf to cover the battle and found the dental convention guarded by men wearing dazzling sky-blue uniforms trimmed with red and gold braid. In an elaborate ceremony, 152 dentists clad in mortarboards and academic robes were solemnly inducted into the American College of Dentists. Amid the pomp and ceremony, battle lines were drawn.

"The Dental Association's going to have to give way," said a spokesman for the city.

"We'll be here," promised a spokesman for the dentists. "We've got a contract."

It was a stalemate, a standoff, a showdown. The American Dental Association and the United States government were standing eyeball-to-eyeball and somebody would have to blink.

The government blinked. On September 14, the city announced that it would hold the Khrushchev luncheon at the nearby Commodore Hotel. Vice President Nixon, arriving for a long-scheduled speech to the ADA convention, delivered the good news to the assembled dentists. "The Russians got to the moon first," he said, "but the American Dental Association got to this ballroom first."

The dentists surged out of their seats, cheering their victory.

News of the dentists' triumph inspired America's headline writers to greater excesses of orthodontic punning:

DENTISTS SHOW TEETH OVER NIK LUNCH PLAN

DENTISTS PULL TEETH OUT OF KHRUSH FÊTE

FIRM-JAWED DENTISTS SNAFU KHRUSHCHEV FÊTE

STRING PULLERS CAN'T BUDGE TEETH PULLERS

For the first time in American history—and perhaps the last—the nation's dentists were authentic American heroes. The ADA was bombarded with fan mail.

"For all of my life, George Washington, John Paul Jones, John Peter Zenger and Roosevelt—Theodore, that is—have been my favorite heroes," wrote Mildred Willand of New York. "Now I must add the members of the American Dental Association to this list."

"Hooray for you for proving all Americans can't be pushed around," wrote a woman who identified herself as Mrs. Average American Who Loves Her Country. "I'll have a lot more respect for American dentists from now on."

Several letters indicated that the courage displayed by America's dentists had inspired courage in their fellow Americans, specifically the kind of courage needed to overcome their heart-pounding, palm-sweating fear of dentists: "I have always dreaded dentists," wrote M. B. Barrett of New Jersey, "but now the stand of the A.D.A. in refusing to be ousted for Mr. Khrushchev has made a convert of me and I expect to visit the dentist hereafter joyfully!!"

33. ARGUE OR PERISH

Nikita Khrushchev arrived in the Commodore Hotel surrounded by a phalanx of cops and bodyguards. They whisked him upstairs to the mezzanine level, and then the dictator escaped.

He slipped away from his protectors and darted out to the balcony. He gazed down at the crowded lobby and smiled. He waved both arms at the people below and they rewarded him with laughter and cheers. For one magic moment, Khrushchev was free. But it didn't last. The police—who'd spent the night searching the hotel after a man with a foreign accent called to say he'd hidden three bombs there—were not about to let the chairman loose. "Grim bodyguards pounced on the premier and led him off into the grand ballroom," the *Times* reported. "But the premier looked content. He had enjoyed his brief spree on stage."

In the cavernous ballroom, 1,200 businessmen sat at tables decorated with red dahlias. It was a "stag luncheon" so all the guests were men—a common phenomenon in 1959.

When Khrushchev arrived in the ballroom, the Meyer Davis orchestra played the Soviet national anthem. Then, as the orchestra launched into the "Star-Spangled Banner," something unexpected occurred: A man began to sing. Softly, hesitantly, in a thin, quivering voice, the little man warbled, "Oh, say, can you see?" People stared at him. Soon a few voices joined in, then a few more. By the time the orchestra reached the anthem's climactic lines, "the land of the free and the home of the brave," the big ballroom resounded with song.

"It was an astounding thing; the emotional impact was tremendous," Wiley Buchanan, the chief of protocol, later recalled. "Some people had tears running down their faces. But everyone was singing. The Russians looked thunderstruck, almost frightened. Then, suddenly, it was all over."

The anthem ended, the crowd cheered, and everybody sat down to lunch. As Khrushchev ate, bending low over his plate to shovel in the chow with gusto, he had no idea that he was about to become the beneficiary—or perhaps the victim—of an educational plan devised by Richard Nixon.

When Nixon returned from Moscow after his verbal brawls with Khrushchev, he outlined a plan for handling the premier in America. Diplomatic niceties don't work with Khrushchev, Nixon told Eisenhower. If you sit quietly while Khrushchev spouts off, he will lose respect for you. You have to take him on and argue with him, especially if a crowd is watching. The State Department was cool to Nixon's idea but Ike took his vice president's advice and instructed Lodge to speak up and correct any erroneous ideas Khrushchev might express.

Nixon called his plan "argue or perish." Later—after the tactic backfired spectacularly in Los Angeles—skeptics coined other names. James Reston of the *Times* called it "a policy of massive verbal retaliation." John Lardner of the *New Yorker* dubbed it "the educate-Khrushchev-after-dessert plan."

Khrushchev's education began at the Commodore after a dessert of vanilla ice cream topped with raspberry sauce. Mayor Wagner stepped to the lectern and started the instruction with some civic boosterism. "Chairman Khrushchev, this is a great city," he said. "We think it is the greatest in the world. We know—you know—there are great cities in your homeland but we think ours is different."

New York is a city of immigrants, "the Irish, the Germans, the Russians, Italians, Poles, Greeks and Jews." They came seeking liberty and opportunity, Wagner said, and they found it. "We know we have some poor, some ill-housed. But more people are living better, healthier and happier here today than any place else, in any previous era, in the world's history."

When Wagner sat down, the crowd stood and cheered. So did Khrushchev. Then Lodge stepped to the microphone. "Here in New York, 8,000,000 people of every race, religion and color live side by side," he said, "and for the most part, all is peaceful."

Lodge knew that Khrushchev was scheduled to make a tour of Harlem the next day, and he could easily imagine the premier spouting off about what the *New York Times* called "the Negro problem." "This is a good place to say a word about the American Negro," Lodge said. "Great progress has been made in establishing justice in this country—as the Constitution tells us to do—for all people, regardless of color. But as long as one individual is discriminated against, a situation exists which we cannot condone."

As Lodge spoke, his country was a place where many states maintained segregated schools five years after the Supreme Court ordered integration; where black people could not sit in restaurants with whites and were systematically denied the right to vote in many places; where a black boy named Emmett Till was murdered for whistling at a white woman and his killers were set free to brag about their crime in a best-selling book. But Lodge preferred to take the long view. "We work without respite to solve the problem," he said. "And there is no doubt at all that, regardless of local obstacles, legal segregation will completely disappear."

After educating Khrushchev on civil rights, Lodge moved on to economics. "The United States cannot be simply described by a reference to the economic system," he said. "And that system, with its intense competition, its wide sharing of earnings, its ever-changing character and its enormous government welfare program, can certainly not be accurately summed up in the one word 'capitalistic.'"

When Lodge took his seat, the audience applauded and so did Khrushchev. Then the premier rose to speak. He thanked Wagner for inviting him to New York. He thanked Eisenhower for inviting him to America. And he thanked Lodge, sort of. "He is making me suffer through this big program that we have," Khrushchev said, smiling. "But at the same time, *he* is suffering, too. That certainly makes my sufferings easier."

The audience laughed.

"I realize that you were prompted in inviting me by the desire to see what sort of a man this Khrushchev is—to see what he's like." He paused a moment. "Well, here I am!" he said, spreading his arms wide like a vaudeville hoofer hearing an inaudible *ta-dah*.

The crowd cracked up.

Khrushchev reminded the audience that he'd listened attentively as Wagner and Lodge praised capitalism and he'd applauded both of them. "So the question may arise: Who am I then? Is it that when I am among Communists, I applaud Communists and when I am among capitalists, I applaud them? People might think, 'This is no politician, this is a weathervane.' So let us just come to an agreement that there is no need for me to exert any effort to make Communists out of you. This would be a waste of effort and I want to save my energy for useful business. And if any of you have any hopes that I might go over to the path of capitalism—well, of course that, too, is a hopeless thought."

He reinforced his point with another of his famous proverbs. "To characterize our attitude toward each other's system, I think the most apt saying is the Russian proverb 'Each duck praises its own swamp,'" he said. "Thus, you praise your capitalist swamp. And as for us . . . "

He paused, mired in a swamp of his own rhetorical making.

"Well, I wouldn't want to say that we are praising our *socialist* swamp because I can't call socialism a swamp, but . . . "

34. STUCK

One of the world's most famous hotels, the Waldorf-Astoria was an international symbol of opulence and celebrity. When it opened in 1931, the magnificent art deco masterpiece was the largest hotel in the world. In 1959, it was home to former President Herbert Hoover, General Douglas MacArthur, the Duke and Duchess of Windsor, and composer Cole Porter, who praised the hotel's famous Waldorf salad in his song, "You're the Top." It was also the place where Mafia boss Frank Costello started hanging out after his psychiatrist suggested that he "get out and meet some nice people."

The Presidential Suite on the thirty-fifth floor, where the Khrushchev family was bivouacking, rented for $150 a day, a princely sum in an era when a motel room could be had for under $10. The tab would be paid, like all the premier's hotel bills, by the State Department. Decorated in colonial style, the suite contained four bedrooms, four bathrooms, and a drawing room where an oil painting of Thomas Jefferson gazed out from above the marble fireplace. The windows offered fabulous views of the Manhattan skyline.

This sumptuous home away from home was just an elevator ride away when Khrushchev arrived in the lobby, and guards conveniently held four elevators open for the premier and his entourage. Khrushchev stepped into one of the lifts, accompanied by Lodge and translator Alex Akalovsky, plus the hotel manager and General Nicolai Zakharov, the Soviet security officer who had earlier informed the Americans that any attack on Khrushchev would result in . . . *Boom!*

The elevator operator, Mary Anna Anemone, closed the metal door and up they rose, past the tenth floor, past the twentieth floor, past the twenty-fifth and then the elevator stopped moving.

They waited. Nothing happened.

Anemone, who'd been operating elevators at the Waldorf for eleven years, told her passengers that she thought the elevator's power had gone out. Akalovsky translated her words to Khrushchev, who nodded and smiled but said nothing.

They waited. Nothing happened. They were stuck.

Somebody suggested that they find out where they were. Anemone opened the door and they all peered out at the dusty darkness of an empty elevator shaft. Above their heads, however, they could see the thirtieth floor of the hotel. They looked at each other. Should they climb out?

They waited. Nothing happened. They decided to climb out.

Anemone slid her beige-upholstered stool to the front of the car. Khrushchev stood on the stool and reached up to the floor above. As Lodge pushed on the dictator's ample rump, the chairman of the Council of Ministers of the Soviet Union hoisted himself to safety. Lodge and the rest of the passengers scrambled up after him, pushing and pulling each other up to the thirtieth floor.

"This," Khrushchev said sardonically, "is the famous American technology."

Before they all plodded up the stairs to the thirty-fifth floor, Lodge turned to Anemone and smiled. "It's history," he said. "You can tell it to your grandchildren."

A few minutes later, power returned, the elevators started working again and a hotel spokesman explained that an overloaded circuit breaker had tripped.

The story of the pudgy Communist dictator crawling out of an elevator in the elegant capitalist hotel was reported all over world, along with Khrushchev's uncharacteristically pithy comment on the incident: "Capitalistic malfunction."

When Renee S. Cushman of Phoenix, Arizona, read the news, she was so incensed that she wrote an angry letter to *Time* magazine, which published it a week later:

"Conrad Hilton, resign! Or should the president of the Waldorf-Astoria hotel now be addressed as *Comrade* Hilton? Khrushchev's having to crawl out of an elevator and walk up five flights is worth half-a-dozen successful U.S. satellite launchings in propaganda. It's bad enough not to be able to get to the moon, but when we fail to reach the 35th floor, it's terrible."

Decades later, Akalovsky had second thoughts about the wisdom of shoving Khrushchev out of the stalled elevator. "It was a risky proposition," he said. "Somebody could have done something to move the elevator and he would have been cut in half." He laughed. "Gruesome!"

35. YOU RULE AMERICA

Memories of cocktail parties tend to fade quickly, leaving only a boozy blur in the brain. But images of the evening when Nikita Khrushchev met America's "ruling class" for drinks at Averell Harriman's Manhattan townhouse lingered long after September 17, 1959.

"Few occasions are etched more vividly on my memory," John Kenneth Galbraith wrote eleven years afterward. "The scene—the very shapeless man in a rather shapeless suit with a very large pink head and very short legs beneath the Picasso—still shines in my eyes."

Khrushchev, who endured countless cocktail parties with innumerable powerful men in his long career, also retained vivid memories of Harriman's gathering: "Tobacco smoke hung in the room like a cloud, and through this cloud people kept coming up to me to exchange a few words," he told the tape recorder that captured his memoir. "Some looked like typical capitalists, right out of the posters painted during our Civil War—only they didn't have the pig snouts our artists always gave them. Others were dressed rather modestly. To look at them you wouldn't know they were the biggest capitalists in America."

W. Averell Harriman was one of the few private citizens in America who could have hosted such a party. Son of E. H. Harriman, a Gilded Age railroad baron who was denounced by President Theodore Roosevelt as one of America's "undesirable citizens," Harriman grew up on an estate that filled nearly thirty square miles of New Jersey. In the 1930s, he ran a New Deal agency for his old chum Franklin Roosevelt. During the war, he served as ambassador to the Soviet Union. Later he became Truman's ambassador to England and commerce secretary. In 1954, he was elected governor of New York. In June 1959, Harriman traveled to Moscow and sat down for a long chat with Khrushchev. To his dismay, Harriman learned that the man who led the small circle of Communists who controlled the Soviet Union held the Marxist belief that a small circle of capitalists controlled the United States—and that they kept the cold war going because they profited from the arms business.

Who are they? Harriman asked.

Khrushchev gave him a playful tap on the arm. "You're one of them," he replied.

Harriman, shocked at the allegation, promptly wrote an essay for *Life* magazine in which he urged President Eisenhower to enlighten Khrushchev by inviting him to America. When Ike did just that, Harriman decided to prove to Khrushchev that America was not ruled by a small group of powerful capitalists by inviting the premier to a cocktail party with a small group of powerful capitalists.

Khrushchev arrived only two hours after he'd escaped from the stalled elevator but he seemed no worse for the wear. Harriman and his wife met the premier at the door and escorted him upstairs to the library, a white room decorated with busts of Benjamin Franklin, Franklin Roosevelt, and Dwight Eisenhower. A large Picasso hung over the fireplace.

Harriman offered Khrushchev some vodka.

"Russian vodka?" Khrushchev asked.

"I am afraid not," Harriman replied. Graciously, he offered his guest a New York State brandy. Courageously, Khrushchev agreed to try it.

Harriman introduced the premier to the other guests—a group that included David Sarnoff, chairman of the Radio Corporation of America, William Herod, president of General Electric, Dean Rusk, president of the Rockefeller Foundation and a future secretary of state, John J. McCloy, chairman of the Chase Manhattan Bank, and John D. Rockefeller III, who needed no further identification.

The least rich and least powerful guest was Harriman's friend Galbraith, the Harvard economist who had become famous in 1958 as the author of *The Affluent Society*, a book that analyzed America's postwar economic boom in caustic prose: "The family which takes its mauve and cerise, air-conditioned, power-steered and power-braked automobile out for a tour passes through cities that are badly paved, made hideous by litter, blighted buildings, billboards and posts for wires that should long since have been put underground. . . . They picnic on exquisitely packaged foods from a portable icebox by a polluted stream and go on to spend the night in a park which is a menace to public health and morals. Just before dozing off on an air mattress beneath a nylon tent, amid the stench of decaying refuse, they may reflect vaguely on the curious unevenness of their blessings."

The book became a best-seller, proving that in the affluent society a man could become affluent by selling the affluent a book mocking affluence.

After the introductions, Harriman and the guest of honor took seats below the Picasso. "This is a cross-section of the ruling circles which you told me in Moscow you think dominate our government and want to continue the cold war," Harriman said.

That got a laugh from the guests.

"But the ruling group is a *secret* one, isn't it?" Khrushchev said, smiling.

That got a laugh too.

Harriman informed the chairman that some of his guests were Democrats and some were Republicans.

Khrushchev repeated his familiar line that there didn't seem to be much difference between the parties. "You rule America," he told the gathering. "You are the ruling circle. I don't believe in any other view. You are clever. You stay in the shadows and have your representatives, men without capital, who figure on the stage."

That comment was met with what Harriman later described as "stunned silence." But the silence didn't last long. Soon the guests were delivering long speeches designed to convince Khrushchev that capitalists were not really so powerful after all.

The first speaker was McCloy, who'd served as assistant secretary of war and president of the World Bank before becoming chairman of Chase Manhattan, the bank of the Rockefeller family. McCloy was "chairman of the Establishment itself," Galbraith wrote years later, wryly praising "the rocklike self-confidence that he always brought alike to truth, error, and even nonsense."

McCloy told Khrushchev that Wall Street's much-touted political power was a myth. Any legislation sponsored by Wall Street, he said, was almost automatically rejected by Congress. He somehow managed to say this with a straight face.

Khrushchev was not convinced. He listened to McCloy's long oration, then responded: "It follows then that those sitting in front of me are the poor relations of the United States."

The capitalists burst out laughing.

Undaunted, McCloy plodded on, informing Khrushchev that it was absurd to think that American capitalists supported the cold war in order to make money in the arms business. "That is a fantastic misunderstanding," he said. "No one among the American people is trying to preserve international tension for profits."

Harriman agreed with McCloy and called on Frank Pace, a former secretary of the Army who was now the chairman of General Dynamics, the huge defense contractor. Pace told Khrushchev that his company would gladly get out of the weapons business if peace suddenly broke out. Unfortunately, his case was not aided by the events of the very next day, when Khrushchev delivered a speech calling for disarmament and the stock market lost $1.7 billion in value, continuing a decline that began the day Ike announced Khrushchev's visit. "Mr. Khrushchev proposed that the world disarm within four years, giving form to the fears that have haunted Wall Street since his trip was planned," the *New York Times* explained. "The financial district wants peace, a spokesman for one large house said, but it also recognizes that any such plan would force unpredictable adjustments in the economic system of this country."

Did that mean that Khrushchev's foolish notion about the power of American capitalists was not completely foolish after all?

President Eisenhower did not attend Harriman's cocktail party and thus couldn't add his thoughts to the debate on the power of Wall Street and the arms industry. But sixteen months later, in his famous farewell address before leaving the White House, Ike warned the American people about the power of what he termed "the military-industrial complex."

"This conjunction of an immense military establishment and a large arms industry is new in the American experience," the old general said. "The total influence—economic, political, even spiritual—is felt in every city, every State house, every office of the federal government. . . . In the councils of government, we must guard against the acquisition of unwarranted influence, whether sought or unsought, by the military-industrial complex. The potential for the disastrous rise of misplaced power exists and will persist. We must never let the weight of this combination endanger our liberties."

36. THE PURLOINED INVITATION

While his father was stuck in an elevator in the Waldorf-Astoria, Sergei Khrushchev soared through the bright blue Indian summer sky over Manhattan in a U.S. Army helicopter.

At twenty-five, he was a thin, handsome man with his blond hair combed straight back, except for a lock that fell raffishly over his forehead. An engineer in the Soviet missile program with a pregnant wife back home in Moscow, Sergei was eager to see America. Flying at an altitude of about 1,000 feet, the chopper cruised over the George Washington Bridge, the United Nations, Coney Island, and the vast canyons of skyscrapers.

"Some of the buildings appeared like spikes," Sergei told reporters when he landed, speaking through an interpreter. "I would not want to live so high."

The chopper ride was fun but what Sergei Khrushchev *really* wanted to see in New York was a butterfly shop in Brooklyn. An avid butterfly collector, he had read about the shop in a magazine and asked if he could visit. At first the State Department balked (Brooklyn was officially off-limits to Soviet visitors), but finally the diplomats relented. Accompanied by a posse of bodyguards and a pack of reporters, Sergei traveled to East Flatbush. "I was very surprised when we left Manhattan to see that New York is a city of small, dirty, dark streets," he recalled years later. "At that time, what was New York to the Soviet Union? It was Broadway and skyscrapers."

Arriving at Butterfly Art Jewelry, Sergei got another surprise: The butterflies were for sale. In Russia, collectors traded butterflies but they couldn't buy them in stores like bread or shoes. "From my understanding, butterflies cannot be commodities. I thought it was a place where you could exchange. Who would buy butterflies?"

Flocks of butterflies, pinned and framed, filled the shop walls to the ceiling, each bearing a price tag. "I saw this butterfly $1, this one $2," Sergei recalls, "and I started counting my money in my mind."

But the shop's owner, Aminadov Glantz, refused to take Sergei's money. "I'm not going to sell them this time," he said. "I'm going to give them to you. And you send me butterflies from your country."

Later Sergei sent Glantz a shipment of Russian butterflies, enlisting his father's foreign minister, Andrei Gromyko, to help transport the insects.

At the butterfly shop—and everywhere else he wandered—Sergei used his little Austrian 8-millimeter, black and white movie camera to capture the strange sights of this strange land: the view of skyscrapers from a window at the Waldorf, a workman unloading boxes from the back of a panel truck, a Coca-Cola sign, a billboard advertising milk: "Borden's—Very Big on Flavor," cars with tail fins so big they looked like rocket ships, the first tollbooth he'd ever seen, topped with a sign reading "Passenger Cars 35 Cents."

In Times Square, Sergei filmed movie marquees, one advertising *Anatomy of a Murder,* another touting a double feature, *Tarzan's Savage Fury* and *She Devil.* He also filmed in a penny arcade where teenage boys with ducktail haircuts blasted away in a shooting gallery, trying to win a kewpie doll. And of course he shot Times Square's famous neon signs flashing in the night sky, and in his black and white home movie they looked like something out of a film noir detective flick.

"There were no such lights in Moscow," he recalled decades later, "because they did not need to advertise."

Returning to his hotel room after one of his rambles around New York, Sergei noticed that the famously efficient staff of the Waldorf-Astoria had cleaned and pressed his black dress suit. Immediately he checked the pockets.

Missing was an invitation to a secret awards ceremony held months earlier in Moscow. Sergei's boss, Vladimir Chelomei, and eleven of his assistants, including Sergei, had been awarded the Lenin Prize for creating the Soviet Union's first cruise missile. The ceremony was secret because the missile itself was a military secret.

On the day he received the prize, Sergei had stuck the invitation in his suit pocket and forgotten about it. When he came to Washington, he donned the suit and discovered the invitation. "At first I wanted to tear it up and throw it away, but then I changed my mind," he remembered. "I knew from detective stories that specialists can easily decipher even burned paper."

Nervously turning the invitation over and over in his hands, he tried to figure out what to do with it. No clever idea occurred to him so he stuffed it back into the pocket.

Now the suit was clean and the invitation was gone. Maybe the dry cleaner had simply thrown it out, he thought. Or maybe not. Maybe it was being scrutinized by the CIA. Sergei said nothing to anyone and hoped for the best.

A few months later, back in Moscow, his father came home from work looking grim and took Sergei aside to ask if perhaps he'd talked too much about his work when he was in America.

Of course not, Sergei replied, irked that his father would even consider the possibility. After all, he said, I'm not a child and I understand the importance of secrecy.

"We caught an American agent here," his father explained. "During questioning, he said that one of his assignments was to find out which project earned Chelomei a Lenin Prize and what Khrushchev's son Sergei was doing in his design bureau."

Instantly Sergei remembered the missing invitation. He confessed, telling the whole story to his father, who looked increasingly glum.

"I felt like a traitor," Sergei recalled.

Ashamed at his foolishness, Sergei could never bring himself to ask his father a question that would linger in his mind for decades: *What did the KGB do to the spy who revealed all this?*

37. HECKLING THE DICTATOR

On their first night in New York, Nina Khrushchev and her daughters accompanied Mrs. Henry Cabot Lodge on a trip to the Majestic Theater to watch *The Music Man,* a smash hit Broadway musical about a con man who travels to Iowa to swindle the rubes in a hick town.

Nikita Khrushchev, who was scheduled to hit Iowa in five days, did not see the show. He was attending yet another banquet with yet another group of businessmen and enduring yet another civics lesson from Lodge, who began by announcing that American capitalists were no longer "robber barons."

"If 'robber baron' is the definition of the word 'capitalist,'" Lodge said, "then we are not capitalists at all."

The modern American economy should not be described as "monopoly capitalism." A more accurate term, he said, is "economic humanism." To support his thesis, Lodge rattled off scads of statistics: Three out of four families own a car. . . . Three-fifths of homes are owned by the families who occupy them. . . . Fourteen million Americans own stocks. . . . One in ten families make over $10,000 a year. . . . Meanwhile, the federal government takes care of the poor, distributing free food to 5 million Americans and sheltering 2 million in subsidized housing.

"We live in a welfare state which seeks to put a floor beneath which no one sinks," Lodge said, "but builds no ceiling to prevent a man from rising."

When Lodge finished, Khrushchev shuffled to the lectern and gazed out over the Waldorf's Grand Ballroom. The place was packed with 2,000 people from the New York Economic Club—an audience that the *New York Herald Tribune* called "one of history's greatest concentrations of capitalists."

After an amiable overture, Khrushchev moved to the question of unemployment in America—specifically the unemployment of his friend Averell Harriman, who was sitting at the head table. Harriman had been out of work since Nelson Rockefeller defeated him in the 1958 gubernatorial election, but Khrushchev volunteered to help.

"I could offer him the job of my advisor," he said, "with good pay and a country home, a dacha, near Moscow."

That got a laugh, so Khrushchev immediately offered jobs to everybody in the room. "You would be paid well and have as good a position as you do in any corporation in this country," he promised. "We value good people, and if any person here wants to try his hand at building socialism in our country, he is welcome to call me up at the hotel and we can come to terms."

That elicited another laugh, although it failed to attract many résumés.

When he finished his impromptu comic monologue, Khrushchev launched into his prepared speech, which touted the glories of the Soviet economy in much the same way that Lodge had lauded the glories of American capitalism.

"Compared with 1913, industrial production in the Soviet Union has increased 36 times over—and only four times in your country . . . "

". . . last year, for instance, we graduated 94,000 engineers while you graduated 35,000 . . . "

". . . our production increased 12 percent in the first eight months . . . "

On and on he droned, citing statistic after excruciating statistic, first in Russian, then in the English translation. It was getting late and people began tip-toeing toward the exits. Finally Khrushchev ended his speech with a plea for trade, brotherhood and peace. Then he agreed to answer questions. That's when the trouble started.

"Mr. Khrushchev, I'd like to ask one simple specific question," said Gardner Cowles, the publisher of *Look* magazine. "Why is it, sir, that you will not allow your people, if they wish, to listen to a broadcast from the United States? And why is it that you do not allow American magazines and newspapers to be distributed freely throughout the Soviet Union?"

"Gentlemen, please understand me correctly," Khrushchev said. "I have come here at the invitation of the president. We have invited your president to come to our country. We agreed that our discussions will not touch upon the affairs of third countries and that there will be no interference in each other's internal affairs. . . "

"Answer the question!" somebody in the balcony hollered.

"Gentlemen . . ." Khrushchev continued.

"Answer it!"

What was this? A dissident in the Waldorf-Astoria?

"You're ducking the question!" somebody else yelled.

Khrushchev was hearing something dictators rarely encounter—the voice of the heckler, the protest from the peanut gallery, the Bronx cheer. Stalin didn't have to put up with this kind of guff, and Khrushchev didn't enjoy it much either. He scowled and his face reddened.

"I'm an old sparrow and you cannot muddle me with your cries," he bellowed. "You might not want to listen to me but surely you must show enough hospitality not to interrupt. If there is no desire to listen to what I have to say, I can go."

But he didn't go. Instead, he took a breath and kept roaring, exploding in rage for the second time in two days. "I have not come here to beg! I come here as a representative of a great people who have made a great October revolution! And no cries can do away with the great achievements of our people!"

He stopped. "I will reply to the question when there are no interruptions."

The audience fell silent. It was a scary moment. The man who'd been doing schmaltzy comedy shtick a few minutes earlier was now throwing a full-blown temper tantrum.

Khrushchev waited while the silence deepened.

"And the reply is this," he said. "The question of what our public listens to or reads should not be decided by any outside government or any outside influence but by our own people and by their government."

His tirade over, Khrushchev was calm enough to add a barbed reference to the treatment of Paul Robeson, the African American singer and actor harassed for his pro-Communist views. "You also jam American voices. For instance, our people and a great many other people in the world like the great singer Paul Robeson. Yet for five or seven years, the

American government would not permit him to tour any other country to sing there. Why is that voice jammed?"

It was a clever retort but it fell flat, overshadowed by the indelible image of a dictator who possessed hydrogen bombs flying into an angry rage over a mildly tough question and some tepid heckling.

"No one who was there will soon forget," wrote *New York Times* reporter Harry Schwartz, "an angry, red-faced Khrushchev waving his fist in the air at the audience."

38. "MAY GOD HAVE PITY ON YOU," SAID THE ATHEIST

When Khrushchev slid into Lodge's limousine for the hundred-mile ride to Franklin's Roosevelt's grave in Hyde Park the next morning, September 18, the premier was still irate at the events in the Waldorf ballroom the previous night, especially the question he'd been asked about Soviet jamming of Voice of America radio broadcasts.

"You would not like people from outside appealing to people here to overthrow the government," the premier told Lodge.

"If such appeals were made on our radio," Lodge replied, "most Americans would simply laugh."

Khrushchev reminded Lodge that dozens of leaders of the American Communist Party had been sent to prison, convicted of violating the Smith Act, which outlawed membership in any group advocating the overthrow of the United States government.

"American communists are committed to overthrow the government by force," Lodge said. "No government, including the Soviet, fails to have laws to protect it against being overthrown by force."

What did those Communists do? Khrushchev asked.

It all happened nine years ago, Lodge said, and he couldn't remember much about it.

But Khrushchev's knowledge of America's Communist Party was sharper than Lodge's, perhaps because he was secretly bankrolling the party. "You can look for nine years," he said, "and you can never find proof that they have done anything wrong."

He gave Lodge a playful nudge in the ribs. "You say you don't like violence," he said. "Did George Washington have an election in order to win the American Revolution?"

As the politicians sparred, their forty-car motorcade left Manhattan and barreled into the Bronx, surrounded by a posse of motorcycle cops. They'd left the Waldorf a half-hour late and were trying to make up time because Khrushchev was scheduled to deliver a speech at the United Nations in midafternoon. Inside Lodge's limousine, Khrushchev boasted about how the Soviet Union would soon surpass the United States in every important way.

"He was definitely trying to tease me," Lodge wrote in his daily memo to the State Department. "He kept coming back to the subject of my grandchildren and that in their future there would be no capitalism."

Lodge tried to avoid provoking the testy dictator but after a while, he could no longer hold his tongue. "You are talking about what my grandchildren will be seeing here," he said. "Maybe you would like to know what I think your grandchildren will be seeing in Russia. I don't think the Soviet Union is static. There is a lot of evolution there."

"Yes," Khrushchev agreed. "Lots of evolution."

"What I think we are going to see," Lodge said, "is a lessening of central bureaucracy and a growth of wider individual freedoms. And my grandchildren's generation and your grandchildren's generation will be very much alike in essentials, although politicians will go on talking a long time in the same old phrases."

It was an optimistic vision of a gradual peaceful convergence of the two competing superpowers. A man possessing diplomatic instincts might have endorsed it, perhaps adding a comment about America evolving toward socialism. Not Khrushchev.

"May God have pity on you," he told Lodge. Then he turned theatrically to his wife. "Isn't it a pity," he asked, "to see a nice man all stuffed up with foolish notions?"

When the motorcade arrived in Hyde Park, Eleanor Roosevelt stood waiting outside the hedged garden where her husband was buried, wearing a blue print dress, a white coat, and a microphone that enabled her conversations with Khrushchev to be heard by viewers watching the live television coverage of the event.

Slightly stooped at seventy-five, Mrs. Roosevelt still possessed the tenacious energy that drove her to become the most active and outspoken First Lady in American history. For twelve years, while her husband was bound to his wheelchair, she served as his "eyes and ears," she said, visiting schools and slums, meeting sharecroppers and soldiers and strikers, and reporting back to Franklin on what she'd seen. After he died in 1945, she kept working, serving as chairman of the United Nations Human Rights Commission, campaigning for Adlai Stevenson and writing a daily newspaper column, a monthly magazine column, and several books. For fifteen consecutive years, polls identified her as "the world's most popular woman," but her critics, who were numerous and nasty, mocked everything from her endless crusading to her buck teeth.

Like most liberals, she supported Ike's decision to invite Khrushchev. "I think he will learn a great deal because he is perceptive and alert," she wrote in her newspaper column. Now she smiled and stepped forward to shake hands with the premier and his wife.

"I felt it an obligation to come here and pay my respects to your husband and his memory," Khrushchev told her. "I did not come for pleasure, but for duty."

It was an ambiguous greeting that could be interpreted several ways, not all of them kindly, but Mrs. Roosevelt, ever the optimist, decided to take it as a compliment. She took both Khrushchevs by the arm and led them through the high green hedge to the rose garden where her husband lay beneath a small marble stone.

With the help of two aides, Khrushchev placed a huge wreath of or-
chids and roses atop the grave and then stepped back and bowed his head
for a moment of what would have been silence except for the clicking and
whirring of countless cameras. After a brief interval, Khrushchev nodded
and then Mrs. Roosevelt led her guests down the road toward the Roosevelt Memorial Library.

During the walk, Lodge reminded Khrushchev that they had scheduled
a tour of Harlem on their way back to the United Nations. Smiling Mike
Menshikov told Lodge that there was no time to tour Harlem because the
chairman wanted to change his clothes before his speech to the U.N.

"In that case, we'll go straight back," Lodge replied.

"Oh, so you don't want Chairman Khrushchev to see Harlem?" Menshikov asked. Then he turned to his boss. "Notice how the Americans
want to prevent you from going to Harlem. This is because they have
something to hide."

Lodge lost his perpetual cool, warning Menshikov not to blame the
Americans for canceling the Harlem trip. Soon the distinguished diplomats were hissing at each other like alley cats while Khrushchev smiled at
the absurd spectacle.

Inside the museum, Mrs. Roosevelt showed the premier a portrait of
FDR done by Stalin's favorite painter, Aleksandr Gerasimov, and some letters that Stalin had written to Roosevelt.

"These might interest you," she said.

They didn't. Khrushchev showed no interest in anything except leaving. "He enjoyed nothing," Mrs. Roosevelt said later. "A man behind him
all the time kept whispering, 'seven minutes, seven minutes.'"

She had provided a lunch for her visitors but Khrushchev, usually an eager eater, ignored it. On his way out the door, he grabbed a roll off the
table and held it up for the photographers. Grinning, he said—in English—"One for the road."

It was a rude spectacle but Eleanor Roosevelt knew exactly what she
was witnessing. She understood the bitter lesson learned by defeated

politicians and the widows of powerful men, who find that a world that once seemed so welcoming has become suddenly indifferent to their charms.

"This gentleman is interested in power," she explained to reporters after Khrushchev left. "And I have no power."

39. RUSSIAN BANDSTAND

Waiting for Khrushchev outside the United Nations building in Manhattan was the usual gaggle of gawkers, protesters, reporters, photographers, and cops—plus a big black bear accompanied by a man wearing a cowboy hat and a fringed buckskin jacket while he strummed a guitar made from pieces of a rail fence, an ox yoke, and the headboard of his grandmother's bed.

The bear was real but stuffed. The man in buckskin called himself Jimmy Driftwood and he entertained the crowd by singing his Khrushchev-inspired version of the old folk song "The Bear Went over the Mountain."

> *The bear flew over the ocean,*
> *The bear flew over the ocean,*
> *The bear flew over the ocean,*
> *To see what he could see.*
> *He saw a friendly nation,*
> *He saw a friendly nation*
> *He saw a friendly nation*
> *And all of our people are free.* *

---

* Copyright Warden Music Company Inc. 1959, renewed 1987. All rights reserved. Used by permission.

Driftwood looked and sounded like a hillbilly from the Ozarks. In fact, he *was* a hillbilly from the Ozarks, and proud of it. He was also a former teacher and school superintendent as well as a songwriter who had authored more than 1,000 songs, six of which were currently riding the pop or country-and-western charts. And that didn't count "The Bear Flew over the Ocean," which had just been released by Driftwood's record label, RCA Victor, the company that had brought him to New York so he could generate publicity by standing in front of the U.N. with a stuffed bear, singing his new song about the visiting Russian bear.

Driftwood wasn't the only songwriter inspired by Khrushchev's visit. Irving Caesar, author of "Tea for Two" and countless other tunes, expressed his views on the trip in a song called "Let's Pow-Wow, Not Kow-Tow." And the team of Dickie Goodman and Mickey Shorr created "Russian Bandstand," a novelty record that managed to answer a question that nobody else had bothered to ask: What would happen if Nikita Khrushchev decided to host a Russian version of Dick Clark's popular rock and roll TV show, *American Bandstand?*

The song began with an emcee speaking in the world's worst fake Russian accent: "Welcome to Russian Bandstand. This is your host, Nikita Clarkchev. In Russia, almost everybody watches Russian Bandstand."

Then comes a blast of machine gun fire.

"Now," Clarkchev says, "*everybody* watches Russian Bandstand. Ha, ha, ha. Next is number one song in Russia."

There's a quick snippet of a rock guitar riff and then the sound of teenagers protesting: "But we don't like that song."

"You've *got* to like that song," says Clarkchev. "It's number one song."

"But we don't like . . . "

Another blast of machine gun fire.

And so on. It wasn't particularly subtle, but it was funny and its portrayal of the traditional Soviet response to dissent was not entirely inaccurate.

Ten years later, in one of history's infinite ironies, Mickey Shorr's seventeen-year-old son Henry, angry at getting suspended from high school for wearing his hair too long, hijacked a plane and flew to Communist Cuba. He died there a year later, one of the more bizarre casualties of the cold war.

40. A SIMPLE, EASY PLAN FOR EVERLASTING PEACE

Returning from Hyde Park in the limo with Lodge, Khrushchev once again bragged about the brilliance of his rocket scientists, the power of his atomic weapons, and the accuracy of his missiles. Then he went to the United Nations to deliver an impassioned speech advocating the destruction of all weapons and the abolition of all armies.

"It would be difficult to devise a weapon more powerful than the hydrogen bomb," Khrushchev said, standing at the rostrum at the U.N. General Assembly, reading the speech that he'd declined to show Eisenhower at the White House three days earlier. "It is hard to imagine the consequences for mankind of a war with the use of these monstrous instruments of destruction and annihilation. If it were allowed to break out, its toll would run not into millions but into tens and even hundreds of millions of human lives. . . . Nor would this war spare future generations. Its poisonous trail in the form of radioactive contamination would long continue to cripple people and claim many lives."

Fortunately Khrushchev had a simple, easy plan to ensure everlasting peace: "Over a period of four years, all states should effect complete disarmament and therefore no longer possess any means of waging war."

What that meant, Khrushchev continued, was that "armies, navies and air forces would cease to exist . . . war ministries would be abolished . . . military training establishments would be closed . . . millions of men would return to peaceful, constructive labor . . . all atomic and hydrogen bombs in the possession of states would be destroyed . . . military rockets of all ranges would be eliminated."

Under his proposal, Khrushchev said, the only armed forces remaining on the planet would be police departments "equipped with small arms and designed exclusively to maintain internal order." If his plan were implemented, he continued, mankind would experience permanent peace, and the wealth wasted on war would be used to feed the hungry and build schools and hospitals. "Human energy," he said, "could be directed to the creation of material and spiritual values beautifying and ennobling man's life and work."

For a moment, it almost seemed as if Khrushchev would end his address by asking members of the General Assembly to hold hands and sing "Kumbaya."

Khrushchev's speech was the most brilliant and beautiful oration ever delivered at the United Nations, according to the reporters who covered it for the Soviet press.

"The first feeling that gripped the audience, regardless of their attitude toward the Soviet Union, socialism and Khrushchev personally, was that they had seldom heard anything more compelling and convincing," wrote a dozen Soviet correspondents in *Face to Face with America,* their collective book on the premier's trip. "If anyone asked what the reason for this effect was, he could sincerely have only one answer: Because everything he says is *the truth.* The whole unqualified, unvarnished truth, as simple and incontrovertible as life itself."

Khrushchev—or, as the Soviet reporters described him, "the indefatigable fighter against the powers of darkness"—had delivered a "profound, strictly scientific and therefore irrefutable analysis" that was "imbued with intense concern for the welfare of humanity." In fact, they concluded, "never in the history of the United Nations had the speech of any statesman made so powerful an impression as that of Khrushchev."

The American press was a tad less laudatory. *Time* magazine called the speech "so absurd and impractical as to be insulting." Columnist Joseph Alsop called Khrushchev's proposals "shameless frauds." The *New York Times* reminded readers that the Russians had first proposed complete disarmament in 1927, "a propaganda vehicle that served the Soviets well."

And Reuben Maury, the feisty editorial voice of the *New York Daily News*, denounced what he called "the butcher's bombshell," adding, "we wonder how the Chinese Reds will feel about disarming and thereby inviting their slaves to massacre them."

American officials were not so quick to reject Khrushchev's proposal. Secretary Herter said the speech "will require very careful examination," and the White House announced that Ike himself was examining it very carefully while vacationing on his Gettysburg farm.

Three days later, Herter told a press conference that Khrushchev's speech merited "very close attention" and that his disarmament proposal should be taken "very seriously." Total disarmament would be "highly desirable," he said, "if it could safely be done."

For a brief moment, Herter came out firmly against skepticism about the premier's proposal: "These are matters, I say, that cannot be treated with skepticism or treated lightly. I have been a little impatient at those who merely waved off Mr. Khrushchev's suggestions as propaganda." A few seconds later, however, Herter himself waved off Khrushchev's proposal as propaganda: "It *is* propaganda. It is in its details something that can be looked at with skepticism."

Of course, the skeptics were correct. The man who had sent tanks to crush the Hungarian rebellion had no intention of disbanding his army. As he later told Arkady Shevchenko, a diplomat who worked at the Soviet mission to the United Nations, his proposal was a public relations ploy.

"Never forget the appeal that the idea of disarmament has in the outside world. All you have to do is say, 'I'm in favor of it,' and that pays big dividends," Khrushchev told Shevchenko, grinning cynically. "A seductive slogan is a most powerful political instrument. The Americans don't understand that. They only hurt themselves in struggling against the idea of general and complete disarmament. What they are doing is as futile as Don Quixote's fighting the windmills."

It was a classic case of bilateral diplomatic posturing. Khrushchev pretended to make a serious disarmament proposal, the Americans pretended to take it seriously, and the arms race continued without pause.

41. SEEN ONE, SEEN 'EM ALL

When Khrushchev left the U.N. after delivering his speech, a mob of anti-Communist protesters charged toward him but the police held them back and the premier slipped into his limo unscathed.

His motorcade roared up Fifth Avenue, heading for the Waldorf-Astoria. Reporters followed. As they hung around the Waldorf lobby, waiting for the premier's next adventure, they watched a tall man with a huge, rugged head walk into the hotel, wearing a rumpled brown suit and carrying an equally rumpled raincoat. Grinning broadly, the man made his way across the lobby, shaking hands, slapping backs and addressing everybody with a cheery cry of "Hiya, fella!"

"Who's that?" a Soviet reporter asked.

"That's Governor Rockefeller," an American reporter replied.

The Russians were stunned. Of course they knew about the Rockefellers, prime symbols of evil capitalism and the subjects of endless propaganda in the Soviet Union, where a book on the Rockefeller dynasty, published in 1957, bore a wonderfully gruesome title—*Ever Knee-Deep in Blood, Ever Trampling Corpses.* But somehow they expected a real-life Rockefeller to look a bit more regal than this rumpled glad-hander.

After working the room like a Tammany ward heeler, Nelson Aldrich Rockefeller, the world's most famous capitalist, stepped into an elevator and went upstairs to greet the world's most famous Communist. They'd met before—at the Geneva summit in 1955, when Rockefeller was a part of Eisenhower's entourage—and the premier hadn't been impressed. "He was dressed fairly democratically and was the sort of man who didn't make much of an impression one way or the other," Khrushchev recalled in his memoir. "When I met him, I said, 'So, this is Mr. Rockefeller himself!' and I playfully poked him in the ribs with my fists. He took this as a joke and did the same thing to me."

Now, four years after that symbolic Battle of the Titans, Rockefeller had emerged as an important figure in American politics—the governor of New York and a man challenging Nixon for the 1960 Republican presidential nomination. But Rockefeller was wary of this meeting with Khrushchev. For some reason, he believed that the premier's entourage contained Soviet psychiatrists who'd been assigned to study the psyches of America's potential future presidents. So Rockefeller was on guard, determined to project an aura of strength to the Soviet shrinks.

When the governor arrived in the premier's suite, Khrushchev offered him a drink and said, "I want to propose a toast to coexistence."

"I won't drink to that," Rockefeller replied. "I don't believe in it."

"What do you mean you don't believe in it?" Khrushchev asked.

Rockefeller said he'd prefer to toast to "cooperation." It didn't make much sense but perhaps Rockefeller thought his refusal would impress the Soviet psychiatrists.

The governor welcomed the premier to New York State, then launched into a speech about "the brotherhood of man under the fatherhood of God" and "love as the greatest force in the world" and the "uniqueness of each individual as a child of God."

Khrushchev listened politely, then mumbled, "We are also deeply concerned for the people."

Rockefeller informed Khrushchev that the population of New York State was 16.5 million, and that a half million of its citizens had come to America from other lands, seeking "freedom and opportunity."

"Don't give me that stuff," Khrushchev replied. "They only came to get higher wages. I was almost one of them."

"If you had come," Rockefeller said, "you would have been the head of one of our biggest unions by now."

The statesmen bantered for about fifteen minutes, then summoned photographers to snap pictures as they hammed it up, pretending to throw punches at each other.

After the photo op, Rockefeller returned to the lobby to regale reporters with his impression of Khrushchev ("he was serious at times and gay at times, but there is always a keen look coming out of his eyes") while the premier headed off to tour Manhattan with Henry Cabot Lodge.

In Lodge's limo, Khrushchev rode past the Brooklyn Bridge, several housing projects, Trinity Church and the New York Stock Exchange. But he couldn't see much out the car window except the roaring, belching police motorcycles that surrounded the limo like a squad of cavalry. "My only impression," Khrushchev recalled in his memoir, "was of a huge, noisy city with an enormous number of signs and automobiles, hence vast quantities of exhaust fumes that were choking people."

The limousine stopped outside the Empire State Building and Lodge took Khrushchev to the top of the world's tallest skyscraper, where the premier could look down on New York City. It was late afternoon on a lovely summer day and the setting sun threw a mellow, cocktail-hour glow over the skyline of Manhattan, inspiring the Soviet reporters who accompanied Khrushchev to pen a paragraph of lyrical prose:

"At the bottom of that canyon of rock, concrete, steel, and aluminum, the stir and bustle of New York could barely be heard," they wrote in *Face to Face with America*. "We could see the flash and whirl of advertising signs for hotels, cinemas, saloons, drinks, cigarettes, patented cosmetics— everything that is bought and sold for dollars, but made by the hands of the toiling millions. The whole seething world of trade, finance, communications, pleasures, sufferings, shattered hopes, crime, wealth and poverty stood sharply etched in the setting sun. The cityscape is impressive, it shows there is no limit to human inventiveness."

Khrushchev's reaction was less poetic. "If you've seen one skyscraper, you've seen them all," he wrote in his memoir. "One thing I'll say for climbing to the top of the highest skyscraper in New York: at least the air is fresh up there. On the whole, New York had a humid, unpleasant climate, and the air is filthy."

The next morning, he rose early, ate a quick breakfast and left the Waldorf with Lodge for the tour of Harlem that Menshikov had demanded so vociferously. At seven o'clock on a Saturday morning, the streets of America's most famous African American neighborhood were nearly deserted, and in the soft morning sunshine, Harlem did not strike Khrushchev as the grim locus of racist oppression that Menshikov described.

"This isn't bad," the premier told Lodge. "We have a lot of areas just like this in the Soviet Union."

From Harlem, Khrushchev sped off to Idlewild Airport, where an American government jet sat on a runway, awaiting the premier and his entourage.

"Good-bye, dear friends," Khrushchev said into the inevitable microphone, then climbed halfway up the jet's ramp, turned around and waved for the photographers.

After forty-six hours in New York, he was headed for Los Angeles, where Hollywood's biggest stars were squabbling for tickets to see him perform.

42. IT KILLED MILTON BERLE AND IT CAN KILL YOU TOO

When Nikita Khrushchev boarded the plane for Los Angeles on Saturday morning, September 19, he had spent less than five days in the United States and already he'd achieved the American Dream: He was the biggest star on television.

"It's Khrush, Khrushy, Khrushchev! The fellow's all over the dials these days," wrote Ben Gross, the TV columnist for the *New York Daily News*. "You can't get away from him on radio or TV. The pudgy Soviet dictator is smiling, laughing, scowling, shaking his forefinger, or clenching his iron fist. Never before has one man been the subject of such an extensive broadcast coverage."

During the day, the three main TV networks covered Khrushchev's comings and goings live. At night, they recapped the action in half-hour news specials—NBC's *Journey to Understanding*, ABC's *Mr. Khrushchev Abroad*, and CBS's *Eyewitness to History*.

Of course, it wasn't just TV cameras that were covering Khrushchev. His journey was also chronicled by more than three hundred print reporters and photographers—the largest traveling media mob yet unleashed upon America, a churning, clamorous horde that encircled the dictator and blocked his view of the country he came to see.

"It was the first of the great media events," recalled Daniel Schorr, who covered the trip for CBS television. "It turned into a media event in part because Khrushchev wanted the attention and in part because TV and radio were still learning how to cover these things."

Schorr, like Harrison Salisbury of the *New York Times*, was a veteran Moscow correspondent. The media gaggle also included the big guns of Washington journalism—Chalmers Roberts of the *Washington Post* and James Reston of the *Times*. But the reporter who came closest to capturing the sheer weirdness of the trip was Murray Kempton of the *New York Post*. Kempton, a former labor organizer who'd briefly flirted with Communism in his youth, viewed the strange events with a skeptical eye and a scathing wit.

"This trip is like one of those tea parties in Dostoyevsky when everyone meets in apparent comity and then, after three or four minutes, Nikolai Nikolaevich for no discernible reason overturns the boiling samovar on the head of Alexander Alexandrovich," Kempton wrote before the pack left New York. "It is a Russian party, elevated only by the possibility that the guest of honor may blow his stack. It is both awesome and deplorable how suddenly Nikita Khrushchev can blow his stack."

The trip was the biggest story of the year, maybe the decade, and nearly everyone with access to a typewriter seemed eager to lay Khrushchev down on the couch for analysis.

"Mr. Khrushchev suffers from a severe national inferiority complex," wrote Erwin Canham in the *Christian Science Monitor*.

"The Soviet premier clearly is a man of huge and urgent self-confidence," noted Andrew Tully in the *New York World Telegram*. "He is like the bucolic wiseacre who suddenly struck it rich and is too overjoyed with his good fortune not to know it."

"He is, in my book, a slow, loutish, ignorant indoctrinaire, who stubbornly deludes himself with wishful thinking, a rural dolt unwittingly proving a case against himself and his system," wrote Fulton Lewis Jr. in the *New York Mirror.*

Columnists compared Khrushchev to nearly everything—a juvenile delinquent, a method actor, a vaudevillian, a country bumpkin. David Lawrence wrote that the premier had "the personality of Adolf Hitler." Doris Fleeson said he had the physicality of Fiorello LaGuardia. And Richard L. Stout called Khrushchev "a mixture of the late gesticulating Mayor Fiorello LaGuardia, of steely-eyed James R. Hoffa, of W.C. Fields, and oddly enough of eloquent Winston Churchill all rolled into one."

"The Chairman, as he likes to be called, looks like your genial host at the neighborhood delicatessen," wrote Charles McCabe in the *San Francisco Chronicle.* "The Chairman also looks as if he could put cyanide in the pastrami, and smile."

"He's an excellent actor," wrote Dorothy Kilgallen. "If you were a Hollywood casting director trying to find a part for him, you might find him perfect for the role of the elderly fat cuckolded husband . . . or you could audition him as a gangster, probably with great success, or as a kindly old fellow who rescued a couple of children."

By the time Khrushchev headed for Hollywood, he'd paraded across America's TV screens for countless hours, stared out from photographs on the front page of every major newspaper, and had been chronicled, quoted, and analyzed as much as any human alive. But this triumph of self-promotion carried with it the danger of a thoroughly modern malady, a disease so rarified that it afflicted only the biggest stars, like Milton Berle. The TV comedian was so popular that he was nicknamed "Mr. Television" until he wore out his welcome and nobody wanted to watch him anymore.

This danger prompted John Crosby, the TV critic of the *New York Herald Tribune,* to issue a friendly warning to the Soviet premier: "Overexposure, Mr. Khrushchev. It killed Milton Berle. It can murder you, too."

43. SOARING AWAY TO NEVER-NEVER LAND

Somewhere over the Midwest, Khrushchev poured Lodge a brandy and proposed a toast to peace. They tossed the shots back, then held their glasses upside down over their heads—Khrushchev's folksy way of showing that a drink was downed, not merely sipped.

Toasting had become a frequent event for the traveling partners, "a symbol of our good relations," Lodge recalled. "And, although it was hardly my usual routine, I survived rather pleasantly."

Even without the glow of alcohol, it was a lovely day, the sun shining brightly all the way across the continent. From the jet's cruising altitude of 31,000 feet, Khrushchev could see for one hundred, sometimes two hundred miles. He saw the skyscrapers of Manhattan and the city's suburban sprawl. He saw the industrial cities of Pennsylvania and Ohio, each cloaked in a cloud of smog. He saw the checkerboard farmlands of the Midwest, the mighty Mississippi, the Great Plains, the peaks of the Rocky Mountains, and the so-called Atomic Mountain, Los Alamos, where the atomic bomb was born. Then, as the plane circled slowly to give him a better look, he gazed at the Grand Canyon, its ancient rocks glowing in countless shades of red in the late morning sun.

Along the way, Khrushchev wandered into the cockpit to chat with the pilot, Air Force Major Jim Lykans. "He patted me on the back and said it was a fine airplane," Lykans said later. "He shook hands with all the crew members. I guess he's a professional politician. We thought he'd never quit talking."

Back in his seat, Khrushchev told Lodge that he liked the Boeing 707 so much that he wanted one. He even offered to trade his pride and joy—the world's tallest plane, the TU–114—for one of these jets. Lodge replied that he wasn't authorized to make such a swap, and Khrushchev said he'd take the issue up with Ike at Camp David.

Flying over the desert an hour east of Los Angeles, Lodge reminded Khrushchev that they had some free time in today's schedule after lunching with Hollywood stars at the Twentieth Century Fox studio. Lodge radioed William Parker, the Los Angeles police chief, and asked if he had any suggestions for interesting things to do in the afternoon. Parker rattled off a few—visit a supermarket, drive through a suburban housing development or tour Disneyland. Lodge told Parker he'd call back after consulting with Khrushchev.

When Lodge laid out the choices, the premier's wife and daughters immediately said they wanted to see Disneyland. Khrushchev agreed, although he had only the vaguest notion of what he'd see at this place he called a "fairy-tale park."

It wasn't the first time Disneyland had been discussed as a possible destination for the premier. The idea had been debated during the pre-trip negotiations and ultimately rejected as too time-consuming. But the Los Angeles newspapers kept speculating about the possibility of Khrushchev touring Disneyland. After all, other foreign leaders—including Sukarno of Indonesia—were among the 15 million people who had visited the amusement park since it opened in 1955 amid massive hype that included live TV coverage hosted by an aging actor named Ronald Reagan.

Lodge called Chief Parker to relay Khrushchev's decision. "Now, Chief, are you sure that you can guarantee security on a trip to Disneyland?" Lodge asked. "Because we will not go anywhere where you do not guarantee security."

Chief Parker assured Lodge that he could.

"Suddenly all the Russians were clamoring to go. Even Gromyko," recalled protocol chief Wiley Buchanan. "The thought of that dour-faced functionary soaring away to Never-Never Land on the Peter Pan sky-ride struck me as almost too good to be true."

Khrushchev's arrival in Los Angeles lacked the pizzazz of his landing in Washington five days earlier—no crowd, no brass band, no twenty-one-gun salute. After touching down, the jet taxied to a remote part of the airport. Police had sealed the site off from the public and penned the press behind a chain-link fence. Looking dapper in a gray summer suit and waving his homburg, Khrushchev stepped down the ramp from the plane to be greeted by a tiny crowd composed mostly of policemen.

At a microphone set up on the tarmac stood Norris Poulson, the mayor of Los Angeles. Poulson's thick glasses and bright smile made him look a bit like Harold Lloyd. Mayor Poulson's most famous accomplishment was luring the Brooklyn Dodgers to Los Angeles in 1957. But he also made headlines by scoffing at the official plans for evacuating Los Angeles in the event of nuclear attack, which basically called for everybody to hop into their cars and drive away. "Even if the bomb failed to explode," he told a congressional subcommittee, "we would probably have a traffic jam that would take weeks to untangle."

Now, standing at the airport waiting to welcome Khrushchev, the mayor was not happy that his job compelled him to be cordial to the leader of world Communism. Consequently he'd planned an ostentatiously unfriendly reception.

"Mr. Chairman," Poulson said, "we welcome you to Los Angeles, the city of angels, where the impossible always happens."

It was a great opening line. Unfortunately, it was the *only* line.

The terseness of the greeting irked Khrushchev, who jettisoned his own prepared speech and ad-libbed remarks that were nearly as brief. "I thank you for this welcome. I am happy to avail myself of the opportunity to visit this city and greeting its representatives and exchanging views with them."

With that, Khrushchev and his entourage climbed into their limos and headed off to the Twentieth Century Fox studios.

That night, Poulson and Khrushchev were scheduled to meet at a civic banquet, and the mayor was already planning another surprise for the premier. "Everybody else has been nice to him, but I'm not going to be," Poulson had told KTLA-TV reporter Pat Michaels the previous day. "You should see my speech. I'm having 200 copies printed up. I'm going to have my fist out there, but it's going to be covered with brocade. And under the brocade, I'm going to have a long, sharp knife. And I'm going to ram it all the way into that son-of-a . . . "

He didn't finish the phrase. He didn't have to.

44. KHRUSHCHEV FEVER SWEEPS HOLLYWOOD

"How the hell are you, Khrush? I'm goddamned glad you're here," said Shirley MacLaine. "Welcome to our country and welcome to Twentieth Century Fox. I hope you enjoy seeing how Hollywood makes a musical. We're going to shoot the Can-Can number without pants."

Unfortunately, MacLaine was not actually talking to Khrushchev. She was chatting with a *Time* magazine reporter on the set of *Can-Can,* joking about what she'd say when Khrushchev visited the set a few days later. Somehow the studio had convinced Khrushchev to drop by and watch the filming of *Can-Can*—an event that promised to be a classic Hollywood publicity stunt.

Staging publicity stunts is—with the possible exception of making movies—what Hollywood does best. In 1947, a PR man named Jim Moran sat on an ostrich egg for nineteen days to publicize a movie called *The Egg and I.* In 1949, a struggling actor named Rock Hudson attracted attention by appearing at the Hollywood Photographer's Ball wearing only skin-tight gold shorts and a coating of gold paint so that he resembled an Oscar statue. The Academy Awards themselves began in 1929 as a cheap publicity stunt for the movie business and evolved over the decades into a far more expensive publicity stunt for the movie business.

Now Fox had lured Nikita Khrushchev to the filming of *Can-Can,* a risqué Broadway musical set among the dance hall girls of fin de siècle Paris. Needless to say, the chairman would be chased by hordes of reporters, photographers and TV cameramen, which guaranteed enormous free publicity for the movie.

The studio sweetened the deal by arranging for a luncheon at its elegant commissary, the Café de Paris, where the great dictator could break bread with the biggest stars in Hollywood. But there was a problem: Only four hundred people could fit into the room and nearly everybody in Hollywood wanted to be there. Soon the stars were scrambling, squabbling and begging for an invitation.

"One of the angriest social free-for-alls in the uninhibited and colorful history of Hollywood is in the making about who is to be at the luncheon," wrote Murray Schumach in the *New York Times*.

Schumach covered Hollywood with an anthropologist's eye and a wry wit, and he enjoyed detailing the delicious ironies that were illuminated when Hollywood was infected with what he dubbed "Khrushchev fever." The lucky four hundred who received invitations had achieved "the greatest prestige in the movie world," he noted, but the rest of Hollywood wallowed in despair. "The ownership of a mansion at Bel Air, of Impressionist paintings, or of a Rolls Royce or membership in an exclusive club could not console a producer who did not receive a telegram permitting him to sit in the Fox commissary with the Soviet premier to eat shrimp, squab chicken, and cantaloupe."

The lust for an invitation to the Khrushchev lunch was so strong that it overpowered the fear of Communism that had reigned in Hollywood since 1947, when the House Committee on Un-American Activities began investigating the movie industry, inspiring a blacklist of Communists that was still enforced in 1959. Producers who were scared to death of being seen snacking with a Communist screenwriter were desperate to be seen dining with the Communist dictator.

Not everyone demanded to attend the lunch. Bing Crosby, Ward Bond, Adolphe Menjou, and Ronald Reagan turned down their invitations as a protest against Khrushchev. "I believe that to sit socially and break bread with someone denotes friendship," Reagan said, "and certainly I feel no friendship for Mr. Khrushchev."

But the handful of stars declining an invitation could not make room for the hordes who demanded one. Hoping to ease the pressure, Twentieth Century Fox announced that it would not invite the stars' agents or spouses. This decree sparked widespread griping, and within days the ban on agents crumbled.

The spouses of stars were less powerful, however, and their protests proved unsuccessful. The only husband-and-wife teams invited were those who were both stars—Tony Curtis and Janet Leigh; Dick Powell and June Allyson; Elizabeth Taylor and Eddie Fisher. Marilyn Monroe's husband, playwright Arthur Miller, could have qualified as a star but he was urged to stay home because he was a leftist who'd been investigated by HUAC and therefore was considered too radical to dine with a Communist dictator.

However, the studio was determined that Miller's wife attend the Khrushchev soiree—dressed in a manner appropriate to her status as America's foremost sex symbol.

"At first, Marilyn, who never read the papers or listened to the news, had to be told who Khrushchev was," Lena Pepitone, Monroe's maid, recalled in her memoir. "However, the studio kept insisting. They told Marilyn that in Russia, America meant two things, Coca-Cola and Marilyn Monroe. She loved hearing that and agreed to go. . . . She told me that the studio wanted her to wear the tightest, sexiest dress she had for the premier."

"I guess there's not much sex in Russia," Marilyn told Pepitone.

She arrived in Los Angeles a day ahead of Khrushchev, flying from New York, chaperoned by her husband's friend Frank Taylor. When they landed, a mob of photographers was waiting.

"She was sitting in the forward lounge, surrounded by cosmetic kits and beginning the familiar ritual with her face," Taylor later recalled. "I told her I would run off ahead as a discretionary measure so no one would wonder who her unfamiliar traveling companion might be. . . . Then I got off and found the waiting limousine. I looked back and saw Marilyn descending the ramp. She ambled down the steps slowly, her pelvis thrown back, her chest thrust forward, her hips swinging rhythmically from right to left and back again. It took all of three minutes for her to reach the bottom."

A reporter asked if she'd come to town just to see Khrushchev.

"Yes," she said. "I think it's a wonderful thing and I'm happy to be here."

That provoked the inevitable follow-up question: "Do you think Khrushchev wants to see you?"

"I hope he does," she replied.

The next morning, she arose early in her bungalow at the Beverly Hills Hotel and began the long, complex process of becoming Marilyn Monroe. First, her masseuse, Ralph Roberts, arrived to give her a rubdown. Then Sydney Guilaroff came to do her hair. Then makeup artist Whitey Snyder arrived to paint her face. Finally, as instructed, she donned a sexy, low-cut black dress.

In the middle of this elaborate beautification project, Spyros Skouras, the president of Twentieth Century Fox, dropped by to make sure that Marilyn, who was notorious for being late, would arrive at this affair on time.

"She *has* to be there," he said.

And she was. Her chauffeur, Rudi Kautzsky, delivered her to the studio before noon. They arrived to find the parking lot nearly empty, which scared Marilyn.

"We must be *late!*" she said, nervously. "It must be over."

It wasn't. For perhaps the first time in her career, she'd arrived at something *early.*

45. THE NEAREST THING TO A MAJOR HOLLYWOOD FUNERAL

Waiting for Khrushchev to arrive at Twentieth Century Fox, Edward G. Robinson sat at table 18 with Judy Garland and Shelley Winters. Robinson puffed on his cigar and gazed out at the kings and queens of Hollywood—the men wearing dark suits, the women decked out in designer dresses and shimmering jewels.

"All of the dames should have been put right down there in front—facing Khrushchev," Robinson said, jabbing his cigar toward the head table, which was not yet occupied. "But I don't think he'll show up anyway. I think it'll be Oscar Homulka."

He was kidding. Oscar Homulka was an Austrian-born character actor who made a living playing Russian generals and spies, and thus wasn't illustrious enough to be invited to this lunch. But Gary Cooper was there. So was Kim Novak. And Dean Martin, Ginger Rogers, Kirk Douglas, Jack Benny, Tony Curtis, and Zsa Zsa Gabor.

"This is the nearest thing to a major Hollywood funeral that I've attended in years," said Mark Robson, the director of *Peyton Place.*

Marilyn Monroe sat at a table with producer David Brown, director Joshua Logan, and actor Henry Fonda, whose ear was stuffed with a plastic plug attached to a transistor radio tuned to the baseball game between the Dodgers and the Giants, who were fighting for the National League pennant.

Debbie Reynolds sat at table 21, which was located—by design—across the room from table 15, occupied by her ex-husband Eddie Fisher and his new wife, Elizabeth Taylor. As every American newspaper reader knew, Taylor had been Reynolds's close friend until she lured Fisher away with her dark, sultry beauty.

Sammy Davis Jr. was there too. So was Nat "King" Cole. "In honor of Mr. Khrushchev there were Negro stars at the luncheon," veteran Hollywood reporter Joe Hyams noted. "Although each star was important in his own right, it's the first time I've seen any of them at a major party."

At table 18, Shelley Winters and Judy Garland sipped the California Chardonnay provided to each table and gazed longingly at the stronger liquids delivered to the head table.

"I'm furious!" Winters said. "I see *vodka* on their table!"

"I think we should all get blind drunk," said Garland, "and hiss and boo and carry on."

They laughed and sipped and speculated on who in the room might be a Secret Service agent.

"I'll bet some of the waiters are," said Robinson. "At least that's the way we'd have done it in pictures."

In fact, the studio swarmed with plainclothes police, both American and Soviet. They inspected the shrubbery outside, the flowers on each table and both the men's and women's rooms. In the kitchen, an LAPD forensic chemist named Ray Pinker ran a Geiger counter over the food.

"We're just taking precautions against the secretion of any radioactive poison that might be designed to harm Khrushchev," Pinker said before heading off to check the sound stage where the premier would watch *Can-Can* after lunch.

As Khrushchev's motorcade pulled up to the studio, the stars watched live coverage of his arrival on televisions that had been set up around the room, their knobs removed so nobody could change the channel to the Dodgers-Giants game. They saw Khrushchev emerge from a limo and shake hands with Fox president Spyros Skouras.

A few moments later, Skouras led Khrushchev into the room and the stars stood to applaud. The applause was, according to the exacting calibrations of the *Los Angeles Times*, "friendly but not vociferous."

Khrushchev took a seat at the head table. At an adjacent table, his wife sat between Bob Hope and Frank Sinatra. Meanwhile, Elizabeth Taylor climbed on top of table 15 so she could get a better look at the dictator.

Henry Cabot Lodge sat next to Smiling Mike Menshikov at the head table and looked out at the audience. It was tough to see through the hot, white glare of the television lights (the luncheon was broadcast live), but he recognized Marilyn Monroe, David Niven, and Maurice Chevalier.

Charlton Heston, the American actor who'd once played Moses, attempted to make small talk with Mikhail Sholokhov, the Soviet novelist who would later win the Nobel Prize. "I have read excerpts from your works," Heston said.

"Thank you," said Sholokhov. "When we get some of your films, I shall not fail to watch some excerpts from them."

Nearby, Nina Khrushchev told Bob Hope that she wanted to see Disneyland. She showed Sinatra and Niven pictures of her grandchildren and bantered with cowboy star Gary Cooper, one of the few American actors she'd actually seen on screen.

"Why don't you move out here?" Cooper suggested. "You'll like the climate."

"No," Mrs. Khrushchev replied. "Moscow is all right for me."

As Lodge ate his squab, police chief William Parker suddenly appeared behind him, looking nervous. During the drive from the airport to the studio, somebody had thrown a big, ripe tomato at Khrushchev's limo. It missed, splattering the chief's car instead. "It indicated to me," Parker noted later, "that not all the Indians were friendly."

Now Parker leaned over and whispered into Lodge's ear. "I want you, as a representative of the president, to know that I will not be responsible for Chairman Khrushchev's safety if we go to Disneyland."

That got Lodge's attention. "Very well, Chief," he said. "If you will not be responsible for his safety, we do not go, and we will do something else."

Menshikov overheard this conversation and immediately got up to tattle. The premier sent a note back to the ambassador: "I understand you have cancelled the trip to Disneyland. I am most displeased."

When the waiters had cleared away the dishes, Skouras stood up to speak. Short, stocky and bald, the sixty-six-year-old Skouras looked a lot like Khrushchev. With a gravelly voice and a thick Greek accent, he also sounded a lot like Khrushchev. "He had this terrible Greek accent—like a 'Saturday Night Live' put-on," recalled *Washington Post* reporter Chalmers Roberts. "Everybody was laughing."

Khrushchev listened to Skouras for a while, then turned to his interpreter and whispered, "Why interpret for *me*? He needs it more."

Skouras may have sounded funny, but he was a serious businessman whose life was a classic American success story. The son of a Greek shepherd, he emigrated to America at seventeen and settled in St. Louis, where he sold newspapers, bussed tables, and saved his money. With two brothers, he invested in a movie theater, then another and another. By 1932, he was managing a chain of five hundred theaters. A decade later, he was running Twentieth Century Fox. "In all modesty, I beg you to look at me," he said to Khrushchev from the dais. "I am an example of one of those immigrants who, with my two brothers, came to this country. Because of the American system of equal opportunities, I am now fortunate enough to be president of Twentieth Century Fox."

Like so many other after-dinner orators on this trip, Skouras wanted to teach Khrushchev about capitalism. "The capitalist system, or the price system, should not be criticized, but should be carefully analyzed—otherwise America would never have been in existence."

Skouras said he'd recently toured the Soviet Union and found that "warm-hearted people were sorrowful for the millions of unemployed people in America." He turned to Khrushchev. "Please tell your good people there is no unemployment in America to worry about."

Hearing that, Khrushchev could not resist heckling. "Let your State Department not give us these statistics about unemployment in your country," he said, raising his palms in a theatrical gesture of befuddlement. "I'm not to blame. They're *your* statistics. I'm only the reader, not the writer."

That got a laugh from the audience.

"Don't believe everything you read," Skouras shot back. That got a laugh too.

When Skouras sat down, Lodge stood up to introduce Khrushchev. While the ambassador droned on about America's alleged affection for Russian culture, Khrushchev interrupted him to plug a new Soviet movie.

"Have you seen *They Fought for Their Homeland?*" the premier called out. "It is based on a novel by Mikhail Sholokhov."

"No," Lodge said, a bit taken aback.

"Well, buy it," said Khrushchev. "You should see it."

Smiling, the dictator stepped to the dais and invited the stars to visit the Soviet Union: "Please come," he said. "We will give you our traditional Russian pies."

He turned to Skouras, "my dear brother Greek," and said he was impressed by his capitalist rags-to-riches story. But then he topped it with a communist rags-to-riches story. "I started working as soon as I learned how to walk," he said. "I herded cows for the capitalists. That was before I was fifteen. After that, I worked in a factory for a German. Then I worked in a French-owned mine." He paused and smiled. "Today, I am the premier of the great Soviet state."

Now it was Skouras's turn to heckle. "How many premiers do you have?"

"I will answer that," Khrushchev replied. He was premier of the whole country, he said, and then each of the fifteen republics had its own premier. "Do you have that many?"

"We have two million American presidents of American corporations," Skouras replied.

Score one for Skouras! But Khrushchev was not willing to concede anything.

"Mr. Tikhonov, please rise," the premier ordered.

At a table in the audience, Nikolai Tikhonov stood up.

"Who is he?" Khrushchev asked. "He is a worker. He became a metallurgical engineer. . . . He is in charge of huge chemical factories. A third of the ore mined in the Soviet Union comes from his region. Well, Comrade Greek, is that not enough for you?"

"No," Skouras shot back. "That's a monopoly."

"It is a people's monopoly," Khrushchev replied. "He does not possess anything but the pants he wears. It all belongs to the people!"

Khrushchev smiled confidently and went on to make another point. Earlier, Skouras had said that American aid helped fight a famine in the Soviet Union in 1922. Khrushchev reminded Skouras that before the Americans sent aid, they sent an army to crush the Bolshevik revolution. "And not only the Americans," he added. "All the capitalist countries of Europe and of America marched upon our country to strangle the new revolution. . . . Never have any of our soldiers been on American soil but your soldiers were on Russian soil. These are the facts."

It was a grim lesson about a less-than-glorious chapter of American history, but Khrushchev said he bore no ill will. "Even under those circumstances," he said, "we are still grateful for the help you rendered."

Khrushchev had fought in the Red Army during the Russian civil war. "I was in the Kuban region when we routed the White Guard and threw them into the Black Sea," he said. "I lived in the house of a very interesting bourgeois intellectual family."

He was an uneducated miner with coal dust still on his hands, he continued, and he and other Bolshevik soldiers, many of them illiterate, shared the house with professors and musicians. "I remember the landlady asking me: 'Tell me, what do you know about ballet? You're a simple miner, aren't you?' To tell the truth, I didn't know anything about ballet. Not only had I never seen a *ballet,* I had never seen a *ballerina.*"

The audience laughed.

"I did not know what sort of dish it was or what you ate it with."

That brought more laughter.

"And I said, 'Wait, it will all come. We will have everything—*and ballet, too.*'"

It was a touching story. Even the tireless Red-bashers of the Hearst press conceded that "it was almost a tender moment." But of course Khrushchev could not stop there. "Now I have a question for you," he said. "Which country has the best ballet? Yours? You do not even have a permanent opera and ballet theatre. Your theatres thrive on what is given to them by rich people. In our country, it is the state that gives the money. And the best ballet is in the Soviet Union. It is our pride."

He bragged that Soviet artists were treated so well that they were getting fat. Then he apologized to Skouras ("my Greek friend") for arguing with him.

"I'm honored," Skouras hollered back, "to have the great premier of a great nation argue with a simple man."

"I am not arguing," Khrushchev said. "I am simply discussing the matter with you. I cannot argue with my hosts."

He rambled on and then apologized for rambling. After forty-five minutes of speaking, he seemed to be approaching an amiable closing. But then he remembered Disneyland.

"Just now, I was told that I could not go to Disneyland," he announced. "I asked, 'Why not? What is it? Do you have rocket-launching pads there?'"

The audience laughed.

"Just listen," he said. "Just listen to what I was told: 'We—which means the American authorities—cannot guarantee your security there.'"

He raised his hands in a vaudevillian shrug. More laughter.

"What is it? Is there an epidemic of cholera there? Have gangsters taken hold of the place? Your policemen are so tough they can lift a bull by the horns. Surely they can restore order if there are any gangsters around. I say, 'I would very much like to see Disneyland.' They say, 'We cannot guarantee your security.' Then what must I do, commit suicide?"

Khrushchev was starting to look more angry than amused. His fist punched the air above his red face.

"That's the situation I find myself in," he said. "For me, such a situation is inconceivable. I cannot find words to explain this to my people."

The audience was baffled. Were they really watching the sixty-five-year-old dictator of the world's largest country throw a temper tantrum because he wasn't allowed to go to Disneyland?

Sitting in the audience, Nina Khrushchev told David Niven that she really was disappointed that she couldn't see Disneyland. Hearing that, Sinatra, who was sitting next to Mrs. Khrushchev, leaned over and whispered in Niven's ear.

"Screw the cops!" Sinatra said. "Tell the old broad that you and I will take 'em down there this afternoon."

Before long, Khrushchev's temper tantrum—if that's what it was—faded away. He grumbled a bit about how he'd been stuffed into a sweltering limousine at the airport, instead of riding in a nice cool convertible on this hot day. But then his anger abated and he apologized, sort of.

"You will say, perhaps, 'What a difficult guest he is.' But I adhere to the Russian rule: 'Eat the bread and salt but always speak your mind.' Please forgive me if I was somewhat hot-headed. But the temperature here contributes to this. Also," he turned to Skouras, "my Greek friend warmed me up."

Relieved at the change of mood, the audience applauded. Skouras shook Khrushchev's hand and slapped him on the back and the two old, fat, bald guys grinned while the stars, who recognized a good show when they saw one, rewarded the duo with a standing ovation.

The lunch was over and Skouras led his new pal toward Sound Stage 8, where *Can-Can* was being filmed, stopping to greet various celebrities along the way. When he spotted Marilyn Monroe, he introduced her to Khrushchev, who had seen a close-up of her face—a clip from *Some Like It Hot*—in a film on American life at the American Exhibition in Moscow. Now the premier shook her hand and looked her over.

"You're a very lovely young lady," he said, smiling.

Later she would reveal what it was like to be eyeballed by the dictator: "He looked at me the way a man looks on a woman." Now she reacted to his stare by casually informing him that she was married.

"My husband, Arthur Miller, sends you his greeting," she said. "There should be more of this kind of thing. It would help both our countries understand each other."

46. MARILYN MONROE TELLS HER MAID WHAT SHE *REALLY* THINKS OF KHRUSHCHEV

When the chairman left the room, reporters swarmed around the stars, fishing for quotes about the historic event and the illustrious guest.

"I wouldn't have missed it for anything," said Elizabeth Taylor. "He's great. I hope it makes for better understanding."

"He seems to have a very agile mind," said Eddie Fisher, "and he can ad-lib with the best of them."

"His speech was interesting," said Kirk Douglas. "Having been a fighter, I know it's smart not to get hit in the clinches. Mr. K never gets hit in the clinches."

"This Khrushchev's an egghead," said director George Stevens. "He tried to hide his intellectual brilliance but he cannot quite do it."

"This guy can really think on his feet," said Charlton Heston. "Ad-libbing with him is like trying to trade gags with Milton Berle."

Shelley Winters said she wasn't impressed with the Khrushchev-Skouras debate: "It sounded like two kids arguing, 'My old man is better than your old man.'"

Bob Hope said he enjoyed lunching with Nina Khrushchev. "She was charming, very sincere, and very sweet," he said. "She seemed very interested in all the people at the luncheon, even though she didn't know who we were."

"She swings pretty good English, too," added Sinatra. "Seriously, she is a darling, charming woman."

"This is about the biggest day in the history of the movie business," said Marilyn Monroe.

Later, when she got back home, Marilyn told her maid what she *really* thought of Khrushchev. "He was fat and ugly and had warts on his face and he growled," she said. "Who would want to be a Communist with a president like that?"

But, she added, he certainly seemed to enjoy meeting *her.* "I could tell Khrushchev liked me. He smiled more when he was introduced to me than for anybody else at the whole banquet. And everybody else was there. He squeezed my hand so long and so hard that I thought he would break it. I guess it was better than having to kiss him."

47. CAN-CAN

While reporters interviewed the stars, Skouras led Khrushchev and his family to Sound Stage 8 and up a rickety wooden staircase to a box above the stage. They sat down, accompanied by Lodge, Gromyko and translator Alex Akalovsky. Sergei Khrushchev took out his movie camera so he could film the show.

Frank Sinatra appeared on stage, wearing a turn-of-the-century French suit—his costume for *Can-Can*. He played a French lawyer who falls in love with a dancer, played by Shirley MacLaine, who was arrested for performing a banned dance called the can-can.

"This is a movie about a lot of pretty girls—and the fellows who like pretty girls," Sinatra announced.

Hearing the translation, Khrushchev grinned and applauded.

"Later in this picture, we go to a saloon," Sinatra continued. "A saloon is a place where you go to drink."

Khrushchev laughed at that too. He seemed to be having a good time.

Sinatra introduced Louis Jourdan and Maurice Chevalier, who arrived to sing the first song. "It's called 'Live and Let Live,'" Sinatra said, "and I think that's a marvelous idea."

When Jourdan and Chevalier finished, Sinatra sang "C'est Magnifique." Then he summoned the dancing girls, whom he identified as "my nieces." They pranced across the stage—sixteen of them, including MacLaine and Juliet Prowse—all wearing long ruffled dresses with low-cut necklines. The view from the box above the stage—preserved for posterity in Sergei Khrushchev's home movie—revealed acres of cleavage. There were also some male dancers, but they were fully clothed and nobody paid much attention to them.

MacLaine recited a greeting in Russian that she'd memorized phonetically the previous night and then somebody stepped to the stage with a bullhorn and said, "All right, roll 'em."

The music swelled and the dancers kicked up their heels, then cartwheeled across the stage, exposing their long, lovely legs, as well as their garter belts and underwear. The male dancers picked the women up and held them over their heads, upside down, and they kicked their long, lovely legs. Jumping back on their feet, the women bent down, flipped their dresses up over their backs and shook their derrieres. Then the men picked them up again and the women wrapped their legs around the men's necks for a moment before bounding back to the stage and dancing some more.

Finally, in the *pièce de résistance*, the men slid under the women's dresses, emerging with lascivious grins on their faces and red panties in their hands.

By then, nobody watching the performance had any doubts why the can-can had once been banned. But many spectators—American and Russian—wondered, *Why did they choose* this *for Khrushchev?*

"It was the worst choice imaginable," Wiley Buchanan later recalled. "When the male dancer dived under her skirt and emerged holding what seemed to be her red panties, the Americans in the audience gave an audible gasp of dismay, while the Russians sat in stolid, disapproving silence."

"From the Soviet point of view, this was bourgeois, dirty, decadent," Sergei Khrushchev said decades later, as he watched his home movie of the performance. "We could not understand why they were showing this to Khrushchev. Maybe they wanted to surprise us or impress us."

Later Khrushchev would denounce the dance as pornographic exploitation, but at the time he seemed to be quite happy with the show.

"I was watching him," said Richard Townsend Davies of the State Department, "and he seemed to be enjoying it."

"I think he was enjoying it," recalled Chalmers Roberts.

"He was enjoying himself," Akalovsky remembered.

Sergei Khrushchev wasn't so sure. "Maybe father was interested but then he started to think, *What does this mean?* Because Skouras was very friendly, father did not think it was some political provocation. But there was no explanation. It was just American life." Sergei shrugged and then added, "Maybe Khrushchev liked it, but I will say for sure: My mother didn't like it."

Columnist Murray Kempton was impressed by Nina Khrushchev's aplomb: "She never once looked at Nikita, as an American wife might, to see if he was about to defect."

When the show ended, Skouras led his guests down the stairs to the stage. Khrushchev shook hands with Sinatra, who introduced him to Maurice Chevalier and Shirley MacLaine. Sweltering beneath the hot lights, MacLaine fanned herself theatrically and addressed Khrushchev in the slow, loud voice Americans use when talking to foreigners who can't speak English.

"Many, many cameras," she said. "Very hot."

A reporter asked Khrushchev if he'd enjoyed the dance and a translator relayed the premier's diplomatic response: "You should ask my opinion of the whole show, not just this element of the picture. I've never been in a cabaret, so I can't be a judge."

Khrushchev shook more hands then moved toward the door, surrounded by a pack of brawny bodyguards. Outside, he encountered Gary Cooper, the cowboy actor, and Clete Roberts, a reporter for KTLA-TV, which was televising the momentous event live.

"You can see from your vantage point, which is better than anywhere in the United States," Roberts told his viewers, "that Mr. Khrushchev is in a long conversation with Gary Cooper."

When the Cooper–Khrushchev summit broke up, the premier headed toward his limo, walking right past Roberts.

"May I shake your hand, sir?" Roberts asked, still speaking into his microphone.

Khrushchev shook his hand.

"I am shaking hands with the Soviet premier," Roberts announced.

Khrushchev climbed into a long, black limousine with huge tail fins and Lodge slipped in beside him. The limo inched forward, then picked up speed as Roberts scooted after it, still prattling into his microphone.

"We shall, of course, continue to stay on top of the story," he promised.

48. G. DAVID SCHINE FINALLY FINDS A COMMUNIST

After leaving Twentieth Century Fox, Khrushchev's motorcade wandered through the vast suburban sprawl of Los Angeles for two hours, which bored Lodge and irked Khrushchev.

Having put the kibosh on Disneyland, Khrushchev's guides were compelled to come up with another plan. Perhaps recalling Eisenhower's desire that his visitor see Levittown, they took the premier on a tour of
tract housing developments. As the motorcade meandered through suburban streets, Sergei Khrushchev pointed his movie camera at the sights
that caught his attention—palm trees, used car lots, and billboards.

The Soviet reporters following Khrushchev around Los Angeles were
as amused by billboards advertising Coca-Cola as the American reporters
who'd followed Nixon around Russia had been amused by billboards
touting Communism. "One-storey houses plastered all over with advertisements are a distinctive feature of Los Angeles," the Soviet reporters
wrote in *Face to Face with America*. "The large letters on them urge you to
buy, ride, eat, drink, smoke, wear, see and read something considered the
very best by the owners of the particular company."

Afraid that somebody might attack Khrushchev, the Los Angeles police
did not reveal the route of the premier's motorcade. But helicopters from
local radio stations hovered over the caravan, broadcasting live, so people
began to gather along the roads to catch a glimpse of the Russian as he
cruised past. Most of them were friendly, but one woman, dressed all in
black, held a black flag and a sign reading "Death to Khrushchev, the
Butcher of Hungary."

Glimpsing the woman out the window of his limo, the chairman demanded that Lodge explain why she was there.

"Well, Mr. Chairman," Lodge said, wryly, "this is a woman who does
not agree with certain aspects of your foreign policy."

"Well, if Eisenhower wanted to have me insulted," Khrushchev replied
angrily, "why did he invite me to come to the United States?"

Lodge was stunned. "Do I understand," he asked, "that you think that
President Eisenhower invited you to come to the United States and then
arranged to have this woman stand on this street corner in Los Angeles so
as to insult you?"

"In the Soviet Union," Khrushchev replied, "she wouldn't be there un-
less I had given the order."

Denied a trip to Disneyland and treated instead to a long, pointless car ride, Khrushchev was in a foul mood. The Americans kept showing him suburban houses and bragging about their prosperity, so he decided to do some bragging of his own, teasing Lodge about the successes of Soviet spies. "Your agents in Europe and the Middle East gave us your code books," he said, "and then we send false information back to you through your codes."

Khrushchev couldn't resist boasting about two secret documents that Soviet spies had recently stolen. One was a confidential letter from Eisenhower to Indian Prime Minister Nehru about India's border dispute with China. The other was a letter from the Shah of Iran to Eisenhower, requesting that Ike pressure Khrushchev to relax tensions with Iran. The documents Khrushchev cited were real, but Lodge told the premier that he knew nothing about them.

"If you wish," Khrushchev said mischievously, "I could supply you with a copy."

When the motorcade finally arrived at the Ambassador Hotel, where Khrushchev would spend the night, the premier was greeted by G. David Schine, the hotel's president. Schine happened to be one of America's most famous Communist-hunters—a young man who'd served as an aide to Senator Joseph McCarthy only to become, as one historian put it, "the agent of McCarthy's doom."

Son of a wealthy hotel magnate, Schine had attended Harvard, where he achieved local renown by hiring secretaries to take notes in his classes. He also wrote a paper about Communism. It contained numerous errors—confusing Marx with Lenin, and Stalin with Trotsky—but Schine was proud of it. After he graduated in 1949, he published it as a six-page pamphlet entitled *Definition of Communism* and his father had copies placed in every room in his hotels, right next to the Gideon Bible.

The pamphlet brought Schine to the attention of Roy Cohn, a brilliant young lawyer who was serving as chief counsel for McCarthy's Red-hunting Senate subcommittee. Cohn was a closeted homosexual and Schine was a strikingly handsome young man. When they met, Cohn was smitten and he offered Schine a job on the committee. Schine accepted, eager for anti-Communist adventures.

"Essentially," historian Ted Morgan later wrote, "Schine was Cohn's dumb blonde."

In the spring of 1953, Cohn and Schine traveled to Europe on a highly publicized seventeen-day search for subversive books in American libraries. When they returned to Washington, McCarthy held hearings on seditious authors, which caused the State Department to send its libraries a list of leftists whose books must be removed, including Langston Hughes, Howard Fast and Jean-Paul Sartre.

That summer, Cohn and Schine were nearly inseparable, living in adjoining rooms in a Washington hotel and taking frequent weekend trips to Manhattan. But the fun ended that fall, when Schine was drafted. Cohn took the news hard and pressured the Army to grant Private Schine extraordinary privileges, including the right to travel to Manhattan by chauffeured limo to meet with Cohn.

Soon stories about Schine's privileges and Cohn's pressure appeared in newspapers. McCarthy responded by accusing the Army of attempting to "blackmail" him by holding Schine "hostage." Obviously, an investigation was required and McCarthy decided that his subcommittee was the perfect venue to investigate the behavior of his staffers.

The legendary Army–McCarthy hearings began on April 22, 1954, and continued for thirty-six days while thousands watched on live television. Viewers watched McCarthy, his face darkened by a perpetual five o'clock shadow, bullying witnesses and bellowing "Point of order!" They also saw Joseph Welch, the Army's patrician attorney, skewer McCarthy with the now famous question: "Have you no sense of decency, sir? At long last, have you no sense of decency?"

By the end of 1954, the Senate voted to censure McCarthy, who drank himself to death in 1957.

Meanwhile, Schine completed his military service, went into his father's hotel business and married a former Miss Universe. They raised five children and avoided politics.

When Khrushchev arrived at the Ambassador Hotel after his long ride through Los Angeles, Schine shook his hand and welcomed him with a smile. Finally the famous Commie-hunter had found an authentic Communist, and he sent him upstairs to the hotel's luxurious Royal Suite.

Schine declined to discuss these ironies with reporters. But Murray Kempton managed to land an interview with Schine's mother, who told him she'd discussed Khrushchev with Spyros Skouras's wife.

"I called Mrs. Skouras—you know we're very good friends—and asked her what the K's were like," Mrs. Schine told Kempton. "She said I would really like them. 'You know,' she said, 'they're very natural people. K says the first thing that comes into his mind—just like Spyros.'"

Kempton used that quote in his column, adding only a single sentence of commentary: "There is the moment when the mind ceases to judge; it simply records."

49. STICKING A FINGER IN KHRUSHCHEV'S EYE

When Lodge read a copy of Mayor Poulson's speech, he begged Poulson to tone it down.

The two men met at the cocktail party preceding the banquet for Khrushchev in the Ambassador Hotel ballroom that night. Lodge didn't know that the mayor had bragged to a local TV reporter that he would skewer Khrushchev with the oratorical equivalent of a "long, sharp knife." But the ambassador had been surprised by Poulson's curt, cold one-sentence welcoming speech at the airport, so he asked the mayor to see a copy of the speech he planned to deliver at the banquet. Lodge was particularly concerned that Poulson was planning to attack the premier over his famous "we will bury you" remark.

Khrushchev had already explained that statement at the National Press Club, Lodge told Poulson. If he hears it again, he'll get mad. Lodge asked the mayor to omit that part of the speech. Poulson refused, saying he'd already distributed the text to reporters.

"Lodge tried to talk him out of it and he got him to take a few gross insults out of the speech," recalled Chalmers Roberts of the *Washington Post*, who knew Lodge well. "But Poulson was going to stick his finger in Khrushchev's eye and the hell with Eisenhower. He was a real right-wing Republican."

The cocktail party ended, and a thousand guests sat down to eat. Poulson rose to speak. He touted the glories of his city then turned his attention to the guest of honor. "We do not agree with your widely-quoted phrase, 'We shall bury you,'" he said. "You shall not bury us and we shall not bury you. We are happy with our way of life. We recognize its shortcomings and are always trying to improve it. But if challenged, we shall fight to the death to preserve it."

The audience applauded. Khrushchev did not. Already irked by the mayor's terse speech at the airport, he assumed (wrongly) that Poulson was also responsible for the canceled Disneyland trip and the long, tedious drive through Los Angeles. Now this man was taunting him about his "bury you" remark. The premier glowered at Poulson, his lips pressed tight. He stepped to the podium and plodded through his prepared speech, which praised Los Angeles, peace and "friendly cooperation." Then he looked up from his text.

"That was the end of my prepared speech, but the speaker that preceded me raised a number of points which I cannot fail to answer," he said. "I turn to you, Mr. Mayor, my dear host. In your speech, you said that we want to bury you. You have shown wonderful hospitality towards me and my comrades and I thank you. I want to speak the truth. Can I do that here? I want to ask you: Why did you mention that? Already while I was here in the United States, I have had occasion to clarify that point. I trust that even mayors read the press. At least in our country, the chairmen of city councils read the press. If they don't, they risk not being elected next time."

The audience laughed. Other pols might have stopped there. Not Khrushchev.

"If you want to go on with the arms race, very well," he said, his voice rising. "We accept that challenge. As for the output of rockets—well, they are on the assembly line." By now, the premier's face had attained its familiar angry redness and seemed headed toward an apoplectic purple. "This is a most serious question. It is one of life or death, ladies and gentlemen, one of war and peace. If you don't understand . . . "

"We understand!" somebody shouted in Russian.

The crowd, which had been laughing only moments before, now sat stunned. "The audience gasped," wrote Relman Morin of the Associated Press. "It was not only the words but the manner in which they were spoken. Two large veins in Premier Khrushchev's forehead bulged as he said this, snarling at Mayor Poulson."

And Khrushchev was not yet finished. "The unpleasant thought sometimes creeps up on me," he said, "that perhaps Khrushchev was invited here to enable you to sort of rub him in your sauce and show him the might and strength of the United States so as to make him shake at the knees. If that is so—it took me about twelve hours to fly here, I guess it will take no more than ten and a half hours to fly back."

He ordered Alexei Tupolev, the son of the man who'd designed his mammoth plane, to stand up. "Isn't that so?" Khrushchev asked him.

"Less than that," Tupolev said.

"I am the first head of either Russia or the Soviet Union to visit the United States," Khrushchev noted. "I can go. But I don't know when, if ever, another Soviet premier will visit your country."

Shocked, the dinner guests wondered if they were witnessing the end of the visit—or perhaps the start of a war.

"It was a terrible moment," wrote Murray Kempton.

"His outburst seemed almost insane," recalled Wiley Buchanan.

"You could see the fuses of nuclear rockets sparking," wrote Harrison Salisbury.

"Needless to say, this sent a tremor—*a tremor!*—through the assembled dignitaries," recalled State Department aide Richard Townsend Davies. "It was very threatening."

"Clearly," Lodge thought, "the Khrushchev visit to America is becoming a horrible failure."

50. FAKING IT

After the banquet, Khrushchev rode an elevator to the Royal Suite and gathered his underlings around him.

"Everyone except Father was confused and depressed by what had happened," recalled Sergei Khrushchev.

The premier took off his suit jacket and sat down on a banquette while his aides slumped into sofas and chairs. "We represent a great power," he told them, "and we don't allow anybody to treat us like a colony."

It was the beginning of a long, loud rant. Bellowing with anger, Khrushchev cursed Poulson, denounced the Disneyland debacle, reviled the long, dull ride through Los Angeles and attacked the State Department for preventing him from mingling with Americans. He threatened to cut the trip short and fly home and again he ripped into the mayor.

"How dare this man attack the guest of the president like that!" he shouted.

The premier seemed so enraged that Andrei Gromyko's wife, Lidia, hustled off to get him a tranquilizer. But it was all an act. Khrushchev was putting on a performance for the benefit of the Americans he assumed were listening to him via bugs hidden in the ceiling.

"At times his voice rose to a scream. His fury seemed to have no limits. Only his eyes, which sparkled with mischief, gave him away," Sergei recalled. "Now and again, father raised a finger and pointed to the ceiling, as if to say, 'This isn't for you; it's for those who are listening in.'"

"I was in full control," the premier wrote in his memoir. "I was giving vent to my indignation for the ears of the Americans accompanying us. I was sure that there were eavesdropping devices in our room and that Mr. Lodge, who was staying at the same hotel, was sitting in front of a speaker with an interpreter and listening to our whole conversation. So, for his benefit, I ranted on about how I wouldn't tolerate being treated like this."

When he finished his bogus tantrum, Khrushchev wiped the sweat from his bald head—his theatrics had steamed him up—and turned to his foreign minister. "Comrade Gromyko," he said, "go at once and tell Lodge everything I just said."

Looking dour, as always, Gromyko dutifully rose from his chair. His wife, who still did not quite understand this charade, blurted out some advice: "Andryusha, be more polite with him."

Sergei Khrushchev glanced at his father. The old man was beaming. If his acting fooled Gromyko's wife, he figured it would fool the American eavesdroppers too.

A few minutes later, a phone rang in Lodge's room. It was after two o'clock in the morning—five o'clock in New York, where Lodge and Khrushchev had started this long, strange day nearly twenty-four hours earlier. Lodge was still awake, not eavesdropping on Khrushchev but dictating his daily cable to Washington. He answered the phone. It was Gromyko requesting to meet with him immediately.

A few moments later, he arrived, accompanied by his translator. When Gromyko sat down and crossed his legs, Lodge noticed that the foreign minister of one of Earth's coldest nations was wearing long underwear on this unseasonably hot day in Los Angeles. Apparently he'd bundled up in an effort to fight a cold.

Lodge started the conversation by suggesting that perhaps Chairman Khrushchev was getting too tired.

Gromyko ignored that remark and launched into a formal diplomatic protest. "I have come in accordance with the wishes of Mr. Khrushchev to state the following: It is now becoming obvious that in almost every place questions are being raised which in our conviction should not be raised if you are guided by good intentions. These questions do not seem fortuitous but designed to complicate the position of the Chairman and negatively affect the outcome of the visit. A typical example was today at dinner but this was not the only one."

Continuing in this formal language, Gromyko complained that the police were preventing Khrushchev from meeting ordinary American citizens. Then he raised a more startling issue: "The next question is whether the trip should not be curtailed entirely and the prime minister returned to Washington to talk to the president."

When Gromyko finished his speech, Lodge took a breath and responded. "I certainly hold no brief for questions that have been asked on various occasions," he said. "But I am sure that on reflection you and Mr. Khrushchev will not think they have been instigated by the United States government to make his visit a failure. I can't believe that you or Khrushchev would believe that. You, Gromyko, know the United States too well to think that. President Eisenhower is not as underhanded or so stupid to do that."

The problem, Lodge explained, was that neither he nor Ike had any control over local politicians. "I have been trying all day to persuade the mayor not to make such an unsuitable speech," he said. "If you had seen what he was going to say and took out, you would realize that I really accomplished something."

The president is not instigating these attacks, Lodge assured Gromyko. Eisenhower wants this trip to be successful. As for the police, he continued, they are simply trying to protect Khrushchev. But Lodge promised to ease up on security and permit the premier to get out of his limo and shake hands with average Americans.

When Lodge finished, Gromyko dropped his diplomatic formality and responded in a conversational tone. The premier believes that the president has good intentions, he said. "But there is a distinction between what the president says and what happens."

Again, Lodge assured Gromyko that Poulson's hostile remarks were not instigated by the White House. "The motive is the personal ambitions of a local politician to have his moment in the limelight," he said. "They see this very eminent man coming into their town and want to get into the limelight for some personal ambition of their own. This is not some plot out of Washington. I hope you, Mr. Gromyko, will explain this to Mr. Khrushchev. He might not believe me because I am an American. Our ways may seem strange. We are a loosely organized country compared with the Soviet Union. We are not directed closely from a central point."

"Maybe I could make a personal suggestion," said Gromyko. "You could say something in your speech. You could point out that Khrushchev is an official guest and that certain conclusions should be made from this with respect to behavior."

Lodge agreed to encourage America's provincial politicians to be nicer to Khrushchev. Gromyko returned to the premier's room to report that Lodge had apologized for the mayor's speech and promised that it wouldn't happen again.

Pleased that his fake tantrum had paid off, Khrushchev went to bed happy.

51. GIVE HIM A BREAK

Marilyn Monroe, Frank Sinatra, Hollywood, Disneyland, dirty dancing, two temper tantrums, an argument with the mayor, a threat to go home, and a hint of nuclear Armageddon—Nikita Khrushchev's twenty-hour sojourn in Los Angeles provided the international press corps with plenty of raw material for punditry and prognostication.

Predictably, Soviet reporters expressed outrage at the U.S. government's unconscionable violation of Khrushchev's inalienable right to visit Disneyland. In *Izvestia*, Khrushchev's son-in-law, Alexsei Adzhubei, re-

vealed the *real* reason why the premier was barred from the Magic King-
dom. It was part of a State Department conspiracy to keep him away
from ordinary Americans, who were drawn to Khrushchev by his love of
peace. "The whole of America wanted to hear N. S. Khrushchev, wanted
to see him, wanted to understand him," Adzhubei wrote. "The whole! It
is not a slip of my tongue."

Adzubei also revealed that the premier was responding to these insults
with a "lofty dignity," a phrase not often used to describe Khrushchev.

Pravda, a newspaper that was not known for whimsy, published a cartoon that showed Mickey Mouse telling Donald Duck, "It seems we represent a danger to the guests of America."

Four enterprising Soviet reporters hustled off to Disneyland to see exactly what Khrushchev missed. They rode the Mark Twain Steamboat,
the Rainbow Caverns mine train and, ironically, the Rocket to the Moon.
"There is nothing like it in the Soviet Union," they reported, adding that
the place seemed perfectly safe to them.

Meanwhile, the British press pummeled Khrushchev's hosts for being
rude to their guest. The *Daily Mirror* mocked those who argued with
Khrushchev as "damn silly Americans," and the *Daily Herald* said the
Yanks were "behaving like a bunch of kids at a Frankenstein movie."

"Give him a break," urged the *Daily Mail*. "It would be a tragedy if
Khrushchev were to go home in a huff. The whole world would feel the
chill."

In the United States, the media responded with its usual cacophony of
conflicting opinions.

"The spectacle of Moscow's top man, one of the two most powerful
figures in the world, ranting at a Los Angeles lunch because he couldn't
go see Disneyland made reporters rub their eyes," Richard Stout wrote in
the *Christian Science Monitor*. "It was all a security snafu but it sounded like
a small boy who couldn't go to a movie."

"Khrushchev has about 10 million kids on his side when he complains
about not getting to see Disneyland," the *Des Moines Register* noted.

"Imagine being in Southern California and not going there. That's what our teenager had to say about it."

Among the journalists and diplomats traveling with the premier, one question was discussed endlessly: When Khrushchev threw his tantrums, was he genuinely angry, or was he just acting?

Daniel Schorr of CBS was convinced that the tantrums were bogus: "another of his skilled tactical moves to cow his hecklers and regain the initiative."

Chief of protocol Wiley Buchanan agreed. "The man was simply trying to frighten us. . . . As for his threat to break off his visit and go home in a fire-breathing huff, I didn't take that seriously for a moment. Khrushchev might be many things, but he was no fool, and he was not going to relinquish the best propaganda platform he had ever dreamed of."

Chalmers Roberts of the *Washington Post* thought Khrushchev was genuinely angry but also putting on a show for the benefit of his Kremlin cronies. "This was a guy who was looking at all these characters back home who were watching him with knives in their pockets. He didn't know whether he was going to come back as Chairman of the Council of Ministers or if he was going to be hung. So I think he blew up just to make his point."

Asked decades later whether his father was really angry in Los Angeles or merely acting, Sergei Khrushchev replied, "He was angry—*and* he acted." The premier was truly enraged at Poulson but his tirade was the product of calm calculation. "He liked to exploit his image as an unpredictable person," Sergei recalled. "He knew what he was doing and what would be the effect."

In this case, the effect was exactly what he wanted: He scared his hosts into changing their behavior. On the morning after the blow-up, Lodge conferred with Tommy Thompson, the American ambassador to the Soviet Union, and President Eisenhower. They decided to jettison the "argue or perish" plan—the Nixon-inspired strategy that called for Lodge and others to debate Khrushchev at every opportunity. Instead, the State Department instructed Lodge to try to keep the premier happy until he arrived at Camp David for the summit with Ike.

Lodge quickly called George Christopher, the mayor of San Francisco, the next stop on Khrushchev's tour, and begged him to refrain from arguing with the premier. And James Hagerty, Ike's press secretary, urged Americans to be nice to Khrushchev: "The purpose of constructive meetings at Camp David is not served by any discourtesies extended to the Chairman during his visit."

On the morning after the tirade that shook the world, Lodge informed Khrushchev about the new plans. "We have decided to manage the trip as though you were a presidential candidate," Lodge told the premier as they prepared to board the train to San Francisco. "We will do some whistle stops."

A whistle stop, he explained, meant that the train would stop in a station so the premier could get out, shake hands and kiss babies. Khrushchev loved the idea.

"Of course, you understand, Mr. Chairman," Lodge added, tongue in cheek, "that some enthusiastic friend may throw a bunch of flowers at you, and you may get scratched."

"I know," Khrushchev replied. "I have had that happen to me in the Soviet Union."

52. MANKIND'S FACE IS MORE BEAUTIFUL THAN ITS BACKSIDE

Khrushchev left Los Angeles without even saying good-bye, walking silently past the microphones set up for his farewell address and boarding the train for San Francisco, looking sullen.

When the train reached Santa Barbara, the first whistle stop, Lodge led Khrushchev down the steps to the platform, which was packed with people. It was a beautiful, sunny Sunday morning and the folks were dressed casually and feeling friendly. Lodge introduced the visitor, the audience applauded and then Khrushchev, grinning happily, waded into the crowd. He shook hands. He slapped backs. He patted the heads of children. He bowed elegantly to the ladies. He even kissed a baby.

For the first time on the trip, Khrushchev was working a crowd and he loved it. The kind of sensuous populist who craves the heady adrenaline high of a cheerful crowd, the premier liked to press the flesh, hear the cheers, feel the love. By the time he climbed back aboard the train, he was a happy man.

Stoked up on what he perceived as the love of the American people, Khrushchev decided to take a stroll through the train so he could chat with the reporters who had stalked him across the continent. A voice on the train's tinny loudspeaker announced that the premier was coming and urged the three hundred reporters to please restrain themselves from mobbing him. This was like asking birds not to fly, fish not to swim.

"He came into the press work car preceded by a Southern Pacific Railroad cop of the bearing, manner, social conscience and type Joe Hill must have died cursing," Murray Kempton wrote. "Then a State Department man, and then Khrushchev and then his translator and then Cabot Lodge."

The workroom was a converted bar car packed with rumpled reporters banging away on typewriters, surrounded by overflowing ashtrays, half-filled coffee cups, and discarded newspapers bearing yesterday's headlines: "Khrushchev, Angry, Interrupts Skouras."

As the dictator waddled into the car, the train bounced and he stumbled. "Now, the American reporters will say Khrushchev lurched because he was drinking," he said, smiling.

Somebody offered him a shot of vodka.

"No, thanks," he said, "it's too hot for vodka."

"Cognac? Scotch? Bourbon?"

"No," Khrushchev replied. "It's too hot."

He didn't need strong liquids. He was already high. "Today, I won my freedom," he announced. "I was able to meet real, live Americans and look them in the eye. I'm happy that the house arrest I was placed under has been lifted."

"You seem in better humor today than you did last night in Los Angeles," Daniel Schorr said.

"You know, Mr. Schorr, when they stick pins in you, you have to retaliate," Khrushchev replied. He illustrated his point by throwing a quick punch toward Schorr's gut, causing the CBS correspondent to flinch and step backward.

Does this mean, Schorr asked, that you've decided not to go home?

"Why should I go?" Khrushchev asked. "Did you see the crowd at the railroad station? Did you see that little girl waving at me? No? There was a little girl, maybe three or four years old, in her mother's arms. Probably her mother told her I was a communist. But she was waving at me. She was waving at communism." He waved his arms to demonstrate.

When Khrushchev reached Kempton's seat, the columnist noted that the chairman "looked as fit as the entire left side of the Baltimore Colts line." Kempton gestured at the exhausted, disheveled reporters around him and asked, "Mr. Chairman, when you were down in that coal mine, did you ever look as tired and dirty as we do?"

Khrushchev responded with an outpouring of spirited Russian that seemed to go on for two full minutes. When he paused for air, the translator distilled his wisdom to a single sentence: "When I was in that coal mine, even there I always sang."

Khrushchev blurted out another long paragraph, which the translator boiled down to a single aphorism: "The secret of my health is that I never let my nose get down."

A reporter asked: Did you enjoy the can-can dance yesterday?

"A man with normal morals cannot be interested in such a dance," Khrushchev replied. "This is a mild form of pornography. The dancing was better than the backsides—but mankind's face is more beautiful than its backside."

He would not, he announced, permit such a movie in the Soviet Union: "The thing is immoral. We do not want that sort of thing for the Russians."

Needless to say, Khrushchev's denunciation of *Can-Can* elated the movie's publicists. Hollywood columnist Joe Hyams gleefully speculated about possible ads: "'See *Can-Can*, the picture that shocked Khrushchev' or 'See *Can-Can* with the dance Khrushchev called immoral.'"

The chairman enjoyed his repartee with the reporters but he had an ulterior motive for his stroll through the train: He wanted to avoid seeing what the State Department desperately wanted him to see—two Atlas missiles aimed at his homeland. "The reason for going on the train was that he was supposed to see Vandenberg Air Force Base, where they had an early generation of missiles," Richard Townsend Davies later recalled. "They were visible from the train window. . . . So the idea was, we'll go by there and these missiles will be up . . . and he'd see them and he'd say, 'Oh, gracious, these people are powerful, I'd better watch it.' . . . Well, as a matter of fact when we went by Vandenberg Air Force Base, Khrushchev made it a point to be giving an interview to a number of correspondents, sitting with his back to the window and he never looked out the window."

There was a reason for Khrushchev's curious apathy—the doctrine of reciprocity. If he looked at the American missiles, then he'd have to let Eisenhower look at Soviet missiles when Ike toured Russia. And Khrushchev knew that he'd been bluffing for years about the quantity and quality of his missiles.

When a reporter informed the premier that two Atlas ICBM missiles were perched on their launching pads right behind his back, Khrushchev did not even glance at them. "I'm not interested in your missiles," Khrushchev said. "We have better ones than you."

Not only did he miss the missiles, he also missed seeing the spiffy logo of the Strategic Air Command, which was posted on a sign. It featured

SAC's official shield—a fist holding an arrow and a bolt of lightning—and its Madison Avenue-style slogan: "Peace Is Our Profession."

When the train stopped at San Luis Obispo, Khrushchev gleefully stepped to the platform, which was mobbed. Grinning broadly, he plunged into the crowd, shaking every hand he could grasp.

"Look at him!" somebody yelled, "Look at him!"

The crowd surged forward, struggling to touch Khrushchev. It was a strange phenomenon. San Luis Obispo was no hotbed of Communism; it must have been the lure of celebrity. Panicking in the sudden crush, the Soviet security guards shoved the people back, slamming elbows into the bellies of those who failed to move fast enough. One of the Soviets shoved Lodge, who promptly shoved him back, hissing, "Don't ever lay a hand on me again!"

Through it all, Khrushchev kept smiling and shaking hands. When the jostling crowd knocked a little boy down, Khrushchev scooped the kid up and cradled him until he stopped crying. A photographer snapped a picture, and the Soviet press published it with a caption that read, "This youngster was the luckiest of them all. He landed in the arms of famous 'Grandpa Khrushchev.'"

The train whistle blew. Lodge and Menshikov linked arms and held the crowd back so Khrushchev could climb up the steps to the train. When they'd all managed to board, the premier reached back to shake more hands as the train began chugging away.

Khrushchev was thrilled to learn of Lodge's fight with the Soviet guard. "I hear you've been beating up one of my security guards," he said, grinning merrily.

"He was obviously delighted," Lodge later recalled, "and his attitude toward me became much friendlier."

The whole crazy scene convinced Khrushchev that *Pravda* was right: The American people loved him. "Now, Lodge," he said, "I want you to notice one thing: The plain people of America like me. It's just those bastards around Eisenhower that don't."

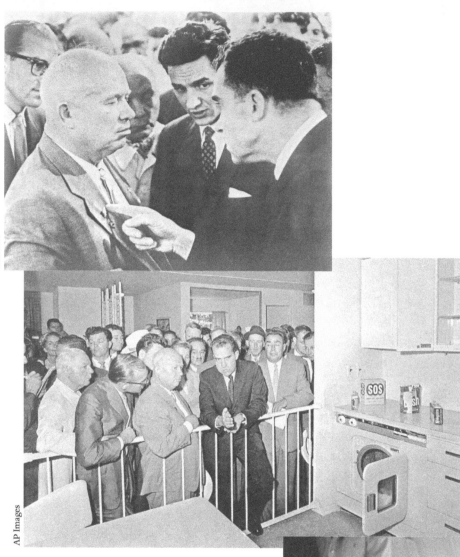

"If war comes, we *both* have had it," Nixon told Khrushchev, jabbing his finger at the premier's chest in their famous "kitchen debate" in Moscow, where SOS was among the items on display. Visiting Nixon's plane, Khrushchev sampled some bourbon. "This is good whiskey, but you Americans spoil it," he said. "You put in more ice than whiskey."

Squeezed between two portly Khrushchevs on the ride from the airport to the White House, Eisenhower looked uncharacteristically glum. He wasn't thrilled to have Khrushchev roaming around the country.

Washington Post

Washington Post

Arriving at the White House, Khrushchev taunted Eisenhower by giving him a model of the Soviet spacecraft that had just landed on the moon—"a strange gift," Ike later called it.

"The turkey certainly doesn't like being handled this way," Khrushchev said as he mugged for photographers on a Maryland farm.

When a cop rescued her from a media mob, Nina Khrushchev patted his hand, saying, "Wonderful American police."

Angry protestors greeted Khrushchev in New York—and every other city he visited—raising fears about possible assassination attempts.

DANGER!!! EVIL MEN AT WORK

Washington Post

At a Hollywood luncheon, Nina Khrushchev dined with Frank Sinatra and Bob Hope, showed them pictures of her grandkids, and told them she was eager to see Disneyland.

CORBIS

As instructed by studio bosses, Marilyn Monroe wore her sexiest dress to the lunch, but she wasn't impressed with the premier. "He was fat and ugly and had warts on his face and he growled," she told her maid.

K blew his top when he was told he couldn't visit Disneyland. "Is there an epidemic of cholera there?" he bellowed into the microphone. "Have gangsters taken hold of the place? ... What must I do, commit suicide?"

The premier looked happy while hobnobbing with Shirley MacLaine after her Can-Can dance, but later he denounced the show as smut. "Mankind's face," he said, "is more beautiful than its backside."

"Now, there's a *real* American," Khrushchev said, patting the impressive pot belly of Jack Christensen, who soon became America's most famous gatecrasher.

Khrushchev howled with laughter when Iowa farmer Roswell Garst threw silage at the obnoxious media mob and kicked a *New York Times* reporter in the shins.

Always an eager eater, Khrushchev gobbled a hot dog in Iowa, bent low to slurp his soup in Washington, and pretended to shoplift a napkin-holder that caught his eye in Pittsburgh.

Returning as an uninvited guest in 1960, Khrushchev played shuffleboard on the boat to New York. At the U.N., he hugged Fidel Castro and pounded his fists on his desk to protest anti-Soviet oratory. He also banged his shoe on the desk, which became the most famous act of his colorful career.

53. THE CITY WITH A FLOWER IN HER BUTTONHOLE

"No matter how far you travel, Big Red, you won't find another city quite like ours," wrote Herb Caen, the legendary *San Francisco Chronicle* columnist, in a piece welcoming Khrushchev to town. "We have been called worldly and provincial, international and insular, tourist-loving and stranger-hating, stuffy and abandoned—the city with a flower in her buttonhole, the city with her nose in the air, the city with her mind in the gutter."

Caen had been lovingly describing the city he called "Baghdad by the Bay," in funny, lyrical columns since 1938, touting San Francisco as a cosmopolitan paradise of witty, wisecracking eccentrics, bohemians, and bon vivants. Caen's San Francisco was romanticized but recognizable. Its rival to the south, Los Angeles, was conservative, Republican, pro-business, and, despite Hollywood, rather staid. San Francisco was liberal, Democratic, pro-union, and quirky. Born as a Gold Rush boomtown, it remained tolerant of vice and fond of eccentricity. Consequently it attracted a colorful array of artists, pseudo-artists, alcoholics, hop-heads, homosexuals, bohemians and writers—from Mark Twain to Ambrose Bierce to William Saroyan to Allen Ginsberg.

In the 1950s, the bohemians hung out at City Lights bookstore, owned by Lawrence Ferlinghetti, publisher of Ginsberg's masterpiece "Howl." These new Bohemians called themselves "beats," but in 1957, Caen dubbed them "beatniks" and the name stuck.

As Khrushchev's visit approached, Caen reported that some local beatniks were preparing to greet "Big Red" in surreal San Francisco style—by hoisting a homemade sign reading "Welcome to San Francisco, Noel Coward!"

"I don't geddit," Caen wrote. "I don't suppose Mr. K will either."

Caen's *Chronicle* colleague, Arthur Hoppe, a feature writer with an impish sense of humor, toured the Royal Suite of the Mark Hopkins hotel, where Khrushchev would be staying. He learned that the premier had requested that the twin beds in the Royal Suite be replaced with a king-size double bed—apparently Nik and Nina wanted to snuggle!

When Hoppe met chambermaid Natalia Heyman—a Russian-speaking Latvian immigrant who'd been assigned to take care of the dictator—he mischievously asked her an absurd question: Do you plan to blow Khrushchev up?

"Goodness no," Heyman replied. "If I blow him up, there's hundreds more like him. Besides, it might cause trouble."

Rolling toward the city with a flower in her buttonhole, Khrushchev ate a big lunch, then settled into a Pullman car for a nap. He slept like a corpse for two solid hours, missing the whistle stop at San Jose. Menshikov took his boss's place on the platform, where the mayor of San Jose presented him with two gifts. One was a plywood key to the city. The other, a box of prunes.

Rested and ready when the train arrived in San Francisco, Khrushchev stepped to the platform and was greeted by Mayor George Christopher.

"Where is your boss?" Christopher asked.

Khrushchev stared back, looking wary.

Christopher smiled. "Both of us are only pretending to be bosses," he explained. "My boss is waiting here for your boss." He introduced his wife, who held a bouquet of roses for Mrs. Khrushchev.

Ah, it was a *joke*! The premier smiled and introduced his wife, and Christopher gave her the bouquet and a hug. Then they all climbed into a limousine for the twenty-minute ride to the hotel. Along the way, Khrushchev commented on the concrete in the roadway—not as good as Russian concrete—and leaned out the window to wave at passersby.

At one point Khrushchev saw Christopher's face staring out from a campaign billboard. "Ah, you are running for election," the premier said. "I will be glad to campaign for you."

"I would prefer," Christopher said with a grin, "that you confine your activities to your own sphere."

Outside the Mark Hopkins hotel, a crowd of 10,000 people gathered to glimpse the guest. Arthur Hoppe of the *Chronicle* worked the crowd, asking people if they planned to applaud Khrushchev. Not a single one answered in the affirmative. "Oh, no," answered one woman. "I don't really think we should for a man like that. I mean . . . "

Then Khrushchev's limo appeared and a few people began clapping. Soon nearly everybody was applauding or waving. Khrushchev stepped out of the limo and beamed. He raised his hands in the air, then joined them over his head like a victorious boxer. He waded into the crowd, shook some hands and hugged a woman.

Amid the cheering crowd, he saw a man holding a sign: "We Hungarians Will Bury You." He smiled at the sight. "So many wise people—and one fool," he said. "That's so we don't get bored."

When Khrushchev finally entered the hotel, Hoppe asked people in the crowd why they'd applauded.

"What's the use of being nasty?" said an old man smoking a cigar. "I mean, where does that get you? We showed *him*, didn't we?"

"Showed him what?" Hoppe asked.

"You know what I mean," the man replied. "We showed *him*."

54. DANCING FOR THE LACKEYS

When Khrushchev walked into the hotel's Golden Empire Room that night to dine with a delegation of American labor leaders, Victor Reuther shook his hand and welcomed him in fluent Russian.

"You speak Russian?" Khrushchev asked.

"Mr. Chairman, have you forgotten that I spent several years in your country?"

"When?"

"In 1933 and 1934."

"Where?"

"In the Gorky automobile plant, named in honor of Molotov," Reuther said, still speaking Russian. "Tell me, Mr. Chairman, is the Gorky plant still named in honor of Molotov?"

It was a loaded question. Vyacheslav Molotov, who'd served as Stalin's foreign minister, was among the Kremlin hard-liners who tried to oust Khrushchev in 1957. They failed. Stalin would have executed them, but Khrushchev merely exiled the plotters to plebian jobs in unpleasant places. Molotov became ambassador to Mongolia, a humiliating post for the man who negotiated the Hitler-Stalin Pact. (Not that the Hitler-Stalin Pact worked out particularly well.)

"*Nyet,*" Khrushchev answered, shooting Reuther a dirty look. "Today we call it only the Gorky Auto Works." Then he turned to meet the other union leaders, including Reuther's brother Walter, who was president of the United Auto Workers.

Walter Reuther was among America's most intelligent and sophisticated labor leaders. Raised in a socialist German family in Wheeling, West Virginia, Reuther moved to Detroit in 1927, at the age of twenty, to become a tool-and-die maker in a Ford plant while attending college at night. Fired for union activity in 1932, he decided to travel around the world with his brother Victor. In Germany, they visited relatives and witnessed the rise of Hitler. They continued on to the Soviet Union where they worked in the Gorky auto plant, which had been constructed with equipment sold to the Soviets by Ford. They spent eighteen months at Gorky during the brutal early years of Stalin's reign of terror and came away with a deep affection for the Russian people and an equally deep loathing of Communism. In 1935, the brothers returned to Detroit, where Walter became an organizer for the fledgling UAW and was brutally beaten by Ford goons while leading the famous sit-down strikes. In 1946, he was elected president of the UAW and hired Victor as his executive assistant. Together, they ran a powerful, progressive and honest union that won excellent benefits for its members. That irritated George Romney, chairman of the American Motors Corporation and a future governor of Michigan, who called Walter the "most dangerous man in Detroit."

After Ike announced that Khrushchev was coming to America, the State Department asked leaders of the AFL-CIO to meet with the premier during their convention in San Francisco. George Meany, the conservative president of the labor federation, refused, declaring that he wouldn't be caught dead in the same room with a Communist dictator. But Reuther agreed to meet Khrushchev and convinced six other union presidents to defy Meany and break bread with the premier. It was a private dinner—just the union leaders, Khrushchev and a few of his aides, but no reporters and no State Department officials, not even Lodge.

When they sat down to eat, Khrushchev found himself in a chair that butted up against a table leg, so Walter Reuther moved him to a more comfortable spot.

"Even though I have shifted you to the right, Mr. Chairman," Reuther joked, "I assure you there is no political significance to it."

Khrushchev laughed. "No matter how much you move me, I will still hold to a basic Communist position," he said. "Everything is fluid and everything progresses toward Communism."

Glasses were filled. Toasts were drunk. The glasses were refilled and reemptied, repeatedly. But Khrushchev noticed that Walter Reuther, who was a teetotaler, was merely touching his glass to his lips. "What is this?" Khrushchev chided. "You are giving only lip service to the toasts?"

"Mr. Chairman, I think you should know," Reuther replied, smiling, "that when the revolution comes to America, there will be at least one sober trade unionist."

Despite copious imbibing, the joviality didn't last long. When Walter Reuther suggested that the United States and the Soviet Union collaborate on foreign aid projects in poor countries, Khrushchev scoffed. "The United States exploits the wealth of other countries, underdeveloped countries, for profit," he said. "England and France do the same. They exploit the wealth of countries that need aid. We do not exploit any country—we only engage in trade."

"You exploit the workers of East Germany," Reuther said.

"Where did you dream that up?"

"If you don't exploit them, why would 3,000,000 of them cross the border into West Germany?"

"You are hopelessly sick with capitalist fever," Khrushchev answered.

"Do you have credentials to speak for the workers of the world?"

"Do you have credentials to poke your nose into East Germany?"

The discussion was beginning to sound like a barroom argument shortly before fists begin flying. And it only got worse when the topic turned to Soviet labor unions.

"Can you give us one single example in which one of your unions ever disagreed with government policy?" Reuther asked.

"Why poke your nose into our business?" Khrushchev replied.

"Freedom is everybody's business. *You* are always expressing your concern for the workers of Asia."

"And what do we call what you represent?" Khrushchev shot back. "Capitalist lackeys."

Reuther, who had been fired, beaten, and shot for his union activities, was amused. "Wall Street says I am an agent of Moscow," he said, "and Moscow says I am an agent of Wall Street."

Paul Phillips of the paper workers union asked Khrushchev why the Soviet Union jammed the broadcasts of Radio Free Europe. Khrushchev had answered that question in New York and he had no desire to do so again.

"What do you prefer to have for dinner?" he asked Phillips.

"Probably roast beef," Phillips said.

"I, borscht," Khrushchev said. "You continue to enjoy roast beef and I, borscht."

"But you insist on borscht for all," Reuther said.

Disgusted, Khrushchev stood up and turned his back to the table. For a moment, it appeared that he was about to storm out of the room in a huff. He wasn't. He was merely changing the subject. Still standing, he bent down, flipped his suit jacket up and started shaking his derriere in a

crude parody of the can-can dance he'd witnessed in Hollywood the previous day.

"This is a dance in which the girls pull up their skirts," he said. "This is
what you call freedom—freedom for the girls to show their backsides. To
us, it's pornography. It's capitalism that makes the girls that way."

"Does the Chairman think that the girls should be prohibited by law
from showing their backsides?" asked Phillips.

"There should be a law prohibiting the girls from showing their backsides," Khrushchev said. "A moral law."

"I may not see it," said James Carey, president of the electrical workers
union. "I may not want to see it—"

"Your children will go see it," Khrushchev said, feigning horror at the
corruption of America's innocent youth.

Khrushchev was certainly not the only politician who ever tried to dis-
tract an audience from a discussion of his shortcomings by denouncing
Hollywood smut, but he may have been the first pol to enliven the distraction with a zesty pantomime of the Hollywood smut he was denouncing.
Unfortunately, no television cameras were present to record the sight of
the Communist dictator shaking his butt at the capitalist lackeys.

The next day, a State Department official interviewed the union leaders
and filed a report that included their description of Khrushchev in mid-
tantrum:

"When K blows top, he begins getting red on back of neck. Red moves
up over head and down face."

55. HOW J. EDGAR HOOVER GOT CAUGHT WITH HIS PANTS DOWN

The next day, Khrushchev escaped.

On Tuesday, September 21, the morning after his meeting with the labor leaders, the dictator arose early and snuck out for an unscheduled
stroll. He emerged from the elevator in the main lobby of the Mark Hop-

kins at 7:35 and ambled outside. Taken by surprise, his bodyguards gave chase, one of them still sticking his shirttail into his pants.

It was a lovely day for a walk, the sun sparkling in the bright blue sky. Khrushchev took a deep breath of autumn air and strolled up California Street, trailed by his bodyguards and a pack of reporters. The dictator wandered through a gas station. He watched two garbage men picking up trash and asked them a few questions about their modern American trash truck. When a cable car rumbled past, he smiled and waved and the passengers waved back. An elderly woman wearing a fashionable hat pulled a camera from her handbag and the premier posed for a picture, smiling like a man saying "cheese!" He paused to admire the Masonic temple, then made his way back to the hotel, clearly thrilled that he'd stolen a few spontaneous moments of unscripted activity.

"I managed to escape the clutches of Mr. Lodge," he told reporters. "While he was asleep, I went walking."

His appetite awakened, he returned to his suite and sat down to a gargantuan breakfast—orange juice, tea, yogurt, French fries, peas, black olives, and a filet mignon, cooked well done.

After breakfast, Lodge took Khrushchev for a tour of San Francisco Bay aboard a Coast Guard cutter. In their limo on the way to the pier, the premier was in a philosophical mood, telling Lodge that the ideals espoused in the Bible were also the ideals of Communism. The difference, he explained, was that Christians believed that the ideal society would come from God, while Communists thought it would be created by man.

Out on the water a few minutes later, Khrushchev's thoughts turned to less ethereal matters. Eyeing a Navy aircraft carrier, he said he felt sorry for the crew because big ships would be sitting ducks if a war broke out: "good targets for rockets." The Soviet navy is scrapping its big ships, he added, and replacing them with submarines.

A reporter asked, How many subs do you have?

"I'd tell you the strength of our submarine fleet but you would only say I was bragging," the chairman bragged. Then he smiled. "Don't worry," he said. "We now use our submarines to catch herring."

"Is your herring-catching fleet concentrated in Vladivostok?" asked Lodge.

"Herrings are not pigs," Khrushchev replied. "You can't breed them where you want to. You have to catch them where they are."

As the ship steamed on, the skipper acted as a tour guide, pointing out the Golden Gate Bridge, Alcatraz, and other sights. Khrushchev basked in the warm sun and savored the salt air. Like countless other tourists visiting San Francisco, he announced that he'd like to come back after he retired.

As Khrushchev enjoyed his cruise on the bay, Mrs. Khrushchev went out shopping with Mrs. Lodge and Mrs. Buchanan. They took her to Sears, where she bought toys, baby clothes, and a dozen pairs of nylon stockings. "She was tickled to death to learn that upon her purchase of a dozen pair of nylons, she was awarded one free pair," the store manager told reporters. After shopping, the ladies lunched at Trader Vic's, where Mrs. Khrushchev ordered the "Chopped New York Hawaiian," which turned out to be a burger topped with pineapple and fried banana.

While she feasted on this strange American dish, her husband's ship headed back to the pier. Khrushchev, feeling mellow, sidled up to Lodge to share his latest thoughts on Mayor Poulson's speech in Los Angeles.

"He tried to let out a little fart," the premier told the ambassador, "and instead he shit in his pants."

Back on dry land, Khrushchev paid a visit to Harry Bridges, president of the International Longshoremen's and Warehousemen's Union—a radical who had been called a Communist almost as often as Khrushchev himself.

When the premier arrived at the union hall near Fisherman's Wharf, trailed by the usual mob of reporters and photographers, Bridges's wife, Noriko, greeted him with a bouquet of roses. As the couple welcomed Khrushchev, Bridges informed the premier that his wife was about to have a baby.

"I hope it grows up in peace," Khrushchev said.

Inside the hall, Khrushchev and Bridges climbed up on a platform to do some speechifying. Photographers asked Bridges, who was tall and thin, to stand behind Khrushchev, who stood a head shorter, so they'd fit in a picture together. "Sure," Bridges said. "I'll stand behind him. He's a good man. I may even give him a job."

A good man? Bridges was the only prominent American labor leader who would dare provide a character reference for a Communist, which is precisely why the government had been trying to deport Bridges for two decades.

Originally from Australia, Bridges ran off to sea at fifteen. He joined a sailors union, participated in a strike, and settled in San Francisco, where he became a longshoreman. It was a tough, dangerous, ill-paid job, and in 1933 Bridges and a cadre of Communist activists organized the dock-workers. In 1934 they struck. When police fired on a group of picketers, killing two men, the San Francisco Labor Council called a general strike that shut down the city for four days.

The longshoremen won their strike and Bridges emerged as America's most renowned radical labor leader. But fame proved a mixed blessing: In 1937, Bridges appeared on the cover of *Time* magazine; in 1938, the federal government began a long crusade to deport him, claiming that he was a member of the Communist Party. He denied the charge, admitting that he supported the party but insisting that he'd never joined it. Between 1939 and 1955, the government made several attempts to revoke his citizenship—all overturned in court.

During this long, Kafkaesque ordeal, Bridges became an expert at identifying, eluding, and tormenting the FBI agents who followed him everywhere. In New York in 1941, he discovered a listening device attached to the phone in his room in the Edison Hotel. He also discovered two FBI agents in the next room, spying on him.

"I sort of settled down," he later told a reporter, "to have some fun with the FBI."

He snuck out of the Edison, dodging his FBI tail, and rented a room in the Piccadilly Hotel across the street. He bought binoculars and invited reporters to his room at the Piccadilly for an FBI-watching party. Then Bridges and a friend returned to his room at the Edison and began to loudly jabber about absurd radical conspiracies while the reporters in his room at the Piccadilly watched the FBI agents listening to the conversation on headphones. Before leaving the Edison, Bridges ripped up a stack of innocuous letters, envelopes, and carbon papers, and left them in the wastebasket. Then he returned to the Piccadilly to watch the FBI agents steal his trash and painstakingly attempt to reassemble it.

When stories of the bizarre incident were published in the newspaper *PM* and in the *New Yorker,* Attorney General Francis Biddle marched FBI director J. Edgar Hoover over to the White House to explain the embarrassing debacle to President Roosevelt.

The president found the absurd tale hilarious. Grinning, he slapped Hoover on the back. "By God, Edgar," he said, "that's the first time you've been caught with your pants down!"

Hoover, never known for a sense of humor, was less amused. Determined to bring down the Red who'd humiliated him, he ordered his men to keep stalking Bridges. By the time Khrushchev arrived in San Francisco, the FBI file on the longshoremen's leader had swelled to more than 37,000 pages.

From the platform in the union hall, Khrushchev addressed a crowd of three hundred longshoremen. "We in Russia use the term *comrades*," the premier said. "May I call all of you here comrades?"

The longshoremen cheered.

"The main wish I want to bring to you workers is peace," Khrushchev continued. "But peace is not enough. There must also be enough work—and a good wage."

The longshoremen cheered again, louder. Khrushchev started shaking hands. One longshoreman took off his white cap and slapped it on Khrushchev's head. Beaming, the premier handed his gray fedora to the worker. "Take mine," he said. "This is an exchange for peace."

Khrushchev wore the white cap for the rest of the day. It gave him the jaunty air of a retired plumber heading for the two-dollar window at the racetrack. All he needed to complete the effect was a copy of the *Racing Form* and a half-chewed cigar.

Three decades later, in 1992, an American historian named Harvey Klehr was granted access to the formerly secret files of the Communist International in Moscow. Klehr found evidence that Bridges had indeed been a Communist. In fact, he'd been a member of the party's central committee in the 1930s. But by 1992, Bridges, who had become a Republican, was dead—and so was the Soviet Union—and nobody really cared anymore.

56. HAIL TO THE IBM

As president of the International Business Machine Corporation, Thomas J. Watson Jr. had lobbied hard to get Khrushchev to tour his fancy new plant in San Jose. He was eager to show his RAMAC computer to the premier—and to the hordes of reporters who'd be following the premier. But he was beginning to wonder if the whole idea was crazy. Everywhere Khrushchev went, he seemed to argue with somebody, and Watson worried that the premier would spoil his publicity stunt by using IBM as a platform to denounce America. What if Khrushchev said something nasty? What should he say in reply? And what about the plant's 2,000 workers? Many were Eastern European immigrants. What if one of them insulted Khrushchev—or worse?

Watson arrived in San Jose a few days before Khrushchev, checked into a hotel and began his preparations. He posted notices on the plant's bulletin boards, announcing that his invitation to Khrushchev was not an endorsement of Khrushchev and offering any employee who objected to the visit two days off with pay. "I figured offering only one day wasn't enough to get potential troublemakers to leave," he later explained. "About twenty employees took me up on the offer."

In a strange way, Watson had much in common with Khrushchev. Both men had succeeded legendary leaders who were also egomaniacal autocrats, and both denounced their predecessors for creating a "personality cult." The man Khrushchev succeeded was Stalin. The man Watson succeeded was his father, Thomas J. Watson Sr., who built IBM into a giant corporation while demanding that his employees sing his praises—literally.

A former traveling salesman, a peddler of sewing machines and cash registers, Thomas J. Watson Sr. took over the Computing-Tabulating-Recording Corporation in 1914, renamed it IBM, and created a bizarre corporate culture that was part benevolent dictatorship and part high school pep rally. Watson instituted a dress code—dark suits, white shirts, no beards or moustaches. He banned drinking and smoking at all IBM events and decreed that a photo of himself would hang in every IBM office, along with signs inscribed with IBM slogans—"Think" and "A salesman is a man who sells" and "There is no such thing as standing still." Watson's picture appeared in every issue of the IBM newspaper, *Business Machines,* and his thoughts appeared in every issue of the IBM magazine, *Think.* He created the IBM Band, the IBM Orchestra, the IBM Men's Glee Club and the IBM Mixed Chorus. He published an IBM songbook entitled "Songs of the IBM" and every morning his salesmen gathered to sing from it.

They sang "March on with IBM" ("With T. J. Watson guiding us/we lead throughout the world"). They sang "Hail to the IBM" ("Our voices swell in admiration/Of T. J. Watson proudly sing"). And they sang a song called simply "To Thomas J. Watson":

> *Pack up your troubles—T. J. Watson's here!*
> *And smile, smile, smile.*
> *He's the genius in our IBM*
> *He's the man worthwhile.*
> *He's inspiring all the time*
> *And very ver-sa-tile.*

If T. J. Watson had been alive when Khrushchev arrived at the IBM plant in San Jose on September 21, 1959, the dictator might have been greeted by 2,000 IBM employees singing "Hail to the IBM" in three-part harmony, accompanied by the IBM orchestra. Unfortunately, that delicious moment never occurred. The old man had died in 1956, and his son was embarrassed by the silly songs and the ridiculous hoopla of what he later called—echoing Khrushchev's secret speech—a "personality cult."

Khrushchev's motorcade arrived at IBM just before lunch. Watson watched as "a funny little round man in a rumpled tan suit" approached. "He had on a bright white longshoreman's cap that he'd just swapped his own hat for at the hiring hall," he remembered later.

A tall, lean patrician with a splendid head of white hair, Watson shook the premier's hand and led him into the IBM cafeteria. That proved to be a brilliant move because Khrushchev was, as usual, hungry. His huge breakfast had been four hours ago and his "comrades" at the Longshoremen's Hall hadn't fed him so much as a Ritz cracker. Now he was famished and in no mood to take a factory tour on an empty stomach.

In the cafeteria, Khrushchev had his first encounter with the concept of self-service. He liked it immediately, perhaps because it allowed him to take as much food as he wanted, which turned out to be quite a lot.

The IBM cafeteria, like many others in America, required the diner to push his tray along a waist-high counter as he passed the sumptuous buffet. Khrushchev had no problems with this procedure but some of his cronies did. "Father pushed his tray along the cases with enthusiasm," Sergei Khrushchev recalled. "Gromyko imitated his example. The rest of the delegation followed. They picked up their trays uncertainly, lowered them warily onto the cafeteria service counter and slowly began sliding them forward, expecting some dirty trick at any moment. Most of them had not moved food from stove to table in a good many years. Waiters, maids, or at worst, secretaries existed for that purpose."

Khrushchev and Gromyko managed to successfully guide their food down the self-service line but somehow Vyacheslav Yeludin, the Soviet minister of higher education, dropped his tray. It landed with a loud crash. As everyone turned to watch, Khrushchev joked that Yeludin would have to go into training because his arms were obviously unaccustomed to work. Mortified, Yeludin stood mute, brushing flecks of cabbage off his pants.

Khrushchev sat down with Watson and dug into his huge load of victuals—fried chicken, potatoes, fruit salad, onion soup, orange juice, and iced tea. The more he ate, the happier he got. "You are well versed in psychology," he told Watson. "You started off our acquaintance by taking me to this dining room."

When the premier was fully refueled, Watson led him on a tour of the plant, showing off his pride and joy, IBM's RAMAC computer. Two months earlier, Watson had taken the RAMAC to the American Exhibition in Moscow, where it answered questions about American life. Back in San Jose, the miracle machine was programmed to perform like an electronic history book. All a visitor had to do was choose any year since 4 B.C. and RAMAC would reveal the key events of that year in ten languages, including Russian.

"This demonstration was dear to my heart," Watson recalled, "because I'd thought it up myself."

Alas, Khrushchev was not impressed. He figured his scientists had plenty of computers. Otherwise how could they hit the moon with a rocket? And besides, he was still marveling at the cafeteria.

"Father was staggered by the IBM cafeteria much more than by its computers," Sergei Khrushchev recalled. The premier loved the concept of self-service and he was already planning to adopt it back home. Now his bureaucrats could carry their own food and they wouldn't have to waste time waiting for waitresses to bring them their meals. The premier was particularly impressed by IBM's cafeteria tables, with their easy-to-clean Formica tops—no more messy tablecloths to launder!

"You brush off the crumbs, wipe it with a cloth, and everything's clean," Khrushchev told Sergei, his voice filled with admiration.

57. A RIOT IN THE CATHEDRAL OF CAPITALISM

Tipped off that Khrushchev would visit Quality Foods, a huge new super-market in suburban San Francisco, *Time* magazine reporter Burt Meyers slipped away from the media pack, hid his press credentials, and sauntered into the supermarket, hoping to pass for a customer.

Meyers was prowling the frozen food section, pretending to study the TV dinners, when he noticed men in sunglasses lurking around the store, trying to look inconspicuous. Secret Service, he thought. That meant Khrushchev really *was* coming.

It made perfect sense to bring him here. The supermarket was the ulti-mate symbol of America's bounty, a cathedral of capitalism, a cornucopia of earthly delights. While the Soviet bloc suffered shortages and ra-tioning, America was building bigger and bigger supermarkets crammed with more and more stuff packaged in brighter and gaudier boxes. No wonder the Russians at the American exhibition had shoplifted as much as they could grab from the faux grocery.

American supermarkets were so awe-inspiring that they scared people. "Housewives typically fall into a hypnoidal trance when they get into a supermarket," wrote Vance Packard in *The Hidden Persuaders,* a huge best-seller in 1957. "The main cause of the trance is that the supermarket is packed with products that in former years would have been items that only kings and queens could afford, and here in this fairyland they were available." Meanwhile, Packard added, the malevolent wizards of Madi-son Avenue had learned to sell their products to these zombified house-wives by packaging the stuff in bright yellow or red boxes that "hypnotize the woman like a flashlight waved in front of her eyes."

A million Americans bought Packard's alarming exposé—packaged in a bright yellow and red cover—but few stopped shopping in supermarkets.

As he waited for Khrushchev in Quality Foods, Meyer noticed that the supermarket was packed. Was it the lure of today's "Fill Your Freezer!" sale or had word of Khrushchev's visit leaked?

A siren wailed. The market's doors swung open and Khrushchev strolled in, trailed by Lodge and the usual mob of bodyguards. The premier headed first for the produce section. He inspected the potatoes and squeezed a grapefruit. He picked up a cantaloupe, sniffed it, thumped it with his thumb, and asked how much it cost.

"There! There's the Russian!" yelled an old lady. "The cute, fat one!"

Shoppers surged toward Khrushchev. Children shrieked. Housewives held their babies up to see the famous dictator. Teenage girls squealed as if they'd spotted Elvis. One of them shook Khrushchev's hand and then screeched, "He touched me!"

Anxious to protect their leader, the Soviet security guards surrounded him and linked arms. That kept the shoppers at bay and also hid Khrushchev from the photographers, who were determined to shoot pictures of the chairman fondling fruit. The cameramen were incensed. They had no choice but to seize the high ground so they could shoot the premier from above. One photographer climbed atop a refrigerated butter case, then slipped down, squishing the butter. Another hopped up on a shelf packed with jars of instant coffee and shot pictures while jars crashed to the floor, spewing shards of glass and granules of coffee.

One shooter scampered up on a checkout counter, only to find that the conveyor belt was moving beneath his feet. "Somebody stop this thing!" he yelled. "It's ruining my shot."

Burton Glinn, a photographer for the Magnum agency, climbed atop a meat counter. The butcher cried, "Hey, get off my chickens!" Glinn ignored him and kept shooting. The butcher grabbed him and tried to wrestle him to the floor.

Carl Mydans of *Life* magazine, one of the great photojournalists of the century, was far too classy to battle butchers. Instead, he paid a teenager five dollars, climbed on his shoulders, and ordered him to head toward Khrushchev. The kid staggered off, trudging beneath his heavy load.

"Faster! Faster!" Mydans commanded, digging his heels into the kid's flanks, until a cop yanked him down and he landed with one foot in a loaf of bread.

Richard Strout, a mild-mannered reporter for the *Christian Science Monitor*, clambered up on a checkout counter. "Come down," ordered a white-coated checkout clerk. Strout ignored him. He was standing in the perfect place to witness one of the first great eruptions of a phenomenon that would soon become a familiar aspect of modern life—the media riot.

Khrushchev left the produce section and walked past the cookie display toward the meat department. A mob of housewives and reporters followed, packing the aisles and knocking over canned goods, which rolled on the floor, tripping people. Teenage boys stood in shopping carts, hoping for a better view, only to tumble out when the carts started rolling. A woman fell into a display of potato chips, causing much crunching.

Stunned, Lodge watched a photographer dashing through a deli counter, wading in Spam and cheese, so he could get a shot of Khrushchev tiptoeing through the spilled food.

A housewife stared in amazement at the mass misbehavior. "I've never seen men act like this before," she said.

But at least one man was still behaving like a gentleman. Standing in the vortex of the insanity, Khrushchev calmly smiled, shook hands with clerks and shoppers, examined the merchandise, and engaged a housewife in a friendly chat about frozen food. The premier would have been the perfect customer except for one thing: He left without buying anything. Perhaps the distraction of the riot had prevented him from succumbing to Packard's "hypnoidal trance."

Outside on the sidewalk, Khrushchev shook the manager's hand and thanked him for his hospitality. "You have a fine store," he said, then he climbed into his limo and the shell-shocked manager shuffled inside to survey the damage.

Dazed and amazed, reporters struggled to capture the strangeness of the scene in the supermarket. Seth Pett of the Associated Press succeeded better than most. "It was like the happy hour in a manic depressive ward," he wrote, "like the year of the locusts, like the bull in a china shop, like the night the dam burst, like, crazy, man."

58. HALFWAY THROUGH THE INTERSTELLAR VOYAGE

Back in his hotel room after the sightseeing tour, Khrushchev found him-self with a couple of unscheduled hours before the evening's inevitable civic banquet. Feeling a bit peckish, he decided to call for room service.

At six o'clock, his snack arrived—clam chowder, abalone steaks, filet of sole, roast pheasants, roast beef, baked potatoes, vegetables, fruit tarts with whipped cream, coffee, tea, and milk. Apparently the chairman felt confident that this would tide him over until the banquet, which was scheduled for 7:45.

Meanwhile, Henry Cabot Lodge pondered the events of the day and concluded that things had gone very well. But the prospect of another banquet darkened his sunny outlook. After all, banquets were the venues where Khrushchev tended to blow his top—at the National Press Club, where he lost his temper over the question about his secret speech; at the Waldorf in New York, where he exploded at hecklers; at the Hollywood luncheon, where he ranted about Disneyland; at Mayor Poulson's dinner, where he threatened to go home. Banquets were starting to make Lodge nervous, so he begged the organizers of this one to avoid inciting Khrushchev.

As it turned out, he needn't have worried. Mayor Christopher and the other speakers at the dinner were exceedingly friendly to their guest and Khrushchev responded with a speech that was a Valentine to San Fran-cisco.

"Your land is excellent, ladies and gentlemen," the premier told a crowd of 3,000, "and your city, San Francisco, is magnificent."

He said he'd spent a "very pleasant day." He thanked the longshoreman who gave him his cap, described Tom Watson as "a very charming man," and noted the "friendly smiles" of people on the street. He praised "your beautiful bay" and "your wonderful roadways" and his "wonderful visit" to the supermarket, and the "wonderful meal" he received at the IBM cafeteria. Then he turned to Mayor Christopher. "I am a little bit afraid of lavishing too much praise upon you because you are in the midst of an election campaign," he said. "I don't want anyone to think that I'm trying to interfere in your elections."

His cup running over with the milk of human kindness, Khrushchev even announced that he had forgiven Los Angeles Mayor Poulson. "Christian teaching tells us to forgive the trespasses of others," the atheist said. "It was just an unhappy incident and let us consider the question to be closed."

For an hour and ten minutes, Khrushchev rambled on like a happy drunk. After World War II, he said, Russian soldiers returned from Bulgaria singing a song that went, "Bulgaria is certainly a very fine country, but Russia is the best of all." Now, Khrushchev said, he wanted to rewrite the words of the song: "All the cities that I visited in the United States are good, but San Francisco is the best of all!"

When he climbed into bed after the banquet that night, Nikita Khrushchev had completed—or maybe the correct word is *survived*—a week in the United States of America. In a mere seven days, Khrushchev's bizarre adventures had boggled the minds of the exhausted reporters traveling with him and left them struggling to conjure up a metaphor that could capture the endless parade of absurdities.

"This is an interstellar voyage," wrote Murray Kempton.

"A traveling spectacle that has long passed credulity," wrote Richard Strout.

"In this grisly political farce being played out under armed guard," wrote Mary McGrory, "the preposterous has now become an hourly occurrence."

"Every once in a while you stop and pinch yourself. This trip of Nikita Khrushchev can't be real," wrote Arthur Edson of the Associated Press. "It seems like a dream, a nightmare. Peel off from the tour for a moment, maybe no longer than to write your story, and when you return, some reporter, his eyes glazed, will say: 'You should have been here. You simply wouldn't have believed it.'"

And it wasn't over yet. Khrushchev was heading to Iowa to visit his friend Roswell Garst, the eccentric millionaire corn farmer, then flying to Pittsburgh to see a steel mill owned by America's most famous party hostess, then continuing on to Camp David to pow-wow with President Eisenhower.

At two o'clock that morning, as Khrushchev slept, Lodge banged out a cable to his bosses back in Washington, updating them on the current state of the premier's mood: "He has been in excellent humor for two days and has come to make a joke of our mishaps in Los Angeles (having at the time been furious). My personal standing with him is really excellent as of this writing. There is no doubt in my mind that as of this moment the gains on this trip definitely outweigh the losses and I can document this in many different ways.

"I can only pray this will continue."

59. PEACE THROUGH CORN

At the Iowa state fair, bands played, ostriches raced, farmers' wives competed to see who made the best pies, and a quarter million people shuffled past 5,000 snorting, snoozing pigs—the biggest swine show yet held in America. Meanwhile, out on the midway, an Indian in full Hollywood headdress struggled to sell bottles of vegetable juice as a cure for the jitters to a crowd of farmers who did not look the slightest bit jittery, and a pitchman touted his amazing patented paring knife as "the greatest thing the world has ever seen—and I can say that without fear of successful contradiction because I've been around the world."

Austin C. Wehrwein jotted down the pitchman's spiel for the readers of the *New York Times*. Generally, the *Times* did not deign to cover the Iowa State Fair, but in 1959, the editors dispatched Wehrwein to Des Moines to chronicle what Khrushchev would miss by arriving in Iowa two weeks after the fair ended:

He'll miss the world's largest farm and livestock exhibition . . .

He'll miss the big meals served in tents by church groups . . .

He'll miss the checker and horseshoe pitching tournaments . . .

He'll miss the essence of Iowa that only a visit to the fair offers . . .

Khrushchev would also miss the Iowans who visited the fair, so Wehrwein described them: "The men for the most part are tanned and smooth-faced and often wear broad-brimmed hats, not quite cowboy style. The women are self-possessed even when their feet hurt, and most are on the substantial side, although some of the 4-H girls look like Miss America."

Weeks before Khrushchev touched down in Des Moines, American journalists went mad over Iowa. It was the symbol of the *real* America, the heartland of the nation, the breadbasket of the world, a place of white picket fences and amber waves of grain. After a week in the sinful cities of Washington, New York, Los Angeles and San Francisco, Khrushchev would finally arrive in small-town America, home of the hard-working, God-fearing yeoman farmer, a place where the air was fresh and the corn was as high as an elephant's eye and people didn't need to lock their doors.

In the days leading up to the premier's arrival, Iowa swarmed with reporters scouring the prairies for simple farm folks and collecting their homespun wisdom about the visit of the Communist:

"I think Khrushchev coming here is a good idea. You never get anywhere fighting with your neighbors."

"I guess it's all right. But we don't think much of not believing in God."

"We should treat the old duffer with respect. . . . The Russians are too big a child to turn over on our laps and spank and say, 'Now you do as I say.'"

"I am getting tired of him yakking all the time. It would be better if he could speak English."

Most Iowans favored the visit, the *Des Moines Register* reported, though it quickly added, "This does not mean Iowans are going overboard in welcoming Khrushchev. They wouldn't vote for him for dogcatcher."

"Iowans will give him a dignified, conservative reception," predicted the secretary of the Greater Des Moines Chamber of Commerce, who bore the patriotic name John Adams. Noting that Khrushchev had complained about the heat in his closed limo in Los Angeles, Adams announced that the Chamber would provide the dictator with a big, powder-blue Cadillac convertible during his visit.

Other Iowans made equally hospitable gestures. A drugstore in Grinnell urged the premier to drop by. So did a rock and roll emporium called the Val-Air Ballroom. And the American Trampoline Company in Jefferson, Iowa, offered to present the premier with a free trampoline if he'd stop by for just ten minutes. Alas, it wasn't to be. There was only one place Khrushchev really wanted to see in Iowa—his friend Roswell Garst's farm in Coon Rapids.

Roswell "Bob" Garst was a big man with a broad back, a gargantuan gut, the huge hands of a farmer who'd spent years milking cows, and a massive head that looked like one of the statues found on Easter Island. Churning with energy, he chain-smoked, chugged coffee, kept up a steady stream of talk—most of it about corn—and frequently burst into song, belting out "Old Man River."

The son of a successful merchant and nephew of an Iowa governor, Garst grew up on a dairy farm in Coon Rapids. He loved farming and was good at it, but his real talent was salesmanship. As a young man in the 1920s he sold real estate in Des Moines and befriended Henry Wallace, the brilliant agronomist and future secretary of agriculture and vice president under Franklin Roosevelt. Wallace had developed a line of hybrid corn that produced strong plants and big yields. Garst tested it, liked it, and volunteered to sell it. He'd stuff ten bushels of the corn in the back of his car and head out across the corn belt. A natural showman, he knew how to draw a crowd. Sometimes he'd lie down on the floor of a crowded hotel lobby and when people came over to see if he was hurt, he'd repeat his dad's favorite motto: "Never stand up when you can sit, never sit when you can lie down." Then Garst would leap to his feet and start talking about hybrid seed corn, pepping up his spiel with colorful proverbs, quotations, and occasional snippets of song.

It worked and Garst became rich. But he wasn't in it just for the money. He was also an idealist who believed in the power of corn. Garst had a vision: He wanted to feed a hungry planet through hybrid corn and modern fertilizers. If everybody on earth had a full belly, he figured, there'd be no more war. He called his dream "peace through corn."

In the 1950s, while Garst was selling, raising and experimenting with corn, Nikita Khrushchev, who also believed in the power of corn, was taking control of the Soviet Union. Soviet agriculture had been ravaged by Stalin's brutal forced collectivization, and Khrushchev believed that the answer was to raise more corn. He established a corn institute in Ukraine, erected a corn pavilion in Moscow, and ordered the crop planted on thousands of acres in the previously untilled "virgin lands" of Kazakhstan.

In 1955, Khrushchev dispatched a delegation to Iowa, the Mecca of corn, to study American agriculture. Garst's farm, already famous among corn aficionados, was not on the itinerary. Eager to exalt the fabled yeoman farmer, American officials wanted to show off small family farms and Garst's operation was too big, too modern, too experimental.

But at a reception, Garst met Vladimir Matskevitch, the head of the Soviet delegation, and pumped his ear full of the famous Garst salesmanship. Even in translation, his spiel was persuasive and Matskevitch asked his American hosts if he could visit Garst's farm. No, they said, the itinerary was set. The next morning, Matskevitch asked the Americans to stop the car he was riding in. He climbed out and refused to return until they agreed to take him to Garst's farm. He spent the day touring the place and listening to Garst's endless theories about corn.

Dazzled, Matskevitch invited Garst to the Soviet Union. Garst accepted and arrived in September 1955. He toured collective farms, lectured on corn production, and offered toasts to "peace through corn." He met Khrushchev at the premier's dacha on the Black Sea and the two hit it off immediately. They both loved to talk, particularly about farming. They chatted all afternoon and continued through a long, lavish dinner and deep into the night.

"He was the sort of man you could profitably listen to and memorize everything he said," Khrushchev gushed in his memoir. "To tell the truth, he usually did all the talking while I just listened."

As the two men drank and talked, Garst asked why the Russians knew so little about American agriculture. American farm journals printed all the techniques that Garst touted. Why didn't you read them? Garst asked. After all, you stole the secret of the atomic bomb in three weeks.

Khrushchev burst out laughing. "It only took us *two* weeks," he said, holding up two fingers. "You locked up the atomic bomb, so we had to steal it. When you offered us all this information about agriculture for nothing, we thought that might be what it was worth—nothing."

The next morning, Garst sold Khrushchev 5,000 tons of seed corn. Then he traveled to Romania and Hungary and sold some more.

In 1959, Garst returned to Russia and spent another day with Khrushchev, talking about corn and arguing about geopolitics.

"Why the hell don't you quit the arms race?" Garst asked.

"How would you like to be surrounded by air bases?" Khrushchev replied, rattling off a list of American bases near the Soviet Union.

"You ought to laugh about those bases," Garst replied, assuring the dictator that America would never attack.

Khrushchev enjoyed sparring with Garst, who was one of the few people the dictator had encountered who wasn't afraid to argue with him. A few months later, when Ike invited him to America, Khrushchev announced his wish to visit Garst on his Iowa farm. It wasn't long before dozens of reporters were swarming over Garst's spread in Coon Rapids.

"How do I know what bedroom we'll put him in if he stays overnight?" Garst grumbled at one of the dumber questions. "I don't know what color the guest towels in the bathroom will be, either. But it's his turn to come to our house and I can just tell you we'll give him a feed that'll be damn good."

He got less grumpy and more loquacious when the subject turned to corn. "Khrushchev is coming here to learn about corn and cattle," he said. "He wants his people to eat less bread, potatoes and borscht and more beef, eggs and sausage. I can give him the answers. I can demonstrate the techniques right here. . . . There is actually no reason why people can't all have lamb chops for breakfast, why people can't all have roast beef for lunch and why people can't all have steak for supper."

Selling corn to the Soviets made strategic sense, he said. "It would be dangerous for the world to have a Russia that is both hungry and has the H-bomb. I never saw a well-fed, contented man who was really dangerous."

Ever the ham, Garst reveled in the attention, giving innumerable interviews and posing for countless pictures, one of them showing him standing in an ankle-length sheepskin coat that Khrushchev had given him. But his wife, Elizabeth, was more bashful. "My husband, he gets me into such complications," she told a reporter, sighing with mock exasperation. "Imagine having the Khrushchevs here for dinner."

With the help of neighboring farm wives, she decorated the house with displays of pumpkins, sunflowers and, of course, cornstalks. And her friend Bertha Keister helped her tidy the upstairs bathroom by making a skirt that hid the soaps and cleansing powders stored under the sink. But Mrs. Garst told reporters that she wasn't going to go overboard spiffing up her six-bedroom farmhouse.

"I don't think I'll even wax the floors," she declared.

As Mrs. Garst prepared for her guests, the state of Iowa dispatched crews to beautify the highways that the premier would traverse on his way to Garst's farm. The crews cut roadside weeds with industrial-size sit-down lawnmowers topped with big red flags. "These flags are not in honor of Khrushchev and have no connection with Communism," the *Des Moines Register* reassured its readers. "The flags are to warn motorists speeding over hilly highways that a slow-moving vehicle is dead ahead."

In Coon Rapids crowds began to gather on Main Street. Church ladies set up tables in a vacant lot next to the library and hawked sandwiches that consisted of two pieces of Wonder bread separated by a slender slice of bologna. The price of this delicacy was a dollar—at least triple the usual rate—and Cokes that usually fetched a nickel were going for a quarter each. Meanwhile, two cute thirteen-year-old twins, Vida and Vicki Peterson, took ears of local corn, which cost almost nothing, decorated them with tags identifying them as "souvenir ears" of the historic Khrushchev visit, and peddled them to tourists for fifty cents apiece, pocketing nearly one hundred dollars in the process.

Apparently Roswell Garst was not the only crafty capitalist in Coon Rapids.

60. HOT DOG

It was a bumpy landing. Caught in a crosswind over Des Moines Municipal Airport, Khrushchev's plane hit the runway, bounced several feet into the air, landed again, bounced again and finally taxied to a stop.

After pleasant greetings from the mayor and governor, Khrushchev hopped into the Chamber of Commerce's powder-blue Cadillac convertible and headed into town. He passed crowds estimated at 20,000, nearly a tenth of the Des Moines population. Most folks were friendly, but one man held a sign reading "We Butcher Hogs, Not People." At the Hotel Fort Des Moines, Khrushchev emerged from the Cadillac and a local radio reporter popped out of the crowd for an impromptu interview.

"Are you tired?" he asked the premier.

"I have no right to get tired," Khrushchev replied. "Life is short. We sleep eight hours a day, so if we live sixty years, we sleep twenty years. Therefore we have to make the best of the other two-thirds and be of as much use to mankind as possible."

It was a noble sentiment but Khrushchev was exhausted, and so was everybody else on the tour. A week of long days, little sleep, and intense pressure had rubbed nerves raw. "We were all getting pretty frazzled," Wiley Buchanan recalled, "and I could feel my own threshold of irritability getting lower by the minute."

The reporters were even more irritable than Buchanan. Most of them had been up long after midnight, filing stories on Khrushchev's speech at the banquet in San Francisco, only to be awakened at four o'clock in the morning so they could stand on a street corner, waiting for a special press bus to the airport to catch the press plane to Des Moines, where they learned that the local hotels were overbooked and their reservations were useless. Irate, the reporters wanted to complain to Joe Reap, the State Department's PR man, but Reap had locked himself in his hotel room and taken his phone off the hook. Another State Department official, the trip's advance man, also collapsed under the strain.

"This poor guy nearly had a nervous breakdown right there in my presence," recalled Reap's assistant, Richard Townsend Davies. "I had to send him off and get somebody to give him a sedative." Davies did the best he could, arranging for reporters to rent rooms in local homes.

Among the irritable was the usually amiable Murray Kempton of the *New York Post*. He'd flown in on the press plane and was promptly herded into a media bus bearing a sign announcing that the ride to town would cost one dollar. But the driver refused to take any dollars until the bus was full. "Then he walked back and collected the fare and sat and counted it— moving his lips—for five minutes," Kempton wrote in his column. "Then he waited until a twin brother of Grandma Moses came into the bus, counted the money again and gave him a receipt."

By then, of course, Khrushchev was long gone. When Kempton finally arrived in Des Moines, he was lucky enough to snag a hotel room but not lucky enough to get lunch. "There was a sign saying restaurant, and there came back the memory of my last meal, which I ate during the Grant Administration," he wrote. "The waitress said I couldn't have steak; it was soup and pink salmon or nothing. I sat down and ordered it. Days passed, and she brought forth a greasy mess of tomato soup soggily fortified with macaroni, but suddenly behind me there was a shaking of pressed flesh; Khrushchev was leaving the hotel to go on his tour. I stood up. The waitress, a Medusa with every snake dyed red, screamed: 'If you don't sit down and eat, I will take away the soup,' presumably to poison the cat. This is why I love Iowa: every waitress is your own wife as avenging angel."

Kempton fled the restaurant and jumped into a car packed with reporters. They chased Khrushchev's limo and caught it at the Des Moines Packing Company. The place smelled like a slaughterhouse, perhaps because it *was* a slaughterhouse. On the steps of the plant, Khrushchev was given a blue thermal smock to keep him warm in the meat freezers. The chairman entered, accompanied by Lodge and followed by a pool of reporters, photographers, and TV cameramen. Guards shooed the rest of the press corps away, and did it with gusto.

"I walked up the steps, and was pushed down them by a State Department security officer," wrote Kempton, who was having a bad day. "I was finished off by an Iowa cop."

Kempton retreated to a trailer where a CBS crew watched the footage their cameraman was shooting inside the plant. It was quite a show. Khrushchev shuffled through the place on a red carpet that, upon closer inspection, turned out to be constructed of red roofing shingles. He met live cows, then saw the room where they were being slaughtered. He wandered through warehouse-size freezers where huge sides of beef swayed on hooks and the photographers struggled to shoot his picture through clouds of frosty mist. He watched a machine squirt out a sausage nearly as long as a garden hose, then he watched blades slice it into hot dogs.

Finally the premier got his reward—a hot dog from a vending machine decorated with the company's logo, which featured Bob-Bee, a grinning kid in a cowboy hat.

With mustard or without? somebody asked.

"With mustard, of course," Khrushchev replied.

His guide slathered the dog with mustard, then a security guard passed a Geiger counter over it. It passed the test. Khrushchev took a bite. He liked it and quickly gobbled it up.

"It's excellent," he said with a smile that crinkled the skin around his eyes. Then he glanced over at Lodge. "Well, capitalist, have you finished your hot dog?"

"Yes," said Lodge, a politician trained in the art of public hot dog munching. "We capitalists get hungry too, you know."

Khrushchev, who'd finished lunch only an hour earlier, ate half of a second dog and asked, "Where's the beer to go with this?"

Alas, none was available. His hosts had remembered the Geiger counter but forgotten the beer.

As they left the plant, Khrushchev surmised that perhaps this tour was nothing but a publicity stunt designed to sell his host's hot dogs.

"Mr. Lodge, that was all just a big promotion, wasn't it?" he asked.

Lodge just smiled.

"Well," Khrushchev said, "you should get a share of the commission since you brought me here."

61. THE COSSACKS ARE COMING!

At the civic banquet in Des Moines that night, Khrushchev caught a glimpse of Roswell Garst across a crowded room.

"The chunky Russian spotted his friend and advanced upon him in a kind of wrestler's crouch, arms wide, grinning broadly," recalled Wiley Buchanan. "Garst arose and made a similar approach until finally they met in an embrace that reminded me of a couple of waltzing bears."

Garst offered his friend a quiet suggestion: Instead of leaving the hotel at 9:00 the next morning, as planned, and traveling with the usual mob, Khrushchev should sneak out of the hotel at 6:30, with just his interpreter. Garst would pick them up in his car and they'd skedaddle off to Coon Rapids before anybody realized they were gone. Khrushchev was amused by the idea but not inclined to attempt this great escape. "If I tried to run off secretly with Garst when he came to fetch me," he later wrote, "it might appear that I'd been kidnapped, like a bride in the Caucasus."

But the premier did ask Lodge if they could change the schedule and leave the hotel at 6:30 the next morning. Lodge nixed that idea but agreed to head out at 8:30. Even that small scheduling change caused a minor panic. Sleepy-eyed reporters scrambled to catch the press buses—there were seven of them—and in the mad rush, Richard Townsend Davies, newly in charge of press logistics for the State Department, missed the last bus. That meant that hundreds of reporters were loose in the Iowa countryside without responsible adult supervision. Fortunately an Iowa state trooper agreed to give Davies a lift to Coon Rapids. "We set off at 110 miles an hour down these straight Iowa highways," Davies later recalled.

Meanwhile, Jack Christensen, a twenty-nine-year-old swimming pool operator from Mason City, Iowa, was also heading toward Garst's farm. He hadn't been invited, which was precisely why he was going. "I've always had a yen to pull off stunts," he later explained. "In the fall of 1953 I turned out for football practice at Mason City Junior College and made the team, although I wasn't a student and had never played football. In 1956, I read that tickets to the Democratic convention were so tight that former President Harry Truman could only get six. So I went to Chicago and wound up sitting with the Pennsylvania delegation."

When newspapers reported that Khrushchev was the most tightly guarded visitor in Iowa's history, one of Christensen's pals teased him, saying, "Well, that's one you can't bust into." Christensen couldn't resist that challenge. But crashing Garst's party wouldn't be easy. The premier was protected by the usual Soviet and American security guards, plus Iowa state troopers, seven hundred Iowa National Guardsmen and nine members of the Green County Pleasure Riders Club, a group of Garst's neighbors who patrolled his farm on horseback. Eluding that army would be the gate-crasher's equivalent of climbing Mount Everest. Christensen decided to try. Early on the morning of Wednesday, September 23, he hopped into his car and headed for Coon Rapids.

Barreling along at ridiculously high speeds, the police car containing Richard Townsend Davies reached Garst's farm shortly after the last press bus arrived. By then, the place was a media madhouse. Photographers were perched in trees. TV crews had erected towers topped with wide-angle cameras. The Associated Press had taken over one barn; United Press International had seized another. TV cables snaked across the front yard, and reporters roamed the grounds peeking into buildings and scribbling notes.

"Everything was wired for sound but the hogs," James Reston wisecracked in the *Times* the next day. And the hogs might have been wired too, but rifle-toting National Guardsmen stood sentry at the pigpen.

Garst was incensed. "Nobody told me you were going to bring all these correspondents," he barked at Davies.

"Gee, Mr. Garst," Davies replied, "Mr. Khrushchev is fairly well known and . . . "

"Well, they can't come on my property."

"Mr. Garst, you tell them," Davies said. "I ain't gonna tell them. *You* tell them."

"I'll get the dogs out here," Garst said.

"Now, Mr. Garst, now really, please," Davies pleaded, invoking the names of reporters too famous to sic dogs on. "There's Scotty Reston here and Bob Considine. Your name will not be Garst, your name will be Mud."

"I don't want them," Garst growled. "They'll tramp down my corn."

It was too late. The reporters were already tramping down the corn, among other crops. Garst grumbled but finally decided to ignore these human locusts and give Khrushchev a tour. First he showed the premier a harvesting machine working in a field of sorghum. Khrushchev studied the scene and asked which brand of harvester Garst preferred—McCormick or John Deere? Garst said he used McCormick and Khrushchev said the Soviets did too.

Khrushchev noticed a strapping young American with a crew cut and a sizable pot belly standing nearby. Impressed with this 240-pound specimen of corn-fed American beefcake, the premier shook hands with the young man, who happened to be Jack Christensen, the gate-crasher from Mason City.

"Now there's a *real* American," Khrushchev said, patting Christensen's ample belly.

"We're both alike," Christensen replied, eyeing Khrushchev's sizable gut.

The premier grinned and patted the gate-crasher's belly a couple more times, so the photographers could get their shots. The next day, a photo of the premier's tribute to the abdominal symbol of American affluence appeared in newspapers all over the world, usually accompanied by his quote: "Now there's a *real* American." Christensen had pulled it off.

When Garst led Khrushchev off to get acquainted with some local hogs and cattle, Christensen followed, boldly determined to push his stunt as far as it could go. He ended up standing in a livestock pen right next to the premier, Garst, Lodge, and Sergei Khrushchev. "I've got to admit that was pretty hairy," he recalled. "But when I still wasn't nabbed, I really got my confidence up."

Christensen spotted a little girl—Martha Jane Thomas, the five-year-old granddaughter of Garst's business partner—and he picked her up and handed her to Khrushchev. "Here," he told the dictator. "The photographers want to take some pictures."

Eager to oblige, Khrushchev hugged the girl while shutters clicked. A week later, *Life* magazine ran that picture in the two-page photo gallery that illustrated Christensen's account of his exploits. Garst led Khrushchev along, eager to show off his silage operation, where corn cobs were chopped and turned into feed for cattle. The vast media multitude, now numbering nearly three hundred uninvited guests, tagged along. At one point, a reporter asked Mrs. Khrushchev if she was enjoying the sights.

"I haven't seen anything yet because of the crowd," she replied.

"There were hordes of people following us, a whole army of journalists—journalists in all directions as far as the eye could see," the premier later recalled. "It reminded me of what Prokop, the gamekeeper on our shooting preserve in the Ukraine, used to say when I asked him how the hunting looked. 'Ducks everywhere, Comrade Khrushchev,' he'd answer in Ukrainian. 'Ducks as far as the eye can see—more ducks than shit.' Well, that's how many journalists there were tramping around after us on Garst's farm."

Garst was not amused. When he saw photographers trampling through his cornfield, he exploded. He yanked a cornstalk out of the ground and jabbed it toward them like a spear.

"Get back!" he yelled. "Get back!"

The photographers flinched but held their ground. These were not raw recruits; they were battle-hardened veterans of the siege of the San Francisco supermarket, and they weren't easily flustered.

"Bring those horses in here!" Garst yelled to the horsemen of the Green County Pleasure Riders Club. "Ride 'em down!" he ordered. "Push 'em back!"

A few of the horsemen obeyed, halfheartedly riding into the media mob. As reporters scrambled out of the way, one wag yelled, "The Cossacks are coming!"

The media hacks might have thought that was funny but Garst did not.

"If you fellows don't get out of the way," he yelled, "I'm going to *kick* you out of the way."

With that, he charged out of the silage ditch, kicking wildly, landing a foot on the shin of Harrison Salisbury of the *New York Times*, the dean of America's foreign correspondents. Then he started scooping up handfuls of wet silage and throwing it at the photographers, who held their ground long enough to snap pictures of the enraged Garst, photos that were published in newspapers around the world.

Khrushchev watched it all, howling with laughter.

Garst drove the photographers a few steps back, but only for a few minutes. As *New York Times* columnist James Reston recognized, a profound but largely overlooked cultural change became visible on Roswell Garst's farm on the morning of September 23, 1959: The mass media had become as important, perhaps more important, than the people and events it covered. "There are so many newsmen reporting this trip that they change the course of events," Reston wrote in his column. "They are not the obscure witnesses of history, but the principal characters in the drama, whose very presence is so ubiquitous that most of the time Mr. Khrushchev is addressing them, or addressing others with them in mind."

The world was becoming a television studio and those who wished to rule it would have to become actors. Khrushchev, a natural ham, instinctively understood this new reality. He recognized that his trip was not just a diplomatic journey; it was an opportunity to put on a TV show starring himself as the folksy, funny populist leader of the dynamic new Communist world.

Perhaps that explains why the premier didn't join his friend Garst in his assault on the photographers. To Garst, they were obnoxious interlopers; to Khrushchev, they were valuable collaborators.

62. GOD AND MAN AND CORN

When Garst led Khrushchev off to eat lunch with one hundred local guests, most of the reporters retreated to Coon Rapids, where they filed stories and grumbled about paying a dollar for the church ladies' meager bologna sandwiches.

But Jack Christensen thought he might as well try to crash Garst's lunch too. Attempting to look like he belonged, Christensen sauntered toward the big brown tent where caterers were serving a country feast of fried chicken and barbequed ribs. A cop stopped him, demanding to know who he was.

"Say," Christensen hollered to a security guard who'd seen him earlier, "I'm having trouble getting in here."

"He's all right," the security guard told the cop. "He's a member of the family."

Inside the tent, Christensen spotted Adlai Stevenson, the former governor of Illinois and Democratic candidate for president. Twice, Stevenson had lost elections to Eisenhower, but he lost with wit and charm and many Democrats consoled themselves with the dubious thought that he'd lost because he was too smart for the American public.

"Hello, Adlai," Christensen said.

"Hello," Stevenson said. "How are you?"

They shook hands and Christensen followed Stevenson through the chow line as if they were old friends. Then the gate-crasher sat down to eat with the Russian security guards, figuring that they couldn't speak much English and consequently wouldn't ask him any embarrassing questions. But Garst spotted him: "Who the hell are you?" he demanded. Christensen mumbled something, then quietly slipped away. The jig was up.

Stevenson sat down with Garst, Khrushchev, and Lodge. They ate chicken, chatted about the world situation, and posed for pictures. Khrushchev ate with gusto and studied the Iowans in the tent. He was impressed by their size, which tended toward the hefty. The premier shared the ancient peasant belief that a pot belly and a plump rump were signs of prosperity, health, and happiness. He was particularly impressed with two zaftig blonde women who obviously had been eating very well.

"I want to meet these slaves of capitalism," he said, smiling. "They are good ads for capitalism. God knows I wish we all looked like that."

After lunch, Khrushchev and Stevenson wandered out of the tent and quickly found themselves facing the inevitable television camera. A reporter asked the two men what they'd discussed during lunch.

Khrushchev, who'd been upstaged by Garst all morning, was not about to be upstaged by Stevenson in the afternoon. "We talked about our hopes for doing away with the great arms burden that presses so hard on the world," Khrushchev answered. Then he turned to Stevenson. "Right?"

"Right," Stevenson replied.

"We decided that the people want to be friendly and it doesn't make much difference whether they are capitalists or communists," Khrushchev added. He turned to Stevenson again. "Right?"

"Right," agreed Stevenson, temporarily reduced to the role of ventriloquist's dummy.

A reporter asked Khrushchev whether Stevenson, who was often rumored to be plotting a third presidential campaign, had said anything about his political plans.

"Can I repeat that little conversation?" the premier asked Stevenson. "It won't reveal any secret? You will not be investigated by the Committee of Un-American Affairs?"

Stevenson laughed.

"*I* will not be investigated, of course," Khrushchev said, "because I am carrying a diplomatic passport."

"You are at liberty to reveal my deepest secret," Stevenson said, smiling.

"Mr. Stevenson said he was a politician in retirement," Khrushchev said. "But in politics, it often happens that a person retires today and tomorrow he may be in the first rank. It all depends on the people."

"It depends on how many times you can retire," said Stevenson, who had already retired twice.

"Honest effort is always rewarded," Khrushchev said.

"My efforts have been honest but they have not always been rewarded," Stevenson replied.

"One must never be discouraged," Khrushchev said, smiling.

"I never knew what it was to be happy until I retired," Stevenson said. "But I don't wish that upon the chairman. But if he ever retires and wants something to do, let me know. Come and live on my farm down in Illinois."

"Do you have a fish pond?"

"No, but I'll dig one for you."

"Don't hurry," Khrushchev said. "I'm not retiring for the time being. I'm not ready for fishing yet."

The two statesmen briefly discussed which fish were best for stocking ponds.

"I have been told," Khrushchev said, changing the subject, "that the Americans want to gobble up the Russians."

"We like them," Stevenson reassured the premier, "but we don't want to eat them."

Before Khrushchev left, Garst led him out to a field where the two men could stand and gaze at Garst's beloved corn, which stood tall enough to hide a full-grown man. As frequently happens when two men ponder a bountiful field of corn, the conversation turned to God.

"I must admit that you are very intelligent people in this part of the world," Khrushchev said. "But God has helped you."

"He's on our side," Garst said.

"Do you think God helps only *you?* He is helping us, too. God is on *our* side."

"God helps those who help themselves."

"We are working so hard that God is on *our* side," said Khrushchev, who couldn't bear to lose an argument, even a theological one. "God helps the intelligent."

63. A COMMUNIST DICTATOR IN HOME EC CLASS

On the way to the Des Moines airport, Khrushchev stopped off at Iowa State University, where he happened to find himself, by some bizarre trick of fate, in a home economics class with a dozen young coeds.

He sniffed the air. He smelled pancakes—*burned* pancakes. He suggested that somebody needed a cooking lesson.

That's exactly what they were getting, explained Dr. Helen R. LeBaron, dean of the college of home economics. These women, she told the premier, were learning to cook and iron and sew in preparation for marriage.

"We don't have such schools," Khrushchev said. "We learn such things from our mothers." Then he asked the dean, "Suppose a man married one of these girls. How can he check to find out her knowledge and efficiency?"

"If she's a graduate of Iowa State University, she receives a certificate," Dr. LeBaron said. "And all graduates of Iowa State have knowledge and efficiency."

"But you can't believe mere words," Khrushchev replied. "How do you know if she can iron or cook? Suppose she has a graduation certificate but she doesn't know how to prepare pancakes?"

The girls in the class laughed and applauded.

Khrushchev, who always enjoyed an appreciative audience, turned to the class. "I think when you get married," he said, "you'll settle that question better with your husband without the help of the dean."

The coeds laughed and Khrushchev offered some advice: "I wish you success, but the main thing is to find a good husband." The girls cheered and the premier walked around the room, shaking their hands.

"I don't know how you feed your people," he said, "but you're very nice girls."

Outside the classroom, male students were peeking in the windows and reaching inside, so they too could shake hands with the dictator. Soviet security guards slapped their arms away, but Khrushchev waved his guards off and reached out.

Khrushchev's guides led him to a building where agricultural students were raising hogs. The premier noticed that the hogs were standing up. "Oh," he said, "I see that the hogs know that they, too, must stand to greet the Soviet premier."

A professor delivered a brief lecture on the school's hog program and mentioned that the anatomy of a pig is quite similar to the anatomy of a human. Khrushchev listened and nodded toward Lodge. "Mr. Lodge thinks the anatomy of a pig is okay for Russians," he said, "but not for Americans."

The chairman got a kick out of teasing Lodge about his aristocratic background. Soon they were wandering through the pigpens, where Khrushchev got a whiff of the pungent aroma that Richard Nixon had told him in Moscow was far worse than horse manure. The premier sniffed the air and announced: "In all his life, Mr. Lodge never experienced such smells as today."

Lodge did not dispute the statement.

Khrushchev may have played the clown at Iowa State, but he also paid close attention to what he was seeing. He was particularly impressed with the agricultural program. The premier thought it was a good idea to locate an agricultural college in farm country instead of a big city, and he was struck by the fact that the American students actually did farm work while they studied—planting crops, raising hogs, shoveling manure. In the Soviet Union, the main agricultural college was located in Moscow and the students didn't perform the dirty work of farming, leaving those mundane tasks to a staff of manual workers. Perhaps, he thought, the Soviets should move their agricultural schools to collective farms.

"When I returned, I insistently began promoting what I had seen," Khrushchev later recalled. "But that wasn't to the liking of either the professors or the students, which is understandable. It's nice to live in Moscow."

Of course, neither the professors nor the students argued with the dictator. Nobody told him that he was wrong to want to move agricultural schools to agricultural areas. "Everyone nodded their heads and agreed," Khrushchev recalled. Yet somehow they just never got around to executing the premier's plan.

Khrushchev had discovered the secret method that common people have used to defy princes, presidents, dictators, and CEOs for innumerable centuries: "The most dangerous form of resistance," he said, "is when they yes you to death."

64. THE HOSTESS WITH THE MOSTES'

It was nearly midnight when the flight from Des Moines arrived in Pittsburgh, but Mayor Thomas J. Gallagher was waiting at the airport to present Nikita Khrushchev with the key to the city.

Khrushchev held up the big bronze key and tapped it with his forefinger. "If anybody's house is broken into tonight," he said, smiling, "I suppose I'll be blamed."

Khrushchev and his fellow travelers had left Des Moines sweaty, exhausted and eager to get back to Washington to prepare for the summit at Camp David. But Pittsburgh was fired up with Khrushchev mania and crowds packed the streets at midnight, hoping for a glimpse of the dictator. "A World Series atmosphere" gripped the city, reported the *Pittsburgh Post-Gazette*, which couldn't resist pushing the sports metaphor as far as it could go: "The Moscow Reds are coming to town. . . . Cleanup man Nikita Khrushchev, the free-swinging batsman who both speaks loudly and carries a big club, is leading his tough teammates into the city."

Mayor Gallagher had arranged an esthetic treat for the distinguished visitor. At the airport, the mayor escorted the premier to a limo and they rode up the nearby hills to the summit of Mount Washington.

"Here's the city!" the mayor said, gesturing toward downtown Pittsburgh, where every light in every skyscraper had been turned on for Khrushchev's edification, and the illuminated city sparkled against the night sky.

"Wonderful," the premier exclaimed. "Wonderful."

Normally, the night sky over Pittsburgh crackled with a different kind of illumination—red and orange lights pulsing in open-hearth steel furnaces. That was a sight that an earlier visitor, Charles Dickens, described as "hell with the lid lifted." But Khrushchev didn't see it because most of the Steel City's steel mills were shut by a strike.

Two months earlier, on July 15, more than 500,000 American steelworkers—nearly 1 percent of the country's workforce—went on strike. On September 24, when Khrushchev arrived in town, they were still striking. They'd be out until November 6, when a presidential decree forced them back to work. It was a long strike in a year characterized by long strikes, as big business and big labor grappled for power. Unlike earlier steel strikes, however, this one was not violent. There were no clashes between pickets and scabs for the simple reason that there were no scabs and few pickets. The steel companies never tried to break the strike by bringing in replacement workers. Consequently the union posted only token pickets at the mills, and many strikers spent their free time fishing or tinkering with their cars. Khrushchev never mentioned the strike, perhaps because such protests were illegal back home in the workers' paradise.

The premier wanted to see an American steel mill in full production, so his hosts booked a tour of the Mesta Machine Company plant, where 4,000 nonunion workers were still on the job. The Mesta plant happened to be the business that provided the fortune that bankrolled the partying of Perle Mesta, who was famous across America as "the hostess with the mostes'." Born Pearl Skirvin in 1890, she was the daughter of a wildcatter who made a fortune in Texas oil. She longed to become an opera singer and she possessed the requisite theatricality and girth but not the voice. Instead, in 1917, she married George Mesta, a handsome steel baron old enough to be her father. He died in 1925, leaving her wealthy, and she reinvented herself in the classic American fashion. She changed the spelling of her name to Perle, fled Pittsburgh, and purchased a mansion on "millionaires row" in Newport, the playground of American high society. She spent a fortune on fast cars and fancy clothes, but in the 1930s she also became active in politics, joining the National Women's Party and lobbying for the Equal Rights Amendment.

Politics led her to Washington, where she bought another mansion and became famous for throwing parties where politicians and powerbrokers ate and drank and sometimes burst into song. Harry Truman played piano at one of her parties. At another, Dwight Eisenhower sang "Drink to Me Only with Thine Eyes."

In 1948, she raised money for Truman's presidential campaign and he rewarded her with an appointment as ambassador to the Grand Duchy of Luxembourg, a country so small that it had never before rated an American ambassador. In 1950, her diplomatic career inspired Irving Berlin's hit Broadway musical *Call Me Madam,* with Ethel Merman playing Perle. In the opening scene, Merman is sworn in as ambassador to a fictitious country called Lichtenburg and promptly asks, "Where the hell is Lichtenburg?" Soon she's belting out the song that gave Mesta her nickname: "I'm the hostess with the mostes' on the ball."

In 1953, the movie version of *Call Me Madam* was released and Mesta returned to Washington, where she was now so famous that society page headlines required only her first name: "Perle Gives a Party" and "Perle Denies a Romance."

She met Khrushchev at Ike's state dinner, which she had attended as J. Edgar Hoover's date. She told reporters that she knew why the Russians wanted to visit the Mesta plant—to engage in industrial espionage: "We make the biggest rolling mills in the world. They're the greatest copyists in the world." Mesta didn't feel compelled to travel to Pittsburgh to escort Khrushchev through the plant. Instead, she stayed in Washington, where she threw a party for Latin American diplomats and denied rumors that she was having an affair with a former Argentine ambassador.

In the absence of "the hostess with the mostes'," Khrushchev was escorted through the plant by Mesta vice president M. K. Powell. The mill, which stretched for a mile along the Monongahela River, was hot and grimy but Khrushchev was impressed. "This is a good plant," he said.

"I'm sure that you have better ones in your country," Powell replied.

"Don't be so sure," Khrushchev said. "We have better ones. We have the same kind. We have even worse. I don't say that all you have is bad and all we have is good. We can learn from you."

As the premier strolled through the plant, a storeroom clerk named Kenneth Jackey walked up and handed him a cigar. Khrushchev didn't smoke but he was touched by the gesture.

"God bless you," he said, and he took off his wristwatch and handed it to Jackey.

Khrushchev's watch turned Jackey into an instant celebrity. He gave interviews, posed for pictures and took the watch to a jeweler to find out how much insurance he should buy. The jeweler told him not to bother: The ruler of the largest nation on earth wore a fourteen-dollar watch.

Khrushchev didn't linger long in Pittsburgh. That afternoon, he flew back to Washington to host a party at the Soviet embassy. Among those invited was Perle Mesta, whose presence was apparently required to make any Washington party official.

She arrived in a chauffeur-driven Cadillac, looking a bit like Margaret Dumont, the actress who played the battle-ax tormented by Groucho Marx in *Duck Soup*. Mesta mingled with the other guests, who included pianist Van Cliburn and Richard Nixon. Utilizing skills honed over decades of diligent partying, she managed to glide through the crowd around Khrushchev and buttonhole the dictator for a brief conversation.

Later she summoned her chauffeur and walked outside to await his arrival. As she knew, reporters were loitering there, eager to talk to departing guests. A TV crew began interviewing her about Khrushchev's tour.

"I certainly think the Americans have been *magnificent*," she said. Then her chauffeur pulled up in her Cadillac. She signaled him to wait and proceeded to regale reporters with the tale of her *tête-à-tête* with Khrushchev. Her goal, she said, was to correct his misconceptions about the power of capitalists.

"I wanted Khrushchev to know," she said, "that my husband had to borrow money to start that plant he visited in Pittsburgh today."

And what was the premier's reply?

"He smiled," she said, and then she slipped into her Cadillac and rode away.

65. *SHANE*

Ten seemingly endless days after Krushchev's arrival in America, the premier's exhausted fellow travelers straggled back into Washington, hollow-eyed survivors of a long, strange trip.

"Whatever the Soviet premier may think, the 300-odd people who went along for the ride were glad it was over," wrote Warren Rogers in the *New York Herald Tribune*. "Diplomats and security guards of both nations, reporters and photographers from all over the world—all dragged their bruised and battered bodies back from what undoubtedly was one of the great stories in modern journalism."

But the trip was merely pausing for a night. The next day, Friday, September 25, Khrushchev and Eisenhower would travel to Camp David for what was, at least theoretically, the main purpose of the premier's visit—a weekend of talks between the two most powerful men in the world.

Henry Cabot Lodge awoke Friday morning and hustled to the White House to brief the president on his travels. The trip was rough at first, he told Ike, but after Khrushchev stepped off the train in Santa Barbara and shook hands with friendly Americans, everything went smoothly. After his brief travelogue, Lodge pulled out written notes and addressed the question on everybody's mind: What makes Khrushchev tick?

Khrushchev is a remarkable, although very difficult man, Lodge reported. He really believes in the religion of Communism, but otherwise he keeps an open mind and he's willing to listen. He repeatedly claimed that nothing he saw on the trip surprised him, but that was mere bluster. Actually, he was much impressed by our factories, our roads, our cars, our people. He probably does not now really think that the Soviets are likely to surpass us—at least anytime soon, Lodge concluded.

When he finished his report, Lodge discussed strategy for the summit with Eisenhower, Secretary Herter and Tommy Thompson, the ambassador to Moscow.

Ike had one simple goal for the meetings: convince Khrushchev to repudiate his ultimatum over Berlin. The premier had issued the ultimatum on November 27, 1958, announcing that capitalist West Berlin was a "malignant tumor" located inside Communist East Germany, and threatening to "do some surgery." He demanded that the Americans, British and French, who had occupied West Berlin since V-E day, withdraw their

troops and turn the city into a demilitarized zone by May 27, 1959. It was
the Soviets' most serious challenge to Western Europe since Stalin block-
aded Berlin in 1948.

Ike had learned of the ultimatum in a little office above the pro shop at
the Augusta National Golf Course, where he was vacationing. Publicly he
vowed to defend Berlin and dispatched more troops to Europe. Privately
he wondered, What does Khrushchev think he's doing?

Khrushchev actually had no intention of going to war over Berlin, or
so he told his son Sergei. He simply figured a deadline would force the
West to negotiate a compromise.

"What if a compromise isn't reached?" Sergei asked.

"Then we'll look for another solution," Khrushchev answered.

And what will happen after May 27?

"May 28," Khrushchev said, laughing.

On May 27, Khrushchev's deadline passed and nothing happened. But
he never repudiated his ultimatum and he periodically riled the West with
blasts of threatening rhetoric about Berlin: "What good does it do you to
have 11,000 troops in Berlin? If it came to war, we would swallow them in
one gulp."

Ike hoped the Camp David summit would produce some kind of
agreement. But what was the best way to get it? Eisenhower asked his
aides if he should raise the issue of Berlin with Khrushchev when they
were alone. Herter thought that was a good idea. Lodge suggested that
Gromyko was a reasonable man who might be a good influence on
Khrushchev. On the other hand, Thompson said, Menshikov was a terrible influence, constantly whispering anti-American comments into
Khrushchev's ear. Lodge agreed. So did Ike, who called the Soviet ambassador "evil and stupid."

Somehow, the president told his aides, Khrushchev needed to let the
world know that he was no longer threatening war over Berlin. It was a
simple and rational request, Ike thought, and if he could quickly convince
the premier to do it, he might take him to the Naval Academy's brand-new

football stadium in Annapolis on Saturday afternoon to see Navy play William and Mary.

Khrushchev arrived at five o'clock, and Ike walked him out to the White House lawn, where two helicopters awaited. Lodge, Gromyko, Herter, Thompson, and the "evil" Menshikov climbed into one. Ike, Khrushchev, and their interpreters and bodyguards boarded the other. The choppers rose slowly into the sky and headed north, toward the Catoctin Mountains. A half-hour later, they landed at Camp David. Ike and Khrushchev stepped out of the chopper and into a Cadillac that dropped them off in front of the camp's largest building, a rough lumber house called Aspen Lodge, where a press pool of seventy-two reporters and photographers awaited.

"It's lucky Mr. Garst isn't here," Khrushchev said.

Everybody laughed and the two leaders spent a couple minutes posing for pictures. Then the journalists were herded off to a makeshift press center in a nearby high school gym.

When the reporters left, Eisenhower escorted his guests into Aspen Lodge and led them to a row of bedrooms—one for Khrushchev, one for Gromyko, one for Herter, and one for Ike. The malevolent Menshikov was relegated to an outbuilding, where he bunked with Lodge and Thompson.

Khrushchev poked around the place and liked what he saw. "On the outside, it looked just like a barracks," he recalled in his memoir, "but on the inside it was luxuriously decorated, yet at the same time very businesslike—typically American. Everything was sturdily built, clean and comfortable."

When the premier had settled in, Ike asked him if he'd like to watch some movies.

"Of course—if they're good ones," the premier replied.

"What kind do you prefer?" Eisenhower asked, flashing his celebrated smile. "Personally, I like Westerns. I know they don't have any substance to them and don't require any thought to appreciate, but they always have a lot of fancy stunts. Also, I like the horses."

"You know," Khrushchev said, "when Stalin was alive, we used to watch Westerns all the time. When the movie ended, Stalin always denounced it for its ideological content. But the very next day, we'd be back in the movie theatre watching another Western. I too have a weakness for this sort of film."

"Good," Ike said. "We'll have some Westerns and other movies."

Eisenhower and his guests sat down to dinner—roast beef and red snapper—and then aides set up a portable screen in the living room. First, Ike showed a 16-millimeter film of the North Pole, shot by the American nuclear submarine *Nautilus*—a not so subtle demonstration of American naval power. Then came the Western—*Shane.*

It was an interesting choice for the evening's entertainment. Released in 1953 and starring Alan Ladd, Jean Arthur, and Van Heflin, *Shane* had a plot that could easily be construed as an allegory of the Berlin crisis:

> *In a beautiful Wyoming valley, a nasty cattle baron named Ryker rides up to a peaceful family of homesteaders and announces that they have to leave their land because he needs to run his cattle on it. Ryker gives them an ultimatum: "You're gonna have to get out before the snow flies."*
>
> *"And supposin' I don't?" says homesteader Joe Starrett.*
>
> *"I could blast you right out of here now," says Ryker.*
>
> *"Now, you listen to me," says Starrett, "the time for gun-blastin' a man off of his own place is past."*
>
> *Ryker rides off, spitting out an ominous reminder: "Well, Starrett, you can't say I didn't warn ya." His henchmen begin to harass the local homesteaders, killing their hogs, trampling their crops. In one confrontation, Ryker proclaims that he has a right to the valley because he fought the Indians for it.*
>
> *"You talk about rights," Starrett replies. "You think you have the right to say that nobody else has any."*
>
> *Starrett and his mysterious farmhand—a reformed gunslinger named Shane—try to settle the dispute peacefully but Ryker forces a fight. When*

it comes, Shane kills Ryker, then rides off into the mountains, wounded,
while Starrett's little boy calls after him. "Shane! Shane! Come back!"

A cruel ultimatum leads to a bloody showdown—the allegory seems too perfect to be a coincidence. But if Ike or his aides chose *Shane* in order to send a message, they never mentioned that fact in their memoirs. And if Khrushchev got the message, he never mentioned it, either.

When Stalin showed Westerns to Khrushchev and the rest of his cronies in the Kremlin, he would frequently follow the screening with a drunken, late-night dinner at his dacha. The paranoid Stalin waited for his underlings to eat first, just to make sure the food wasn't poisoned. Sometimes he'd amuse himself by ordering Khrushchev to dance the *gopak* and chuckling while his portly deputy dutifully squatted on his haunches and kicked his feet.

At Eisenhower's dacha, the postmovie experience was less frightening. When *Shane* ended, the two tired leaders knocked back a quick nightcap and trudged off to bed.

66. IMPASSE

The next morning, a thick fog shrouded Camp David. Khrushchev rose early to take a walk in the woods with Gromyko, so they could discuss strategy without being overheard by the eavesdropping devices they assumed were hidden in their rooms.

When they returned to Aspen Lodge, Khrushchev spotted Herter and Lodge eating breakfast. "You two fellows are trying to eat up all the food before I get here," he joked. Then he sat down and tucked into a breakfast of four eggs, eight sausages, and six strips of bacon. When Lodge kidded him about the gargantuan meal, Khrushchev responded with the rationale uttered by countless hungry travelers through the ages. "I'm not usually allowed to eat this much," he said. "When I'm away from home, I give myself a good time."

Soon Eisenhower arrived at the table and the premier began regaling the president with war stories. Khrushchev had been a political commissar during World War II and now, sitting at the breakfast table with his bulbous bald head poking out of an embroidered white shirt, he recounted horrific tales of waging war under Stalin.

During the battle for Kharkov in 1943, Stalin, who was safe in Moscow, ordered his army to attack the German invaders. But both Khrushchev and the commanding general, who were on the scene, believed that an attack would destroy their 300,000-man army. Khrushchev called Stalin in the Kremlin to ask him to alter his orders. Marshall Zhukov, who was Stalin's top general, took the call and said that Stalin demanded an attack. Khrushchev begged to speak to Stalin so he could explain the situation, but the tyrant refused to get on the phone. So the order stood, and the Red Army attacked. The Soviets lost 300,000 soldiers—a figure that was, as Eisenhower knew, only about 105,000 less than the *total* number of American deaths during the war.

But there was more to the story, Khrushchev told Eisenhower. Five years later, Stalin and his underlings were sitting around drinking, and Khrushchev's friend Mikoyan, who was half drunk, started teasing Stalin about his blunder at Kharkov, reminding him that Khrushchev had been right. Mikoyan was too tipsy to notice that Stalin was getting angry, so Khrushchev tried to calm the situation. "Don't worry, Comrade Stalin," he said, "we would have lost those 300,000 men whether we defended or attacked." Given Stalin's propensity for executing his underlings, Khrushchev's soothing words might have saved Mikoyan's life—and maybe his own.

Ike enjoyed the war stories but he wondered why the premier was telling them. "I was not sure," he later recalled, "whether Khrushchev was trying to make me understand Stalin's weaknesses or, possibly, his own skill in handling his master."

After breakfast, the two leaders and their aides and interpreters moved to the terrace of the lodge to begin the official talks. Eisenhower started by announcing that Berlin was his primary concern. "If we could ease tensions with respect to this problem," he said, "we could make progress on other questions." Khrushchev's ultimatum had alarmed Americans, Ike continued. The United States didn't want to occupy Germany forever, but it would never consent to being evicted from Berlin by force.

Khrushchev replied that the war was long over but the Soviet Union still did not have a peace treaty with Germany. It was time to settle the question of Germany's future.

Ike said he didn't mind if the Soviets signed a peace treaty with East Germany as long as it did not affect West Berlin.

Khrushchev said that was an impossible condition. But, he added, Berlin was only one problem. The real issue was disarmament. If the West agreed to his U.N. proposal on complete disarmament, the Berlin problem would be solved automatically.

If we can't reach agreement on Berlin, Ike replied, we can't even discuss disarmament.

For nearly two hours, they went back and forth, getting nowhere. Finally they took a break and Ike led Khrushchev and their interpreters on a stroll through the woods. They ended up in Camp David's bowling alley, where the world's most powerful men watched Navy yeoman John Halferty roll five strikes and a spare, racking up a score of 218. Khrushchev, who'd never seen bowling, watched curiously, although he seemed less interested in the game than he was in the magic of the automatic pin-setting machine.

The two leaders autographed Halferty's scorecard then walked back to the Aspen terrace, where they sat at a card table with only their interpreters, discussing Berlin while everyone else began eating lunch. Again, they failed to reach an agreement. Khrushchev didn't know it, but his bullheaded intransigence had ruined the only chance he would ever get to watch a Navy–William and Mary football game.

Seeing no progress, Ike led Khrushchev to the lunch table, pausing on the way to whisper something to Andrew Goodpaster, his staff secretary. Goodpaster listened, then scrawled one word in his notebook: "Impasse."

Looking glum, the two leaders sat down to a lunch of hot dogs and beans. When Khrushchev saw Nixon at the table, he started needling him, grumbling in a nasty voice about the American exhibit in Moscow and the idiotic "miracle kitchen" that Nixon foolishly thought would lure the Soviets down the capitalist road.

Eisenhower tried to ease the tension by changing the subject. He liked to take vacations, he said, but he could never seem to escape the constant ringing of the telephone. Khrushchev responded as if Ike had insulted the Soviet Union.

"We haven't got as many telephones as you do *now*," he said angrily, "but we're going to have *more*."

Ike excused himself, announcing that he was going to take a nap, and the lunch broke up.

"Everybody was very much depressed," White House aide George Kistiakowsky wrote in his diary. "There was a general feeling that the meeting will end in a complete failure."

67. SCRUBBING SPOTS AND CHASING BUTTERFLIES

While the premier and the president wrestled with the fate of mankind, Nina Khrushchev watched a stain-removal expert demonstrating the proper way to scrub a spot off a wedding gown.

Wives were not invited to the summit at Camp David, so Mrs. Khrushchev had to settle for something slightly less interesting—a tour of the National Institute of Dry Cleaning. The idea for the tour came from the nimble mind of John Jay Daly, a young public relations man at the institute, which was a trade group for the dry cleaning industry. Daly's job was to publicize dry cleaning and he performed this plebian task with Promethean zeal, promoting a program in which America's dry cleaners agreed to launder any American flag for free—a promotion with the delightfully patriotic name "New Glory for Old Glory."

When Daly heard that Premier Khrushchev was coming to America, his brain went into overdrive, struggling to find a way to link the historic trip to the dry cleaning business. He did some research and learned that there was no dry cleaning in the Soviet Union—a tragic situation that compelled American diplomats in Moscow to stuff their dirty clothes into diplomatic pouches and ship them to Western Europe for cleaning. Daly decided to promote his industry by announcing that Khrushchev and his family would get free dry cleaning all across America.

That got some publicity, but Daly wanted more. When he learned that Khrushchev was going to Camp David, he was struck with a flash of inspiration: He figured that Mrs. Khrushchev would be stuck at Blair House with nothing to do, so he invited her to take a tour of the National Institute of Dry Cleaning. Then he started working the phones, making dozens of calls—to the State Department, to the Secret Service, to Mrs. Henry Cabot Lodge. Much to his amazement, Mrs. Khrushchev actually accepted his ludicrous invitation.

"I remember the Secret Service saying, 'Okay, she'll come but don't tell anybody about it,'" Daly recalled decades later. "We said, 'OK, sure.' But somehow the Associated Press and *The New York Times* heard about it." He burst out laughing. "I don't know how that happened, but it did."

Mrs. Khrushchev arrived at the institute on Saturday morning, accompanied by Mrs. Lodge and trailed by a mob of reporters and photographers.

"Our executive director, George Fulton, who has since gone on to the dry cleaning plant in the sky, greeted her limousine," Daly recalled, "and then walked her through the plant."

She observed the lab where experts analyzed dry cleaning errors. She saw the institute's menagerie of moths, which were used to test experimental moth-proofing techniques. And she watched spot removal expert George Purdy working his magic on a soiled wedding gown. Before she left, Fulton presented her with an autographed copy of *Focus on Fabrics,* a foot-thick book of fabric swatches and instructions on how to clean them.

The *Today* show aired film of Mrs. Khrushchev touring the plant and the *New York Times* ran the story on page one, along with a photo of the Soviet First Lady smiling enigmatically at the sight of the newly spotless wedding dress.

"We were ecstatic," Daly recalls.

Not everybody was quite so happy. When Daly and his colleagues arrived at work Monday morning, they found that somebody—presumably somebody opposed to Mrs. Khrushchev's visit—had broken all the institute's windows with rocks plucked off the B&O railroad tracks behind the building. But that, Daly figured, was a small price to pay for the kind of publicity that money can't buy.

Uninterested in the glories of dry cleaning, Sergei Khrushchev had arranged for a different kind of adventure that weekend.

"I have my butterfly net," he told his contacts at the State Department. "Maybe it is possible to go somewhere to catch butterflies."

They told him they'd try to arrange something, but they didn't want a mob of reporters chasing Sergei while Sergei chased butterflies. "For some reason, they did not want to expose me and my butterfly net to these journalists who were following us everywhere," Sergei said forty-seven years later, laughing at the memory. "One of them called and said, 'Let's go. Take the net but don't take it openly.' So I put the net into a bag and we went to the White House. There was a small door and we opened this door and there was an escape tunnel, and then we appeared in some underground place and there was a hidden door and a car, and they brought me to somewhere on the outskirts of Washington."

The car stopped at a meadow. Sergei climbed out and looked around, accompanied by three or four State Department security guards. He could see the last butterflies of summer fluttering around the field. He

was eager to catch them but he felt a bit self-conscious about chasing butterflies in front of the security guards.

"I asked them how they were feeling about this and they said, 'We
don't care. We see so many different people with different requirements
and you are not the worst.'"

Reassured, Sergei handed his movie camera to one of the security
guards, who filmed a sequence that looks like a scene from a dream—or
maybe a Buster Keaton movie: A handsome young man wearing a suit
and tie and horn-rimmed glasses scurries through a scruffy field of scrag-
gly weeds, holding a net over his head, chasing the bright elusive butterflies of America.

68. THE FIRST TO BE SHOT

After Eisenhower awoke from his nap, he invited Khrushchev to visit his
farm in nearby Gettysburg, Pennsylvania.

"I'd be delighted," the premier said.

Before the two leaders boarded a helicopter for the brief flight to Ike's
farm, Eisenhower called his son John, who lived in a house adjacent to the
farm. John's wife Barbara answered the phone and the president told her
that he and Khrushchev were dropping by for a visit. "Have the kids
cleaned up and ready," he said. Barbara rounded up her children—David,
11, Barbara Ann, 10, Susan, 8, and Mary Jean, 3—and quickly scrubbed
them into reasonably presentable shape.

"We got about a half-hour's notice before the helicopter landed," Susan
Eisenhower recalled decades later. "They were at Camp David and they'd
reached an impasse, so my grandfather decided to give Khrushchev the
family treatment. My grandfather had the experience of living in Europe—as well as Asia and Latin America—before he was president, and he
knew foreign cultures well. He knew that there is something very special

about being taken home to meet the family. It frames everything in a completely different way. I think that's what this was about."

The chopper landed, the two leaders emerged, and Eisenhower escorted his guest around the farm. When Khrushchev expressed admiration for the president's Black Angus cattle, Ike smiled and offered to give him one as a gift. Khrushchev thanked him and promised to send some Russian birch trees to plant on the farm "as an expression of gratitude."

Ike led his guest into the farmhouse. It was a comfortable but hardly luxurious home, far less opulent than Khrushchev's regal dachas, and the premier was impressed with his host's unpretentiousness. "Eisenhower," he concluded, "was a reasonable and modest man." Ike whisked the chairman past the formal dining room and out to the sun porch, a homey room with a lovely view of the countryside where Union troops fought Confederates in a monumental battle ninety-six years earlier. While the two men sipped tea, John and Barbara Eisenhower arrived with Ike's grandchildren. Khrushchev's face lit up. He greeted the kids one by one, asked them their names and informed them what they'd be called in Russian. (Except for Susan: He couldn't think of a Russian word for Susan.) Then he reached into his pocket and pulled out a handful of red star badges and pinned one to each kid's lapel.

"He sort of struck me like Santa Claus without the red suit," Susan recalled. "He was very round and there was that unforgettable smile—he had a gap in his teeth as I recall. I was very intrigued by him."

Khrushchev turned to the president. "When you come to Moscow," he said, "you must bring your grandchildren with you."

Ike's "family treatment" had worked its magic. When the two leaders climbed back into the helicopter, Khrushchev was far friendlier than he'd been at lunch a few hours earlier.

Back on the sun porch, Ike's grandchildren immediately began asking if they could go to Russia. "We were very excited about the idea," Susan remembers, "and we were lobbying our parents like mad." Their parents were less eager. They wanted the kids to know that the man they'd just met might not be as jolly as he seemed. There was, Susan recalled, a brief tutorial on the cold war and the evils of Communism. This man, her parents said, is not a friend of the United States.

"I remember thinking, 'If he's not a friend of the United States, then why did he come to our house?'" Susan recalls. "Of course, all during this time, we were having duck-and-cover drills at school. So all this was hanging over our heads, which I never quite associated with Khrushchev until this conversation."

As soon as the president's helicopter lifted off, carrying the two leaders back to Camp David, Barbara Eisenhower confiscated the red star badges Khrushchev had pinned on her children and threw them away. But she must have missed one: A couple days later, John Eisenhower caught his son David wearing a red star to school.

"If Khrushchev could take us over," he told the boy, "guess what family would be the first to be shot?"

69. MORE EISENHOWERS THAN YOU KNOW WHAT TO DO WITH

In Wheaton, Illinois, that day, celebrated evangelist Billy Graham called a press conference to offer advice for the president of the United States in his dealings with Khrushchev. "I certainly hope that President Eisenhower will invite him to church tomorrow," Graham said. "Khrushchev is his house guest and if he should refuse to go, it would put Khrushchev on the spot."

The next morning, a Sunday, Eisenhower invited Khrushchev to accompany him to the Gettysburg Presbyterian Church but the premier declined, explaining that his appearance in church would be too much of a shock to his people.

So, while Ike attended the 8:30 service, Khrushchev remained at Camp David, discussing trade issues with undersecretary of state Douglas Dillon. The discussion didn't go well. When Dillon suggested that perhaps the Soviets would like to buy American shoes, Khrushchev exploded.

"Shoes?" he bellowed. "Look at my shoes! We make the best shoes in the world! We don't need any shoes!"

A year later, in what would become his most famous act, Khrushchev would demonstrate to the United Nations that Soviet shoes could, in a pinch, be used as a gavel to drown out unwanted anti-Communist rhetoric.

When Eisenhower returned from church, he invited Khrushchev to take a walk in the woods—just the two of them and an interpreter. Ike had noticed that the premier was more friendly and accommodating when Gromyko and Menshikov weren't around, and he figured the best way to reach an agreement over Berlin was to do it in private.

On their walk, the two leaders compared notes on how their generals lobbied for more money. As Khrushchev recounted in his memoir, their conversation went like this:

Eisenhower: "My military leaders come to me and say, 'Mr. President, we need such and such a sum for such and such a program. If we don't get the funds we need, we'll fall behind the Soviet Union.' So I invariably give in. That's how they wring money out of me. They keep grabbing for more, and I keep giving it to them. Now, tell me, how is it with you?"

Khrushchev: "It's just the same. Some people from our military departments come and say, 'Comrade Khrushchev, look at this! The Americans are developing such and such a system. We could develop the same system but it would cost such and such.' I tell them there's no money; it's all been allocated already. So they say, 'If we don't get the money we need, and if there's a war, then the enemy will have superiority over us.' . . . I mull over their request and finally come to the conclusion that the military should be supported with whatever funds they say they need."

Eisenhower: "That's what I thought. You know, we really should come to some sort of agreement to stop this fruitless, wasteful rivalry."

The two leaders did not manage to craft an agreement on that issue, but as they strolled through the woods of Camp David, they did reach an accord on Berlin: Khrushchev agreed to end his ultimatum. In return, Eisenhower pledged to convene a Big Four summit where Khrushchev and Ike would discuss the future of Germany with French President Charles De Gaulle and British Prime Minister Harold Macmillan. Eisenhower also agreed to visit the Soviet Union in the spring of 1960.

While their aides drew up the joint communiqué that would inform the world of their agreement, Ike and Khrushchev sat down to lunch with their senior advisers. On Saturday, Khrushchev had been surly and obnoxious at lunch; on Sunday, he was charming. As he passed around a box of chocolates that pianist Van Cliburn had given him, he praised American candy. When Menshikov muttered in Russian that Soviet chocolate was better, Khrushchev turned to his interpreter and said, "Don't translate that remark!"

After lunch, as the leaders examined the draft of the communiqué, Khrushchev suddenly demanded that his promise to end his Berlin ultimatum be removed from the statement.

Eisenhower was shocked. "This ends the whole affair," he snapped. "And I will go neither to a summit nor to Russia."

Quickly Khrushchev explained his action, telling Ike that he could not announce his concession until he had time to explain it to his Kremlin colleagues. If Ike would wait until Tuesday to reveal that part of the agreement, Khrushchev would immediately confirm it in Moscow.

Eisenhower agreed. He'd already waited ten months for the premier to end his ultimatum; he could wait two more days. And he'd learned a valuable lesson about Khrushchev. Unlike Stalin, he wasn't confident enough in his power that he could afford to ignore or bully his Kremlin cronies.

It was midafternoon, and Khrushchev had to hustle back to Washington for a final TV appearance before he flew home to Moscow that night. So the president and the premier slipped into Ike's limousine and raced toward the capital at 90 miles per hour, escorted by police cars with screaming sirens.

In Washington, Eisenhower dropped Khrushchev off at Blair House, just as he'd done when the chairman arrived thirteen days earlier. As the two leaders shook hands on the steps, Khrushchev reminded the president to bring his grandchildren with him when he came to Russia in the spring.

"I'll bring the whole family," Ike said. "You'll have more Eisenhowers there than you know what to do with."

70. CHIHUAHUAS FOR KHRUSHCHEV

In his dressing room at the NBC studios in Washington, Khrushchev shooed the makeup artist away.

Makeup? Was this some kind of capitalist trick? Were the Americans trying to make him look like a fool? They told him that everybody wore makeup on TV, that without it his face would look red and light would flash off his bald head whenever he moved. But the premier didn't care. He was not going to let anybody swab him with makeup.

"Good evening, American friends," he said when the show began, speaking live to those Americans who had chosen to watch a Communist dictator deliver a speech in Russian when they could have been enjoying *Gunsmoke* or *Have Gun, Will Travel.* "I am glad for the opportunity to talk to you before leaving for my country. We liked your beautiful cities and fine roads but most of all your amiable, kind-hearted people."

Reading a few paragraphs, then pausing for the translation before reading some more, he praised President Eisenhower, denounced the cold war, plugged his plan for total disarmament, and bragged that Soviet Communism had ended unemployment and provided free education and health care for everyone.

"It will not be long before we abolish—I repeat, *abolish*—all taxation of the population," he said, uttering the most popular promise a politician can make.

He ended with a few words in English: "Goot-bye and goot lock, friends!"

Watching the speech on a color TV at the Blair House, Sergei Khrushchev concluded that his father had done well. "The only problem," he thought, "was that his face appeared unusually red and his bald head gleamed with every movement."

After the show, Khrushchev returned to Blair House, where the steps were piled with Soviet suitcases, plus lots of American shopping bags bearing the names of such prominent capitalist enterprises as "Woodward & Lothrop" and "Saks Fifth Avenue."

There was also a box that emitted strange, high-pitched yelps. It contained two Chihuahua puppies—a gift for Khrushchev's grandchildren from California businessman Alexander Lieb. Suspicious of any American who would give puppies to a Communist, the FBI investigated Lieb, compiling a twelve-page dossier that included his photo, his unlisted phone number, his bank balance, his college major (accounting), his company's finances, and the rumor that during his seven-year career as a Los Angeles cop in the 1940s, Lieb was a "chronic complainer" and "critical of superior officers." Of course, the FBI also checked with its informants inside the Communist Party, who reported that they'd never heard of Lieb.

The dossier contained no information, however, on the political views of the Chihuahuas.

The Soviets' luggage filled three Army trucks, which hauled it out to Andrews Air Force Base, where the premier's gigantic TU–114 plane had spent six hours refueling. When Khrushchev arrived, Nixon presided over a farewell ceremony that echoed the arrival ceremony thirteen days earlier—a long red carpet, a twenty-one-gun salute, an exchange of friendly speeches.

"From the bottom of my heart, I thank you for your kind hospitality, for your bread and salt," Khrushchev said. "I would like to wish that we more and more frequently use, in the relations between our countries, the short and good American word—*Okay.*"

Carrying a huge bouquet of red roses, he climbed into the world's tallest plane, which sat at one end of Andrews's 7,200-foot runway. The door closed and the TU–114 inched forward, burdened by the enormous weight of its fuel, luggage, countless American consumer goods and, of course, the two Chihuahuas.

The plane lumbered down the runway, slowly picking up speed. It had almost run out of pavement by the time it finally managed to lift off, rising like an overstuffed goose. As spectators on the ground gasped, it just barely cleared the treetops and headed toward Moscow, 5,000 miles away.

71. STORMY APPLAUSE

Ten thousand Russians cheered when Khrushchev emerged from the plane at an airport near Moscow. Thousands more cheered as his motorcade passed through the city on its way to Lenin Stadium, where a crowd of 17,000 applauded when the premier stepped across a stage decorated with a bright red banner bearing the catchy slogan, "Long Live the Peaceful Policy of the Communist Party and the Soviet Government."

The sight of the premier home from his travels caused a sustained outbreak of what *Pravda* liked to call "stormy applause." Nikita Sergeyevich Khrushchev took a seat and listened as speaker after speaker rose to extol his greatness.

First, the mayor of Moscow: "Allow me, Nikita Sergeyevich, to express on behalf of all present at this meeting and on behalf of all the working people of Moscow, our warm gratitude for your tireless activity in the name of peace and the happiness of the Soviet people."

That bit of rhetoric inspired what the official transcript described simply as "*(Applause)*."

Then a machinist spoke on behalf of Soviet workers: "Nikita Sergeyevich is crushing the ice of the Cold War with the strength of an atomic icebreaker and striking the enemies of peace with the accuracy of the Soviet moon rocket!"

That sparked an outbreak of (*prolonged applause*).

Then came a worker from a collective farm, speaking for the peasants: "We most heartily wish you, an outstanding champion of peace and friendship among nations, many years of life."

(*Prolonged applause.*)

Then a college student, speaking for Soviet youth: "We assure you, Nikita Sergeyevich, our Party, and all Soviet people, that we shall always and everywhere act as most loyal and tireless fighters for the great cause of communism!"

More (*Prolonged applause.*)

Finally it was time for Nikita Sergeyevich to speak. As he stepped forward, the crowd stood and greeted him with (*stormy, prolonged applause*). "Dear comrades," he said, "we have just stepped off the plane which made a nonstop flight from Washington to Moscow!" (*Applause.*) "We have come straight to this meeting, dear Muscovites, in order to share our impressions with you."

He promised to be brief, but dictators are notoriously poor judges of time, particularly when addressing crowds that keep bursting into (*prolonged applause*). He told the story of his great odyssey at great length, beginning with his arrival in Washington: "We were accorded a reception worthy of our great country, our great people." (*Prolonged stormy applause.*) He reported that he'd addressed the United Nations in support of "complete disarmament." (*Stormy applause.*) He related how the mayor of Los Angeles tried to "use the Communist bogey to frighten people" and how Khrushchev had stood up for "the cause of peace." (*Prolonged applause.*)

He described the friendliness of Harry Bridges and his longshoremen. (*Stormy applause.*) He hymned the joys of Iowa: "We drove out to the corn fields so dear to my heart." (*Animation, applause.*) He reported that President Eisenhower "sincerely wishes to see the end of the cold war." (*Stormy applause.*) But he warned that some "evil forces" in America were working against peace. "They must be dragged into the open, exposed and publicly flogged," he said. "They must be roasted like devils in a frying pan." (*Laughter, prolonged applause.*)

He described his trip to Eisenhower's farm: "I couldn't very well visit the president without having a look at his corn, could I?" (*Animation.*) He reported that he'd met Ike's grandchildren and invited them to Russia. (*Laughter, applause.*) Finally Khrushchev approached his grand finale, building to a crescendo that drove the crowd wild: "Long live the great Soviet people who are successfully building Communism under the leadership of the glorious Party of Lenin! (*Prolonged applause.*)

"Long live Soviet–American friendship!" (*Prolonged applause.*)

"Long live the friendship among all the peoples of the world!" (*Stormy, prolonged applause. All rise.*)

The crowd stood cheering while Khrushchev smiled. America had its charms, of course, but it was nice to be back in Moscow, where all the crowds are friendly, all the speakers are flattering, and all the applause is stormy and prolonged.

72. A SOAP BUBBLE OF HOPE

"With Khrushchev gone," wrote columnist Fletcher Knebel, "life will be as empty as a silo without corn, TV without wrestling or the trumpet without Armstrong."

In a single sentence, Knebel captured the postpartum depression suffered by the reporters who'd tailed Khrushchev across America, covering the biggest story of the decade. But now it was time for mere reporters to step aside and let America's vast army of columnists, commentators, editorial writers, and pundits explain What It All Meant.

"The U.S. saw Nikita Khrushchev and Nikita Khrushchev saw the U.S.," *Time* magazine began. "The meeting turned out to be one of the grand confrontations of the cold war and of all time."

Actually, this "grand confrontation" didn't produce much in the way of tangible results. Khrushchev had lifted his Berlin ultimatum and Eisenhower had agreed to convene a Big Four summit, then travel to Russia. That, most analysts agreed, constituted only a modest diplomatic success.

"Was the Khrushchev visit worthwhile?" asked a *Washington Post* editorial. "Despite the absence of tangible moves to crack the icecap of the Cold War, the answer must be yes."

The Los Angeles Times agreed, and said so in an editorial that began with a delightfully mixed metaphor: "Mr. Khrushchev left behind him a soap bubble of hope and our government is trying to preserve the fragile fabric in a steamy gas of optimism."

The statesmen's failure to resolve other vexing issues—particularly the arms race—must have pleased the kind of capitalists Khrushchev had accused of profiting off the cold war. "Wall Street is breathing a bit more easily," reported the *Christian Science Monitor*, because "there are no signs that the administration will reduce its current defense outlays of $41,000,000,000 a year."

But commentators who evaluated Khrushchev's visit solely on the basis of official diplomatic agreements were missing much of the point. The trip was more than a summit conference; it was a two-week nonstop cultural exchange, a chance for the world's two superpowers to peek behind their comfortable myths and observe each other up close. After seeing the country for himself, Khrushchev could no longer view America as a nation riven by Marx's inevitable class conflicts and ripe for revolution. And after watching Khrushchev, a man bursting with familiar human quirks and foibles, Americans could no longer see the Soviet Union as a nation of brainwashed automatons led by a faceless, malevolent Big Brother. The trip was, if nothing else, a victory for nuance.

"We know now that he is no buffoon reeling drunkenly through the Kremlin but a shrewd, tough and able adversary," *Newsweek* concluded.

Pundits agreed that Khrushchev was wowed by America's bounty but disagreed on exactly what wowed him most. Columnist Bob Considine thought the premier was amazed at America's rich Corn Belt and "the sheer girth and quiet confidence of the farm folk." Stevenson thought Khrushchev marveled at the sight of "working people riding in their automobiles along great, gleaming highways." Only Murray Kempton, writing with tongue at least partly in cheek, suggested that the premier might be impressed by something less lofty: "The gaudiest image he has seen is of our fools, our vast national surplus of the comic and the excessive. We tend to think of our country as having become gray and characterless, but Nikita Khrushchev comes here and who does he meet in quick succession but Spyros Skouras, a drunken CIO vice president, Bob Garst, and the American photographer, all abounding with idiot delight."

One aspect of Khrushchev's trip was obvious only in retrospect: It had been the television debut of the now-familiar phenomenon of the nonstop, round-the-clock, multiday media circus—a story reported, recorded, and inevitably distorted by an anarchic mob of reporters, photographers, and TV cameramen, who end up dominating the event they are ostensibly covering.

Of course, Khrushchev had been an eager participant in that circus. He'd designed his trip for maximum media exposure. (Why else would he go to Hollywood?) Two years later, in his famous book *The Image*, historian Daniel J. Boorstin coined a word to describe this phenomenon— "pseudo-event"—an event that existed "for the immediate purpose of being reported." Boorstin predicted that America would witness more and more pseudo-events. Needless to say, he was right.

The day after Khrushchev departed, the House Committee on Un-American Activities announced that it had determined that the Russian dictator was definitely un-American. The committee released a transcript of the testimony of Eugene Lyons, an ex-Communist now working as a *Reader's Digest* editor. "The new Soviet boss, despite his homespun exterior, is one of the bloodiest tyrants extant," Lyons said. "Those of us who roll out red carpets for him will soon have red faces."

"Sir, what did you think of Mr. Khrushchev?" a reporter asked President Eisenhower at his press conference the day after the premier left.

"Well, he is a dynamic and arresting personality," Ike replied. "He is a man that uses every possible debating method available to him. He is capable of great flights, you might say, of mannerism and disposition from one of almost negative, difficult attitude to the most easy, affable, genial type of discussion."

That was Ike's public view of the premier. The next day, he expressed his private views in a letter to British Prime Minister Harold Macmillan: "The most I can say at this moment is that the meeting with Mr. Khrushchev did not end up on the truly sour note that it well could have. I believe he is sincere in his desire for helping to arrange a program of disarmament. He talked to me at great length about costs in armaments and the sacrifices that their manufacture demands of citizens everywhere. Moreover, I believe he is genuine in his anxiety that there should be no general war."

In Moscow, Khrushchev was far more exuberant in his praise of Eisenhower. The premier publicly extolled Ike's "wise statesmanship" and his "courage and determination," and he expressed confidence that "the president is prepared to exert his efforts and his will to bring about agreement between our two countries."

Khrushchev's rhetoric was part of a propaganda campaign to polish his image as a peacemaker and pump up enthusiasm for Eisenhower's upcoming visit. But he also backed his words with actions, scrapping plans for new warships and reducing Soviet armed forces by 1.2 million men—decisions that were highly unpopular in the Soviet equivalent of the military-industrial complex.

That fall, Khrushchev sent Eisenhower a gift—a collection of Christmas tree ornaments. "Some of them were astonishingly beautiful—little hand-painted figurines of women with these beautiful angelic faces," Susan Eisenhower later recalled. "But there were a number of bulbs—I seem to remember that they were blue—that featured a Soviet missile going to the moon with an American rocket behind it."

The president displayed many of the ornaments on the family Christmas tree, his granddaughter recalled with a laugh, but somehow the moon rockets "got eradicated from the collection."

Meanwhile, Khrushchev was secretly preparing another gift for Eisenhower: He ordered the construction of the Soviet Union's first golf course, so his American friend could play his favorite game when he visited Russia in the spring.

the
BANGING
of the **SHOE**

73. THE TRAP

Soaring 60,000 feet over the Soviet city of Sverdlovsk, American pilot Francis Gary Powers heard an explosion and saw a flash of orange. Suddenly the U–2 spy plane he was piloting began to shake. Then its wings broke off and it dropped like a stone.

"My God," Powers thought, "I've had it now!"

As he struggled to free himself from his seat belt, he was blown out of the cockpit and over the U–2's nose. About three miles above the earth, his parachute snapped open and he began drifting slowly toward the ground, watching shattered chunks of his plane falling around him.

Powers's descent took twenty minutes, which gave him plenty of time to ponder his fate as an American spy captured by the Soviets: "The worst things that can happen to a person are what they're going to do to me." He reached into his pocket and pulled out the silver dollar given to U 2 pilots by their CIA superiors. In a hidden hole in the edge of the coin sat a pin containing a powerful poison. In the event of capture, U–2 pilots were encouraged, but not ordered, to kill themselves. Powers removed the poison pin and tossed the silver dollar away. He stared at the pin and considered using it. But he didn't. He decided to wait. He slipped the pin into his pocket in case he needed it later.

It was the morning of May 1, 1960—seven months after Nikita Khrushchev had left the United States, two weeks before the Paris summit was scheduled to begin, and six weeks before Ike was due to arrive in Moscow for his tour of the Soviet Union.

Powers's flight was not the first time a U–2 had flown over the Soviet Union. Since 1956, the spy planes had cruised through Soviet airspace two dozen times, photographing industrial and military sites so clearly that CIA director Allen Dulles bragged that "I was able to look at every blade of grass in the Soviet Union." The photos revealed that Khrushchev's boasts about producing missiles "like sausages" were wild exaggerations. In fact, the Soviets lagged behind the United States in both missiles and long-range bombers.

The Soviets issued angry protests about the first few U–2 flights. After that, they kept silent because Khrushchev was embarrassed to admit that he possessed neither planes capable of flying high enough to intercept the U–2s nor missiles capable of shooting them down. If the premier had asked Eisenhower at Camp David to stop the flights, the president might have agreed. But Khrushchev couldn't bring himself to ask; it was too humiliating. Instead he seethed, feeling "infuriated and disgusted" that the U–2 flights proved that he was impotent, unable to protect his nation from enemy aircraft.

Khrushchev and Eisenhower agreed about one aspect of the U–2: They both wanted to keep it secret from their people. The premier refused to admit that he couldn't shoot down enemy planes, and the president refused to inform even the top leaders of Congress about the U–2, despite the fact that the information the spy planes gathered might have quelled Democrats' angry rhetoric about America falling behind the Russians. "You can almost say," CIA deputy director Richard Bissell wrote years later, "that the U.S. and U.S.S.R. governments collaborated in keeping this program secret from the U.S. and Russian publics."

Reporters for the *Washington Post*, the *New York Times* and the *Cleveland Plain Dealer* learned about the U–2, but editors killed their stories at the request of Allen Dulles. Only one American periodical dared to publish a story on the U–2—*Model Airplane News,* which printed drawings of the plane in 1958, along with an article reporting an "unconfirmed rumor" that "U–2s are flying across the Iron Curtain taking aerial photographs."

After Khrushchev's trip to America, Eisenhower suspended the U–2 flights, fearing that they would jeopardize the summit. But Dulles begged the president to allow another flight, and Ike relented. On April 9, a U–2 flew out of Pakistan to photograph the Soviet missile site at Tyura-Tam. A Soviet MiG–19 fighter plane chased the U–2 but failed to catch it and then crashed, killing the pilot. Khrushchev was incensed. He couldn't believe his friend Eisenhower would do this. It must be the work of Dulles, he told his son Sergei. But he didn't protest. "Why give our enemies the satisfaction?" he said bitterly.

Dulles asked Eisenhower for one more flight. Ike balked—it was getting very close to the summit—but he finally agreed, with one restriction: "No operation is to be carried out after May 1."

At six o'clock on the morning of May 1, Khrushchev awoke to the ringing of the secure phone on his bedside table. When he answered, his defense minister informed him that another U–2 had entered Soviet air space. Khrushchev ordered him to shoot it down.

A few hours later, as Khrushchev prepared to preside over the annual May Day parade, an antiaircraft missile exploded just behind the U–2, close enough to blow the wings off.

Powers landed on a collective farm, where he was soon surrounded by curious Russians. They quickly realized that he was a foreigner.

"Are you Bulgarian?" someone asked.

Powers was flown to Moscow and interrogated by KGB officers in Lubyanka prison, the infamous site where the Soviet secret police murdered thousands during Stalin's purges. The pilot admitted that he was a civilian employee of the CIA but he refused to reveal anything about the U–2. When his captors found the poison pin that he'd slipped into his pocket while falling from the sky, he warned them to be careful.

"It contains a very active poison," he said. "A prick from this needle brings instant death."

Later the KGB tested the pin by stabbing it into a dog. Within ninety seconds, the poor pooch was dead.

Khrushchev was perched atop Lenin's tomb in Red Square, watching the May Day parade, when the commander of Soviet air defenses arrived to tell him the news: We shot down the U–2 and captured the American pilot.

"Well done!" Khrushchev exclaimed.

He came home happy that night and told his son that he'd devised a trap for the Americans: He would make a speech announcing that the Soviets had shot down an American plane but he wouldn't reveal that they'd captured the pilot and his photographs. That way, the Americans would respond with their usual story about an innocent plane that accidentally strayed off course. Then he'd produce the pilot and the pictures and show the world how the Americans lied.

A few days later, in the Great Hall of the Kremlin, Khrushchev addressed the 1,300 deputies of the Supreme Soviet, as well as the American ambassador, Tommy Thompson, who unexpectedly found himself seated in a place of honor in the front row of the balcony. For two hours, Khrushchev droned on, delivering a dull recitation about the wonderful things his government had accomplished. Then he paused theatrically, looked up at Thompson in the balcony, and announced that the Americans had sent a spy plane over the Soviet Union on May Day and that he'd ordered the minister of defense to shoot it down.

"This assignment was fulfilled," he reported. "The plane was shot down!"

The deputies cheered wildly. Thompson, who now realized why he'd received such a good seat, struggled to maintain a poker face.

"Just imagine what would have happened if a Soviet aircraft appeared over New York, Chicago or Detroit," Khrushchev continued. "How would the United States have reacted?" He looked up at Thompson and posed a sarcastic question: "What was this—a May Day greeting?"

The deputies laughed and cheered. Khrushchev basked in the moment, theatrically denouncing the Americans. But he was careful to leave open the possibility that the U–2 wasn't the fault of his friend Eisenhower. Perhaps, he told the deputies, this outrage was "performed by Pentagon militarists without the president's knowledge" in an effort to scuttle the upcoming summit. "I do not doubt President Eisenhower's sincere desire for peace."

Eisenhower learned of Khrushchev's revelation while he was engaged in a doomsday drill, meeting with aides in the Blue Ridge mountain bunker where they were to gather if Washington was obliterated in a nuclear attack. Dulles reported the details of Khrushchev's speech and Ike ordered his aides to concoct a cover story.

Assuming that the U–2 pilot had either died in the crash or committed suicide, Allen Dulles and undersecretary of state Douglas Dillon came up with a story designed to provide an explanation that was at least vaguely plausible: "A weather research plane based at Adana, Turkey, piloted by a civilian, has been missing since May 1. During the flight of this plane, the pilot reported difficulty with his oxygen equipment. . . . It is entirely possible that, having a failure in the oxygen equipment which could result in the pilot losing consciousness, the plane continued on automatic pilot for a considerable distance and violated Soviet airspace."

It was exactly the kind of lie that Khrushchev had been expecting. On May 7, he again addressed the Supreme Soviet. Smirking, he read the State Department's explanation and a statement by NASA explaining that the U–2's mission was to photograph clouds. Then he announced that he would reveal a secret: "When I made my report two days ago, I deliberately refrained from mentioning that we have the remnants of the plane—and we also have the pilot, who is quite alive and kicking!"

The deputies cheered. Khrushchev informed them that the pilot was Francis Gary Powers, a former Air Force officer employed by the CIA. The premier held up photographs taken by Powers, which were not pictures of clouds but aerial photos of a Soviet air base. "Look at this!" he bellowed. "Here are the airfields! Fighters in position on the ground! Here they are!"

Khrushchev told the story of Powers's suicide pin: "He was to jab himself with this poison pin, which would have killed him instantly! What barbarism!" He held up a photo of the pin. "Here it is—the latest achievement of American technology for killing their own people!"

Grinning, he displayed photos of other items that Powers had been carrying—7,500 Russian rubles, two dozen gold coins, two watches, and seven women's rings. "What did he need all this for in the upper layers of the atmosphere?" he asked as the party hacks hooted and cackled. "Perhaps the pilot was to have flown even higher—to Mars—and intended to seduce Martian ladies!"

Khrushchev rejoiced in his triumph. Just as he'd hoped, the world was appalled at the sight of the Americans caught in a pathetic lie.

"The Americans have made fools of themselves," the British *News Chronicle* concluded.

"This country was caught with jam on our hands," said the *Washington Post*.

"Mr. Khrushchev has us on the run in the propaganda battle now, making us look sick," said Senator Hubert Humphrey.

With characteristic hauteur, French President Charles De Gaulle pronounced the affair "a bad comedy in questionable taste."

In the White House, the president seemed depressed, muttering to his secretary, "I would like to resign." Eisenhower's son urged him to fire Allen Dulles. So did Ike's brother Milton. But the president refused. That would be "hypocrisy," he said. To blame his underlings would simply confirm Khrushchev's suggestion that he wasn't in control of his own government, and cause people around the world to fear that some low-level official could set off World War III.

Instead, Eisenhower called a news conference on May 11 and announced that he would read a statement about the U–2 incident. After that, he quickly added, "I shall have nothing further to say."

His statement suggested, but did not quite admit, that he'd ordered the U–2 flights: "Ever since the beginning of my administration, I have issued directives to gather, in every feasible way, the information required to protect the United States and the free world against surprise attack." Spying is "a distasteful but vital necessity," he said, and the U–2 flights were required because Soviet society was so secretive. "In most of the world, no large-scale attack could be prepared in secret, but in the Soviet Union, there is a fetish of secrecy and concealment. This is a major cause of international tension and uneasiness today."

Eisenhower pointedly did not promise to stop the spy flights. Instead, he announced that he'd bring to the Paris summit a proposal for an "open skies" agreement to allow U.N.-supervised aerial surveillance of both the United States and the Soviet Union—an idea that Khrushchev had rejected in Geneva in 1955.

"After reading this statement in his Kremlin office, Father simply flew into a rage," Sergei Khrushchev recalled. The premier was incensed that Eisenhower didn't apologize for the flights or promise to halt them. Khrushchev had been snared in his own clever trap. Ever since he returned from the United States, he'd praised Eisenhower as a peacemaker and used his friendship with Ike to justify huge cuts in his military budget. Now he'd caught Ike in a lie and made himself seem naive to the Kremlin hard-liners who had opposed those cuts. And after making such a fuss over U–2 flights that he'd ignored for years, how could he now negotiate with Ike as if nothing had happened?

That day, Khrushchev visited Gorky Park, where his government had displayed the wreckage of the U–2 plane, along with Powers's now famous poison pin and his collection of rubles and rings.

"I was horrified to learn that the president had endorsed the acts," he told the mob of reporters who followed him through the exhibit. "If the U.S.A. has not yet suffered a real war on its territory and wants to start a war," he added, "we will fire rockets and hit their territory a few minutes later."

"Do you still want President Eisenhower to come to the Soviet Union?" a reporter asked.

Khrushchev pondered the question for a long moment. "What do you want me to say?" he asked. "You know my attitude toward the president. I have often spoken about it. I am a human being and I have human feelings. I had hopes and they were betrayed. . . . So how can I now ask our people to turn out and welcome the dear guest who is coming to us? They will say, 'Are you *nuts*? What kind of dear guest allows a plane to fly over us to spy?'"

Two days later, Khrushchev flew to Paris, determined to wreck the summit he had been so eager to arrange.

74. PRIDE AND DIGNITY

When Charles de Gaulle escorted Khrushchev into the elegant green and gold conference room in the Élysée Palace in Paris on the morning of May 16, 1960, the premier shook hands with Harold Macmillan but only nodded to Eisenhower.

"We are gathered here for the Summit Conference," De Gaulle said after the leaders and their aides had taken seats around a large square table. "Does anyone therefore wish to say anything?"

"Yes, I would like the floor," Khrushchev said, leaping to his feet.

"I would also like to make a short statement," said Eisenhower, who remained seated.

De Gaulle suggested that Eisenhower speak first but Khrushchev objected. "I was the first to ask for the floor," he said, "and I would like my request to be granted."

De Gaulle raised his eyebrows in a subtle Gallic protest, then glanced at Eisenhower. Ike nodded grimly.

Still standing, Khrushchev donned his reading glasses and pulled a thick manuscript from his pocket. As his hands trembled and his left eyebrow twitched, he read a long, vociferous attack on the "aggressive" U–2 flights and the "ridiculous" cover story and Eisenhower's failure to "condemn this provocative act." As he read, his voice grew louder and angrier.

Finally, de Gaulle interrupted. "The acoustics in this room are excellent," he said, dryly. "We can all hear the chairman. There is no need for him to raise his voice."

Khrushchev glared at de Gaulle over his reading glasses but lowered his voice, at least temporarily. "We want to participate in the talks on an equal footing," he continued, "and that is only possible if the United States declares that it will not violate Soviet borders, that it deplores the acts undertaken in the past and will punish those directly guilty of such actions."

On the American side of the table, translator Alex Akalovsky watched Eisenhower's face get redder and redder.

Khrushchev continued his tirade. He announced that he was canceling Eisenhower's visit to the Soviet Union, and he urged that this summit conference be postponed for six to eight months—in other words, until Ike was out of office. "We regret that this meeting has been torpedoed by the reactionary circles of the United States," he said. "Let the disgrace and blame for this rest with those who have proclaimed a bandit policy toward the Soviet Union."

After nearly forty-five minutes, Khrushchev finished. The room was silent, except for the soft ticking of a gold clock in the center of the table.

Now it was Eisenhower's turn to speak. He was livid but remained calm. There was "no aggressive intent" behind the U-2 flights, he said. They were undertaken "to assure the safety of the United States and the free world against surprise attack by a power which boasts of its ability to devastate the United States and other countries by missiles armed with atomic warheads."

But, he added, he had suspended all U-2 flights, and he promised that they would not be resumed. He urged that the summit continue. "I see no reason to use this incident to disrupt the conference."

When Eisenhower finished, Macmillan said he hoped the summit could proceed. So did de Gaulle: "It would not serve humanity to break up on the basis of a parochial incident."

"We cannot agree to this," Khrushchev replied. Eisenhower had not apologized for his "aggressive act" and therefore the Soviets would not participate in the summit. "We will allow no one—*no one*—to violate our sovereignty."

"Yesterday," de Gaulle said, "that satellite you launched just before you left Moscow to impress us overflew the sky of France eighteen times without my permission. How do I know that you do not have cameras aboard which are taking pictures of my country?"

"Our latest sputnik has no cameras," Khrushchev replied.

"Well," de Gaulle said, "how did you take those pictures of the far side of the moon which you showed us with such justifiable pride?"

"In that one I had cameras."

"Ah, in *that* one, you had cameras," de Gaulle said, archly. "Pray continue."

For the first time, Khrushchev addressed Eisenhower directly. "We don't understand what devil pushed you into doing this provocative act to us just before the conference. If there had been no incident, we would have come here in friendship." He raised his hands: "As God is my witness, I come with clean hands and a pure soul."

When Eisenhower heard that line, he nearly choked, he later told aides. But he stifled his gag reflex and reported, once again, that he had grounded the U–2: "The flights will not be resumed—not only for the duration of this conference but for the entire duration of my term."

"For us, that is not enough," Khrushchev replied. Without an apology, he could not participate in the summit. "Otherwise the Soviet people will think the United States has forced the Soviet Union to its knees."

Eisenhower did not apologize. The meeting adjourned.

The next day, de Gaulle convened another session of the summit. Eisenhower and Macmillan attended. Khrushchev refused. Instead, he held a raucous press conference for 3,000 journalists from all over the world. Answering questions for two hours, Khrushchev was alternately funny, angry, and frightening. When he heard heckling from West German reporters, he pounded the table so hard that he knocked over his mineral water. Calling his hecklers "fascist bastards we didn't finish off at Stalingrad," he issued a belligerent warning: "If you boo us and attack us again, *look out!* We will hit you so hard that there won't be a squeal out of you!"

A reporter asked why the premier didn't ask the president at Camp David to stop the U–2 flights.

"I will answer that question with pleasure," Khrushchev said. "When I was talking at Camp David with President Eisenhower, I almost opened my mouth to make that statement. The atmosphere was so convivial, with the president telling me to call him *my friend* in English and calling me *moi drug* in Russian. Like a brother he was. It was then that I wanted to tell my friend that it was not nice to fly over a friend's territory without his permission. But then I thought better of it and decided, 'No, I am not going to tell him. There is something stinky about this friend of mine.' I did not broach the subject. And it turned out that I was right in my doubts because we caught the American spy—like a thief, red-handed! We told the Americans that they act like thieves and they say, 'No, this is our policy. We have flown and will keep on flying over your territory.' It's their thief-like policy, that's all!"

Soon Khrushchev was waving his fist and bellowing threats: "We shall shoot such planes down! We shall deal shattering blows to the bases where they came from—and at those who set up the bases!"

"Khrushchev has lost his mind," West German chancellor Konrad Adenauer told *New York Times* columnist C. L. Sulzberger. Poland's ambassador to France, Stanislaw Gajewski, agreed, telling Sulzberger that the premier was "a bit unbalanced emotionally."

"Khrushchev engaged in inexcusable hysterics," Anastas Mikoyan, the premier's Kremlin colleague, said years later. "He was guilty of delaying the onset of détente for fifteen years."

In his memoirs, Khrushchev explained his state of mind in Paris: "My anger was building up inside me like an electric force which could be discharged in a great flash at any moment. . . . Frankly, I was all worked up, feeling combative and exhilarated. As my kind of simple folk would say, I was spoiling for a fight."

For the rest of his life, Khrushchev insisted that he was right to respond to the U–2 by sabotaging the summit: "Our pride and dignity would be damaged if we went ahead with the meeting as though nothing had happened."

75. OBLIGATORY SEX SCENE

On August 17, 1960, Francis Gary Powers went on trial for espionage. He faced a possible sentence of death.

His wife, Barbara Gay Powers, flew to Moscow to attend the trial. She was a headstrong, high-spirited woman from rural Georgia, and she got so drunk the night before the trial that she took a cab to Lubyanka prison at 3:00 in the morning in an unsuccessful attempt to visit her husband.

A few hours later, she sat in a private box in the ornate Hall of Columns, where victims of Stalin's purges were tried and inevitably convicted. A bell rang and her husband was brought into the room, wearing a Russian suit that was far too big for him.

"Defendant Powers, do you plead guilty of the charge?"

"Yes," Powers replied.

In most places, a guilty plea makes for a very short trial. But this was a classic Soviet show trial, televised for maximum propaganda. For two days, a prosecutor presented evidence, lingering over Powers's now famous poison pin and his collection of rubles, gold coins, and rings.

When the prosecutor finished, a defense attorney described Powers as a mere "tool" of the American aggressors and urged the court to display the "humaneness" of the Soviet system in contrast to the "reactionary forces of the United States, who sent him to certain death and wanted his death."

The three judges deliberated for five hours and then delivered their verdict: "Out of socialist humaneness, the sentence of the defendant Powers is limited to ten years of confinement."

Later two Soviet officials escorted Barbara Powers to visit her husband in his prison cell. She recounted what occurred there in *Spy Wife*, her delightfully uninhibited 1965 memoir. The passage turned out to be what was known in those days as the "obligatory sex scene," or as novelist Vladimir Nabokov called it, "the OSS," a scene that provides an erotic *frisson* for readers whose tastes are not purely literary.

Here, verbatim, is *Spy Wife*'s obligatory sex scene, complete with the author's own ellipses, italics, and eccentric paragraphing:

> With the preliminaries over, Gary and I began to make mad love.
>
> In nothing flat, Barbara Gay Powers was standing stark naked in a Russian prison cell . . .
>
> And just that quick we were bouncing up and down on Gary's cot, enjoying the true union of man and wife.
>
> *We had intercourse three times in those three hours!*
>
> Gary hadn't been able to bathe for twelve days, and he smelled like a Billy Goat!
>
> But I didn't mind. I was swallowed up by our passion.
>
> It felt like my husband was *raping* me.
>
> Once, between love sessions, Gary whispered—
>
> "You do realize the guards may be watching?"
>
> "I don't give a good damn!" I retorted.
>
> Furthermore, I felt that the Russians, at least in this instance, had gone out of their cotton-pickin' way to make us happy.
>
> And this was a mighty nice going-away present, which they had served us on a silver platter—er, I mean *cot*.

As Powers stood trial in Moscow, Nikita Khrushchev was vacationing at his dacha on the Black Sea, where he watched the trial on television and prepared for his next great adventure: *He was going back to America!*

He'd conceived the idea after the Paris summit: He would appoint himself head of the Soviet delegation to the United Nations, so he could

travel to the U.N. General Assembly in New York, where he could torment the Americans on their own turf with the whole world watching.

He was, as his son later recalled, "simply bursting to do battle."

"By suddenly announcing that the Soviet delegation would be headed
by Prime Minister Khrushchev," the chairman wrote in his memoirs, "we
poured oil on the fire which had been started by the U–2 affair."

The Soviet announcement quickly elicited an announcement from
the Americans: For his own protection, Premier Khrushchev would be
restricted to the island of Manhattan for the duration of his visit to
America.

At a reception shortly before he left for New York, Khrushchev saw
Tommy Thompson and began to berate the ambassador about the U–2.
Just in case that didn't get his message across, he stomped on Thompson's
foot, then said, "If you do that, you should say, 'Excuse me!'"

76. ROSES ARE RED, VIOLETS ARE BLUE

Khrushchev made the trip to New York by sea because the world's tallest
plane, the TU–114, was under repair, and he couldn't bear the humiliation of flying in a smaller plane that would have to stop in England to re-
fuel. Instead, he traveled aboard the *Baltika*, a 429-foot passenger ship that
the Soviets had seized from the Germans after the war. The *Baltika* set sail
on September 9, 1960, carrying a cargo of Communist dictators, the
rulers of a few of Khrushchev's Eastern European colonies—Janos Kadar
of Hungary, Todor Zhivkov of Bulgaria, and Gheorghe Gheorghiu-Dej of
Romania. With such an august collection of Communists aboard,
Khrushchev worried that a NATO ship might try to sink the *Baltika*.

"The Atlantic Ocean is an enormous space, with plenty of room to
sink a ship without anyone's ever being the wiser," he thought. "With all
the witnesses dead, NATO could always say that the ship had accidentally
hit a mine left over from World War II."

Despite Khrushchev's paranoia, the weather proved more dangerous than NATO. For days, a savage gale pummeled the ship, causing an outbreak of seasickness that felled most of the passengers and much of the crew. But Khrushchev was unaffected, which pleased him immensely. He ate and drank heartily and strolled the ship, happily taunting his miserable comrades when they stumbled from their sickbeds, looking green and groggy.

The storm subsided after a few days and Khrushchev settled into a pleasant routine. In the mornings, he'd sit on deck in a rocking chair, dictating drafts of the speeches he would deliver at the U.N. or listening while an aide read him the latest news cabled from Moscow. He was particularly interested in reports from the Congo, where the Soviets supported leftist Prime Minister Patrice Lumumba against an American-backed general, Joseph Mobutu, and other rebels. When Khrushchev learned that U.N. Secretary-General Dag Hammarskjold had refused to support Lumumba, he exploded. "I spit on the UN," he roared. "That good-for-nothing Ham is sticking his nose into important affairs which are none of his business. . . . We have to get rid of him." With that, he began plotting how to oust—or at least harass—Hammarskjold.

But shipboard life wasn't all work because Khrushchev had become a shuffleboard buff. He'd never seen the game before he set sail but soon he was hooked, playing with the enthusiasm of a Florida retiree and eagerly attempting to beat his fellow dictators by as many points as possible.

"We couldn't get enough of this game," he reported in his memoirs.

The excitement of shuffleboard was enhanced by the consumption of large quantities of alcohol. "Khrushchev drank hugely—vodka, wine and cognac—but he did not become intoxicated easily," recalled Arkady Shevchenko, a young bureaucrat in the Soviet foreign ministry who traveled aboard the *Baltika*. "Sometimes, in the evening, after he had been drinking hard all day, he would indulge in pranks and jokes without inhibition."

Half drunk one night, Khrushchev turned to Nikolai Podgorney, his party boss in Ukraine, and said, "Why don't you dance a *gopak* for us?"

Podgorny looked stunned. He was an old man and the *gopak* was a strenuous dance. But Khrushchev insisted and finally Podgorny squatted down and kicked out his feet in an awkward attempt to boogie.

"Well done!" Khrushchev said, laughing condescendingly, just like Stalin used to do.

After ten days at sea, the *Baltika* steamed into New York harbor on the rainy morning of September 19, 1960. Escorted by a U.S. Navy submarine, a fleet of tugs, and a flock of police helicopters, it passed a flotilla of charter fishing boats packed with men holding picket signs:

CRUMMY KHRUSHCHEV GO HOME!

THERE'S PLENTY OF GARBAGE FLOATING IN THE RIVER TODAY

One sign displayed a poem:

ROSES ARE RED
VIOLETS ARE BLUE
STALIN DROPPED DEAD,
HOW ABOUT YOU?

Standing on deck in a yellow rain slicker, Khrushchev peered through binoculars at the protesters, who were members of the International Longshoreman's Association, the same union that had welcomed the premier so warmly in San Francisco a year earlier.

Much had changed in that year as the optimism of Khrushchev's first visit curdled into bitter hostility. Americans were outraged when the Soviets shot down the U–2, and appalled when Khrushchev sabotaged the Paris summit. The mood worsened in July, when the Soviets shot down an American RB–47 spy plane as it flew over the Barents Sea near the northern coast of Russia, killing four airmen and capturing two. The U.S government claimed that the plane had been flying over international waters; Khrushchev said it had violated Soviet air space and he threatened to try the captive fliers for espionage.

When he arrived in America a year earlier, Khrushchev had been greeted by a military band, a twenty-one-gun salute, and President Eisenhower. This time, there would be no band, no salute, and no Eisenhower. Vice President Nixon also declined to greet the premier. So did Governor Rockefeller and Mayor Wagner. And the longshoreman's union announced that its members would refuse to dock the *Baltika*: "Those bums will have to unload the ship themselves."

Time magazine reported that Khrushchev was "about as welcome in the U.S. as the Black Plague." The reason, the magazine explained, was that "he has about as much interest in reducing tensions and promoting world order as the Three Stooges."

On the night before the *Baltika* arrived, a crowd of 2,000 protesters marched to the Soviet U.N. mission on Park Avenue, led by a truck bearing a gallows with a hanging effigy of Khrushchev. When they arrived at their destination, the protesters charged the mission, exchanging blows with a squad of fifty riot police. "Soviet HQ Is Clobbered Even Before K Arrives," read the headline in the *Daily News,* and New Yorkers worried that the violence would only escalate when K actually appeared. Radio announcers instructed listeners on what to do if bombs exploded.

The next morning, in a heavy rain, the *Baltika* sailed past the Statue of Liberty, past the boats of jeering longshoremen, past Con Edison's coal-burning power plant, where four smokestacks pumped black soot into the leaden sky. Finally it arrived at Pier 73 on the Manhattan side of the East River at 25th Street. With the longshoremen refusing to dock the vessel, the *Baltika*'s crew tied the boat to the pier with some awkward assistance by low-level Soviet diplomats.

From the deck, Khrushchev peered at the pier and beheld a dilapidated ruin. Water poured through huge holes in the roof and puddled on the cracked concrete floor. The premier was infuriated. "Another dirty trick the Americans are playing on us," he growled to his aides.

Actually, the squalor of the scene was Khrushchev's own fault. He'd ordered his ambassador not to waste money on a fancy pier: "Bargain for the cheapest place there is!" he commanded, and his ambassador obeyed.

"Well," Khrushchev grumbled, "we got the cheapest all right."

A wall of cops held back a crowd of demonstrators who began howling at the first sight of the unwanted guest. "When Khrushchev's bald dome was seen moving from the *Baltika* to the pier," the *Daily News* reported, "the crowd let loose a volley of names—in English and assorted tongues—that would have blanched Captain Kidd."

As Khrushchev stepped to the pier, not a single representative of the federal, state, or city governments was on hand to welcome him. But there *was* a red carpet. Spread across the pier by workers from the Soviet mission that morning, it had become thoroughly soaked with rain. As Khrushchev walked across it, water squished from beneath his shoes.

He ignored it, stepped to a microphone, and smiled. He pulled a speech from his pocket and began to read to the wet crowd of protestors, reporters, and cops. He'd come to New York for "the good of peace," he said, as raindrops falling through the holes in the roof bounced off his bald head.

77. THAT SON OF A BITCH RICHARD NIXON

Khrushchev and his shuffleboard partners from Eastern Europe were not the only heads of state visiting New York. The city teemed with an unprecedented array of presidents, premiers, prime ministers, princes, and other assorted panjandrums.

The 1960 session of the U.N. General Assembly was the largest yet. Decolonization had added fourteen new members to the United Nations, thirteen of them newly liberated African nations, and many world leaders decided to attend the historic session. Eisenhower and Macmillan were

there, along with Sukarno of Indonesia, Nasser of Egypt, Tito of Yugoslavia, Diefenbaker of Canada, Nehru of India, Nkrumah of Ghana, Si-
hanouk of Cambodia, and Castro of Cuba. It was, the *New York Times*
reported, "the most momentous diplomatic gathering in history," and
Time magazine could not resist the temptation to roll out its most purple
prose: "Not the pomp of ancient Rome or the jeweled brilliance of the
great courts of France could shadow the moment: The eye of history
could scarcely encompass the spectacle of so many potentates, presidents
and dictators."

New York's cops were less thrilled. Faced with what the *Daily News* described as "the biggest security headache in U.S. history," the police com-
missioner cancelled vacations and holidays, extended shifts to twelve
hours, and assigned 8,000 cops to protect the various potentates from
people who detested them, frequently with good reason.

The streets of Manhattan swarmed with protesters. Everybody
seemed to be mad at somebody. Yugoslavian dissidents hollered at Tito;
students from British Guyana chanted anti-English slogans; a Ukrainian
immigrant burned a Soviet flag; anti-Castro Cubans fought pro-Castro
Cubans with fists, picket signs, and beer bottles; two Hungarians demonstrated their hatred of Communism by chaining themselves to a lamp-
post; four pacifists protested the arms race by staging a public hunger
strike; and a local Manhattan woman paced 44th Street with a sign that
read, "Americans Awake—Germ Warfare Has Begun."

At the United Nations, so many people were protesting so many injus-
tices that the cops herded them into "picket pens"—barricaded spaces that
held twenty-five dissidents each. At the Soviet mission on Park Avenue,
where Khrushchev was living, demonstrators pelted Soviet limousines with
eggs and tomatoes, threw firecrackers under the hooves of police horses,
and made so much noise at night that residents began retaliating against the
protesters by dumping buckets of water on them from high windows.

But neither dissenters nor disturbances could stop the world's leaders
from visiting each other. Macmillan visited Nkrumah, who visited Tito,

who visited Nehru. Nkrumah breakfasted with Nehru, who lunched with Macmillan and Diefenbaker. Macmillan met with Nasser and Khrushchev. Khrushchev met with Tito, Nehru, and Nasser. Eisenhower met Macmillan, Tito, Nehru, Nasser, and Nkrumah.

The only two major leaders who did not meet were Khrushchev and Eisenhower, who were still seething about the U–2 and the Paris summit. Khrushchev refused to meet with Ike until the president apologized for the U–2, and Ike refused to meet Khrushchev until the premier released the captured American RB–47 fliers. Consequently the two most powerful men on earth took great pains to avoid accidentally running into each other as they scurried around Manhattan meeting other leaders.

The other leaders were appalled that two men armed with atomic weapons were so angry at each other that they wouldn't even shake hands. The situation, said Sukarno, "threatens the world with grave consequences." Sukarno and four other neutralist leaders—Nehru, Nasser, Nkrumah, and Tito—sponsored a resolution asking the United Nations to officially request that the president and the premier meet. The two men could "break the ice," Nkrumah said, "if they could only meet and shake hands."

When reporters asked Khrushchev about the resolution, he responded with one of the most absurd evasions in the long history of political question-dodging. "I have not yet thought it over," he said. "It is a big question and it requires much thinking. The fact is that yesterday I went to bed intending to think over that problem, but when I did, I fell asleep."

The neutralist resolution angered Eisenhower. "At best it seemed totally illogical," he later wrote, "at worst it seemed an act of effrontery." If the proposal passed, Ike realized, he would find himself with a terrible choice: refuse to comply with a U.N. resolution or meet with a man he now loathed. It was, he noted, an "impossible situation."

Behind the scenes, they both maneuvered to defeat the resolution and, working toward their common goal, they succeeded.

Privately Eisenhower wondered why Khrushchev had bothered to come to New York. "Perhaps," Ike thought, "he hoped in some way to influence our presidential election."

The presidential campaign was in full swing when Khrushchev arrived, and he soon found that the main issue was . . . Khrushchev. The Republicans had nominated two men famous for jousting with the premier—Richard Nixon and Henry Cabot Lodge—and they missed few opportunities to remind voters that they had more experience handling Khrushchev than their opponents, John F. Kennedy and Lyndon Johnson. Nixon charged that Kennedy was "the kind of man Khrushchev will make mincemeat of."

When the premier landed in New York, Nixon unleashed a ploy that illustrated why he'd earned the nickname "Tricky Dick." He announced that as long as Khrushchev remained on American soil, all candidates had a "responsibility" to avoid criticizing America's foreign policy or saying anything else that "would encourage Chairman Khrushchev." And if Kennedy refused to comply, Nixon added, "the American people will hold him accountable."

Kennedy refused to accept Nixon's "campaign truce" and responded with some demagoguery of his own: He repeated his claim that America had fallen behind the Soviets militarily, which the U–2 had shown to be untrue, and he blamed Nixon for Fidel Castro's 1959 Cuban revolution. "Those who say they will stand up to Mr. Khrushchev," he said, "have demonstrated no ability to stand up to Mr. Castro."

Khrushchev followed the campaign closely. He was rooting for Kennedy, not because he liked the senator but because he detested Nixon. "He's a typical product of McCarthyism, a puppet of the most reactionary circles in the United States," he told his aides, adding that he'd figured out a way to influence the election. The Americans were pressuring him to release Francis Gary Powers and the RB–47 fliers, he said, but he wouldn't do it until after the election. "We would never give Nixon such a present!"

Later, after Kennedy won a narrow victory, Khrushchev bragged that his decision had "cast the deciding ballot" that defeated "that son-of-a-bitch Richard Nixon." But Khrushchev kept his preference for Kennedy carefully hidden while he was in New York.

"Who would you like to see take President Eisenhower's place after this election?" a reporter asked on September 21, two days after Khrushchev's arrival.

"I don't see any difference in these two candidates or the two parties," Khrushchev replied. He was standing on the balcony above the front door of the Soviet mission on Park Avenue, wearing a white shirt and green tie but no suit jacket, bantering with the mob of reporters and photographers who loitered on the sidewalk below, waiting for him to do something newsworthy. As usual, he did not disappoint them.

"Are you pleased with your progress here in America?" a reporter asked.

"I am not seeing America," Khrushchev replied, as his interpreter, Victor Sukhodrev, translated. "This is America?" He gestured out at the scene before him—the traffic-jammed street, the squad of cops guarding him, a handful of protesters. "I'm under house arrest. This is the only place I can stroll. Prisoners in prison have more space to stroll in."

The reporters scribbled in their notebooks and hollered more questions.

"Are the RB–47 pilots going to be tried?"

"That is a matter for the courts to determine."

"Don't you think you are being unfair to Mr. Nixon and Mr. Kennedy by keeping them off the front pages?"

"I don't think they will be offended."

"Do the people elect the government in Russia?"

Khrushchev dodged this question with a ludicrous non sequitur. "Didn't you know that in our country people have no trousers?" he said, grinning. "Really. Run quick. You will see them."

A motor scooter roared past, carrying two young men who each raised a hand to his nose and wiggled his fingers at the premier. Khrushchev responded by raising his own hand over his head and making an enthusiastic thumbs-down gesture, like a Roman emperor condemning a gladiator. Across the street, the protesters booed.

"What do you think of the booing?" a reporter asked.

"These must be the wisest people in America."

"Why?"

"Those who shout the loudest are the wisest," he said, smiling. Then he pointed to the traffic on Park Avenue. "You see how many cars are passing? They make no hostile manifestations. Many of them wave friendly greetings. They are the real Americans."

"You think the demonstrators aren't real Americans? What are they?"

Khrushchev smiled and pointed to a policeman on a horse. "They are what is under the feet of that horse over there."

Again, the motor scooter buzzed past, having circled the block. Again, the two riders thumbed their noses at Khrushchev. Again, the premier grinned and jabbed his thumb toward the ground. "My friends, they go around and around," he said, laughing.

"Why don't you come down and have a chat?" a reporter asked.

"We are on different levels, don't you see?" Khrushchev replied.

When somebody asked about the death threats he'd received, the premier stuck his chin out pugnaciously, puffed up his chest, squeezed his right hand into a fist, and unleashed a ferocious uppercut at an imaginary assassin.

Across the street, students from Hunter College began singing "God Bless America."

"Let them sing," Khrushchev said. "In Russia, we also sing." With that, he launched into a chorus of the rousing radical anthem, "The Internationale."

"Arise ye prisoners of starvation," he warbled in Russian, "Arise ye wretched of the earth!"

78. RENDEZVOUS IN HARLEM

On the morning of September 20 Khrushchev bounded out of the Soviet mission on Park Avenue and headed for his Cadillac limousine.

"Where are you going?" reporters asked.

"We Communists don't tell our secrets," Khrushchev replied. "Watch for the newspapers. They will tell you where I'm bound."

He slid into the limo and sped off, followed by a caravan of police cars and a fleet of taxis carrying reporters. A few minutes later, amid screaming sirens, Khrushchev emerged from the limousine at the Hotel Theresa on 125th street, which was surrounded by a mob of cops, reporters, curious Harlem residents, and rival groups of demonstrators who chanted "Long Live Castro!" and "Death to Castro!" in both English and Spanish.

That morning, Khrushchev had learned that Cuban leader Fidel Castro had theatrically moved his entourage from the Hotel Shelburne in bourgeois midtown Manhattan to the Hotel Theresa in Harlem. Khrushchev decided to visit him there—a gesture that would enable him to show his solidarity with both the charismatic Cuban revolutionary and with the oppressed black people of Harlem.

Khrushchev had not yet met Castro but seven months earlier, in February 1960, he'd dispatched Anastas Mikoyan to Havana to size up the young dictator, who hadn't yet announced to the world that he was a Communist. "Yes, he is a revolutionary," Mikoyan reported upon his return to Moscow. "Completely like us. I felt as though I had returned to my childhood." After that, Khrushchev sent a shipment of oil to Castro and announced that the Soviet Union was willing to use its nuclear missiles to defend revolutionary Cuba against Yankee aggression.

At the Hotel Theresa, Khrushchev was surrounded by a scrum of police who bulled their way through the crowded lobby. The premier was appalled at the hotel—it was dirty and smelly, he recalled—but he was impressed with Castro: "He was a very tall man with a beard and his face was both pleasant and tough at the same time." Khrushchev hugged the Cuban and they chatted for twenty minutes, and then Castro walked him back out to his limo.

A few hours later, at the opening session of the U.N. General Assembly, Khrushchev bounded over to Castro and gave him a big bear hug as photographers snapped pictures that showed Khrushchev beaming as Castro loomed over him, tall enough that his beard could dust the premier's pate.

"The photograph of Premier Khrushchev embracing Premier Castro at the United Nations on Tuesday will doubtless become famous," the *New York Times* predicted. "One can read into it all kinds of symbolisms, not the least being that a bear hug can be lethal." The *Times* clearly thought Khrushchev was a danger to Castro, but a man calling himself "Chautauqua Hermit" wrote to the *Daily News* suggesting that the scruffy Cuban was a danger to the Russian: "I understand Khrushchev woke up scratching the other morning. He should be careful whom he embraces."

Six days before Khrushchev hugged Castro at the Hotel Theresa, two other men met in another New York hotel to talk about killing the Cuban leader. On September 14, 1960, in the Plaza Hotel, James O'Connell, the number two man in the CIA's Office of Security, met Sam "Momo" Giancana, the number one man in the Chicago mob, to discuss a matter of mutual interest—the assassination of Fidel Castro. O'Connell wanted to kill Castro because the CIA believed the Cuban dictator was a Communist. Giancana agreed to help because Castro had shut down the mob's casinos in Havana.

The CIA wanted Giancana's gangsters to kill Castro in classic mob style, gunning the dictator down in a restaurant or on a Havana street. Giancana didn't think that would work—Castro was well guarded—and suggested something more subtle, like poison. So the CIA's chemists created poisoned cigars, poisoned handkerchiefs and poison pills. Giancana opted for the pills and his henchmen delivered them to their contacts in Havana, but none of the would-be assassins managed to get close enough to Castro to slip the poison into his drink. Finally the CIA gave up on the idea of poisoning Castro and set about raising an army of anti-Castro exiles and preparing to invade Cuba at a place called the Bay of Pigs.

Castro knew nothing of these CIA plots during his week at the Hotel Theresa, where he thoroughly enjoyed himself—at least according to a delightfully lurid *Daily News* article entitled "Cubans Go Native with the Girls."

"All through the day and all through the night since Fidel and his band made the long trek to Harlem, girls, girls, girls have marched into the

Cubans' suites," the *News* reported. "There have been blondes, brunettes, redheads and—a detective said—many known prostitutes. . . . A hotel employee said Fidel himself had a visitor from 2 A.M. to 3:30 A.M. yesterday—an attractive bosomy blonde. The employee did not know whether they had discussed high international policy."

79. THE GUEST WHO WOULDN'T LEAVE

Khrushchev's first speech at the 1960 session of the U.N. General Assembly lasted two hours and twenty minutes. And that was just the first.

A year earlier, when he spoke at the U.N. on his first trip to the United States, Khrushchev was a cuddly Santa Claus proposing a utopian plan for total disarmament and eternal peace. This time, he was a gruff bully spoiling for a fight. He attacked the United States for sending spy planes over his country—an act that could "plunge mankind into a third World War." He praised "courageous Cuba" for nationalizing American businesses and denounced the United States for threatening Cuba with "attacks, intrigues and subversion." He demanded that colonialism be ended "immediately" and rattled off a long list of colonies to be liberated, including Puerto Rico. He excoriated Secretary-General Hammarskjold for "pursuing the line of the colonialists" and proposed eliminating the office of secretary-general and replacing it with a trio of officials—one from the West, one from the Communist bloc, and one representing the neutral nations. And he urged that the United Nations be moved out of the United States, where delegates from African nations were, he charged, subjected to "racial discrimination" and "attacks by gangsters."

If the U.N. wanted to move to Moscow, he added, he could guarantee that African delegates would not suffer because of "the color of their skin."

On and on he went, plodding through a 19,000-word harangue that drove many diplomats out of the hall and into the delegates lounge, where a TV was showing the speech with the sound turned mercifully low.

"Premier Is Harsh," read the headline in the *New York Times*, and the *Daily News* called the speech "a fist-waving Communist super-tirade." Secretary Herter described the oration as "a real declaration of war against the structure, the personnel and the location of the United Nations."

The bad reviews didn't bother Khrushchev. Bantering with reporters, he promised to deliver ten more speeches before he went home. "I want to justify my expense account," he explained, smiling. As it turned out, he wasn't joking. Over the next three weeks, he really *did* deliver ten more speeches, none quite so long as his first but many just as nasty.

Speaking in support of a resolution to admit Communist China to the United Nations, he began reasonably enough, pointing out that a country containing nearly a quarter of the human race ought to have U.N. representation. But soon he soared into a full-blown rant, attacking Taiwan's dictator Chiang Kai-shek as a "political corpse," berating Hammarskjold as a "loyal servant of monopoly capitalism," and denouncing racism in the United States: "Negroes are lynched and hanged only because they are black. . . . Negro children cannot attend schools together with whites. Is this not a shame for a civilized society?"

When Khrushchev called Spanish dictator Francisco Franco "the butcher of the Spanish people," Frederick Boland, the Irish president of the General Assembly, rapped his gavel and instructed the premier to restrain from "offensive remarks of a personal character."

"Why didn't you stop the representative of the United States when he slandered China?" Khrushchev demanded, referring to American attacks on Mao's regime.

Like many a populist demagogue before and since, Khrushchev fancied himself as a rare straight talker who dared to utter plain truths in a place full of mealy-mouthed pedants. His harangues were designed to advance two goals—to court the newly liberated nations of the Third World and to force Hammarskjold out of office for opposing Khrushchev's wishes in the Congo. Neither plan succeeded. The General Assembly overwhelmingly rejected a Soviet motion to censure Hammarskjold. On that issue, and many others, most Third World nations voted with the West to defeat the Soviet-backed resolutions. Except for one symbolic victory on a vote against colonialism, the delegates rejected all of Khrushchev's proposals.

He did not lose graciously. When his proposal for general disarmament was defeated, he launched into a frightening tirade, beginning with his familiar boast that the Soviets were churning out rockets "like sausages," then denouncing the Western nations that attacked the Soviet Union in 1918. "We routed their troops and threw them out like scum from our sacred soil. Should the imperialists repeat their aggression now, we shall defeat them again, but on a more advanced level," he bellowed. "Some gentleman will immediately jabber that Khrushchev is threatening somebody. No, Khrushchev is not threatening anybody, but is forecasting your real future. . . . Should war break out, many of those sitting here will be among the missing."

Khrushchev wasn't the only statesman to deliver long, combative speeches to the General Assembly. His new friend Fidel Castro took the podium, announced that he would "endeavor to be brief" and then delivered a four-hour attack on various enemies of humanity, including "monopolists," "imperialists," and the New York City police.

Khrushchev sat patiently through Castro's oratory and told reporters he'd be delighted to hear more. But he wasn't so patient with speakers who opposed him. When Hammarskjold addressed the Assembly, Khrushchev began pounding his desk with both fists. Watching from the next seat, Gromyko felt obliged to begin beating his desk too, although with noticeably less *brio* than his boss. Soon Communist delegations around the hall were pounding their desks in unison with Khrushchev's drumming—proving their status as Soviet puppets. Three days later, Khrushchev again pounded his fists on his desk, this time to protest a speech by Macmillan that nearly everyone else thought was rather tepid. And when Macmillan stated that the world was disappointed at the failure of the Paris summit, Khrushchev leaped to his feet. "You send your planes over our territory!" he shouted. "You are guilty of aggression!" Boland banged his gavel and Khrushchev sat down.

Sergei Khrushchev claims that his father drummed his desk and heckled his opponents because he'd read that "fights and mutual insults were normal conduct among Western legislators." But there is another possible explanation, one that's familiar to the parents of unruly two-year-olds: Perhaps the premier got cranky because he needed a nap. During the 1959 trip, Henry Cabot Lodge noted that Khrushchev's tantrums tended to come when he got tired. In New York in 1960, the premier was perpetually tired. His problem was the noise outside the Soviet mission.

"I had to listen to the nerve-racking unceasing roar of the motorcycles," he recalled in his memoirs. "These belonged to the policemen who were protecting me. They kept changing shifts all through the night. You can't imagine what a racket they made. . . . It would first sound like people clapping, then like gunfire, then like artillery shells exploding—and all right under my window. It was impossible to sleep. No matter how tired I was, I'd lie there awake, either listening to one shift leaving or waiting for another shift to arrive."

It was enough to make even the most diplomatic dictator a bit irritable.

By the end of September, most of the other heads of state had returned home, but Khrushchev remained in New York, perhaps just to irritate the Americans who were obviously eager to see him leave. He was, he later admitted, getting bored. He was a dictator, accustomed to issuing orders, and he wasn't cut out to be one member of a large legislature, particularly a legislature that kept voting against him. As he sat through the long, tedious debates, his mind wandered, drifting into strange fantasies. He stared at the bald head of the Spanish delegate sitting in front of him and remembered that he'd promised Dolores Ibarruri—the famous Spanish Communist known as La Pasionaria, now exiled in Moscow—that he'd do something to torment her enemies, the Spanish fascists. "In my thoughts, I was pecking away at the bald spot on his head with my nose," he revealed in his memoirs, "and I imagined the face of my friend Dolores Ibarruri beaming with pleasure."

Let the record show that he did not act on that bizarre fantasy. But one day, as he walked back to his seat after delivering a speech, he noticed that the Spanish delegation was not applauding him. He stopped in the aisle and screamed insults at them, shaking his finger in the face of a Spanish diplomat. The Spaniard responded by standing up and shaking his finger at Khrushchev and the two men proceeded to yell at each other until security guards hustled in to separate them before they came to blows.

By then, Khrushchev had become a modern version of a classic comic character—the obnoxious guest who will not leave. He understood that role and he enjoyed playing it for laughs. When a reporter asked when he was leaving, he replied, "No longer than two weeks after the session ends." Stunned, another reporter asked if he was kidding. "I was very much in earnest," Khrushchev replied. "I just might throw in another week."

On October 6, Khrushchev's eighteenth day in New York, CBS reporter Daniel Schorr interviewed the premier at a reception in the Soviet mission. "Is this your farewell?" Schorr asked. "Are you leaving soon?"

"Would you like me to leave?" Khrushchev asked.

"Speaking purely personally and frankly, of course," Schorr said, "you are a guest in my home . . . "

"No, you are a guest in *my* home," Khrushchev replied, referring of course to the Soviet mission.

"All right, I am a guest in *your* home, which is situated in *my* homeland," Schorr said. "I want you to stay as long as you like, but I have to stay as long as you do and I have some important business in Europe."

"That's frank enough. I get the point," Khrushchev replied. "I'll think it over."

"You know, I am a slave of both capitalism and communism," Schorr said. "You would consider me a capitalist slave but I am also a slave of communism because I have to wait for you to go so I can go."

"You'd better get used to being a slave of communism," Khrushchev replied. "It's growing, you know, and there will be more of it."

Finally, on October 10, the Soviets announced that the premier would fly home on October 13. That news generated palpable relief among U.N.

delegates, State Department officials and the overworked New York police. But as it turned out, Khrushchev would stay long enough to stun the world with what would soon become the most famous act of his life—the banging of the shoe.

80. THE BANGING OF THE SHOE

The day of the legendary shoe banging, October 12, 1960, began calmly enough.

Khrushchev arrived at the United Nations in a jolly mood and paused in the foyer to banter with reporters. When an Indian woman wearing a colorful sari approached, the premier smiled, pressed his hands together prayerfully, touched them to his forehead, and bowed deeply. Somebody shouted a question about disarmament and Khrushchev started clowning.

"If I were to disarm every day, I'd be totally disarmed," he said, and then patted his pockets like a cop frisking a suspect. He pulled an eyeglass case out of one pocket. "This is my only weapon," he announced, but then he found a small penknife in another pocket. "I have this," he said, grinning. "Can you puncture a sack such as Wadsworth with this?"

James J. Wadsworth was the American delegate to the U.N.

Pleased with his spontaneous shtick, Khrushchev strolled into the General Assembly chamber, where he delivered a speech in support of a Soviet resolution condemning colonialism. It was a short speech, at least by Khrushchev's standards, but he managed to include not only the requisite attacks on "the imperialists and the colonialists" and their "policy of plunder, rapine and murder" but also a spirited denunciation of the United States for exterminating Indians, enslaving Africans, and barring black children from attending school with whites.

"Such is the true face of the 'civilization' that the colonialist powers boast so much about!" he snipped. "A fine sort of civilization, indeed!"

It was, the *New York Times* reported, "a relatively calm speech." So far, the premier was, as the *Daily News* put it, "on his good behavior." But that lasted only until a Filipino delegate had the audacity to suggest that the Soviet Union might not be entirely innocent of the sin of colonialism.

Lorenzo Sumulong stood at the podium to announce that the Philippines would vote for the Soviet resolution on colonialism. But the resolution should be expanded, Sumulong suggested, to include the people of Eastern Europe, "who have been deprived of their political and civil rights and have been swallowed up by the Soviet Union."

Khrushchev leaped to his feet, waving his hand and demanding a chance to respond. Frederick Boland, the Irish president of the General Assembly, agreed. Khrushchev walked to the podium and waved Sumulong away with a contemptuous flick of his hand. Then he denounced the Filipino as a "fawning lackey of the American imperialists." Without even bothering to defend the Soviet occupation of Eastern Europe, he stormed back to his seat.

Sumulong stepped back to the dais and resumed his speech. He detected hypocrisy, he said, when he heard the Soviets "bleeding over the plight of colonial peoples while being the greatest colonial power in the world."

Enraged, Khrushchev jumped up again, his face beet red. He had something in his hand and he waved it like a club. It was his right shoe, a tan loafer. For a moment, *Washington Post* reporter Murrey Marder thought Khrushchev was going to throw it at the podium. But he didn't. Instead, the premier sat down and began banging the shoe on his desk. His first few blows were mere taps, but then he pounded harder and harder, louder and louder. Soon the other delegates were turning around, craning their necks to see who was making such a racket.

"He banged to a regular rhythm, like the pendulum of a metronome," his bodyguard, Nikolai Zakharov, later recalled. "That was the moment that entered world history as Khrushchev's famous shoe. A sensation was born right before my eyes."

Sitting next to Khrushchev, Andrei Gromyko watched with a pained look on his face. He knew what he had to do but he wasn't happy about it. He reached down, slipped off one of his shoes, and began to tap it on his desk, as quietly and unobtrusively as possible.

Khrushchev kept banging away, grinning with glee. What was he thinking? He never explained his action in his memoir, simply noting that "I took off my shoe and pounded on the desk so that our protest would be louder." But his son Sergei later ventured an explanation: "Father categorically disagreed with the words coming from the rostrum and decided to show how indignant he was. Such a little devil always lurked inside him. It peeped out now and pushed Father into some minor hooliganism."

After a few moments, Khrushchev slipped his shoe back on his foot and stood up to demand another chance to reply to Sumulong. The long-suffering Boland agreed and Khrushchev took the podium for the third time that afternoon. He didn't even mention his outburst. Instead, he offered a painfully condescending "defense" of Sumulong: "He is not a bad man," Khrushchev said, but he's an American puppet, and his country, which had been an American colony until 1946, is not yet truly independent. "It has to be peered at through a microscope, this independence," he said sarcastically. He invited Sumulong to visit the Soviet Union to "understand what freedom is" and then ambled back to his seat.

The debate continued. Other delegates rose to make speeches, including Francis O. Wilcox, America's assistant secretary of state. "Everyone here in this Assembly hall," Wilcox said, "is fully aware of the sad fact that there are a number of states in Eastern Europe which do not have their complete independence."

At that, a Romanian delegate, Eduard Mezincescu, stood up and demanded the right to answer this "slander and calumny." Khrushchev stood too, and once again he held a shoe in his hand. Apparently he'd slipped it off again. But this time he refrained from banging it and sat back down to watch Mezincescu take on Boland.

"Where are we?" the Romanian bellowed. "Are we sitting in the Senate of the United States?"

Boland pounded his gavel. Mezincescu yelled louder. Boland pounded harder. Mezincescu shouted something about "the Irish people" and Boland smashed the gavel down so hard that it cracked and its head went flying over Boland's shoulder.

That was it. Boland called a recess. The most bizarre and tempestuous day in the history of the United Nations was over.

On his way out of the hall, Khrushchev told a reporter that the broken gavel was symbolic. "It shows how shaky the UN is," he said without betraying even a hint of shame.

81. I FEEL VICIOUS, MALICIOUS, AND LOW!

Khrushchev's cronies felt obliged to congratulate him on his brilliant performance but privately they were appalled at the sight of Lenin's heir hammering his shoe on a desk in the United Nations.

"We were stunned at Khrushchev's behavior," recalled Arkady Shevchenko, the young Soviet diplomat who'd met the premier on the *Baltika*. "At the Mission at the close of the session, everyone was embarrassed and upset. Gromyko, noted for his strict, impeccable behavior, was white-lipped with agitation. But Khrushchev acted as if nothing at all had happened. He was laughing loudly and joking. He said that it had been necessary to 'inject a little life into the stuffy atmosphere of the UN.' He did not seem to realize or care what the other UN members would think about him in the wake of this escapade."

When Khrushchev learned that his aide, Oleg Troyanovsky, hadn't seen his latest performance, he expressed his condolences. "Oh, you really missed something! It was such fun! The UN is a sort of parliament, you know, where the minority has to make itself heard one way or another. We're in the minority for the time being, but not for long."

At dinner that night, Hungarian Premier Janos Kadar worked up enough courage to kid Khrushchev about his behavior. "Comrade Khrushchev, remember shortly after banging your shoe, you went to the rostrum to make a point of order? Well, at that moment our foreign minister, Comrade Sik, turned to me and said, 'Do you think he had time to put his shoe on, or did he go barefoot?'"

Around the table, Khrushchev's colleagues snickered, and Troyanovsky thought that maybe his boss finally realized that he'd gone too far.

But if Khrushchev felt embarrassed, he didn't show it the next morning at the U.N. When Boland took the podium, the delegates greeted him with an ovation and Khrushchev protested by thumping his fists on his desk.

The premier was wildly misjudging his audience. He thought the Third World delegates would appreciate his belligerent tactics toward the colonialist West. But the new delegates were proud to be part of this prestigious world legislature, and they resented Khrushchev's attempts to mock it. Sekou Toure, the leftist president of Guinea, rose that morning to deplore the previous day's tantrums as misguided attempts "to feed the fires of discontent and disturbance in this place." And a representative from Nepal attacked Khrushchev's behavior, denouncing anything "which has the effect of lowering UN prestige and dignity."

Compounding his folly, Khrushchev protested the Nepalese delegate's speech by drumming his fists on his desk once again.

That morning, Khrushchev won his only victory of the session when the General Assembly passed the Soviet anticolonialism resolution. In the afternoon, he waddled to the podium one last time to make a farewell speech that turned out to be as belligerent as the rest of his oratory. He demanded that the Assembly condemn the United States for the U–2 flights. When Wadsworth, the American representative, rose to remind him that the Security Council had already rejected that proposal twice, Khrushchev flew into a rage, calling the Security Council "a spittoon." He denounced the U–2 affair as an "insolent act of aggression," called Eisenhower a liar, and promised that another spy flight would mean war.

"If you want a war," he bellowed, "keep on provoking us and you will get a war."

When a British representative protested the premier's remarks, Khrushchev informed him what would happen to England in a nuclear holocaust. "Britain," he said, "will cease to exist the first day of the war."

After that he calmed down, concluding his speech with something approaching an apology: "I beg you not to be offended if I said anything in not quite the way I should have." He even alluded to the previous day's tantrums: "I hurt the Filipino representative a little and he hurt me. I am a young parliamentarian; he is an old hand. Let us learn from each other."

Five minutes after his U–2 resolution was defeated, he was out the door, never to return again. That night, he flew to Moscow on the TU–114, opting for a quick trip home over the prospect of ten days of shuffleboard on the *Baltika*. He'd already been away for thirty-five days—ten of them at sea.

When he landed in Moscow, he was greeted by the usual delegation of dignitaries. He hugged his comrades from the Presidium, shook hands with the Cuban ambassador and then greeted Tommy Thompson, the American ambassador.

"Did you enjoy your trip?" Thompson asked.

"Certainly, certainly," Khrushchev said, grinning and pumping Thompson's hand. Then, perhaps recalling that Thompson had accompanied him on his 1959 trip across America, he added, "But it wasn't the same at all—not like last time."

Returning home in 1959, Khrushchev had hustled from the airport to the sports stadium to deliver a long, lyrical account of his adventures in America. In 1960, his report to the crowd in the stadium was relentlessly grim. "Today, the United States is a reactionary state dominated by monopoly capital," he said, and he described New York as a vision of hell: "It seems to embody the ugliness and degeneration of capitalism. . . . The streets are literally jammed with a vast number of automobiles. And automobiles, as is known, use gasoline for fuel. That is why the entire atmosphere is poisoned. To put it in a nutshell, New York is a horrifying city."

He did not mention his shoe-banging but assured the crowd that he had represented his country "with honor and dignity."

The Soviet media also refrained from informing the citizenry about Khrushchev's novel use of his footwear, although *Pravda* included a cryptic allusion to the event: "A fresh wind rushed into the East River building. The devils squirmed and wriggled as the head of the Soviet delegation, brushing aside all subtleties of protocol, put his foot on their tails."

Perhaps the Soviets were wise to avoid mentioning the incident. In the United States, the banging of the shoe soon became the most famous act of Khrushchev's life, an indelible image that captured the absurd excesses of his outsize personality—his hot temper, his childishness, his churlishness, his buffoonery. It was an image that was both hilarious and frightening—a pudgy, bald dictator armed with atomic bombs banging his shoe like a petulant two-year-old.

In late November 1960, a few weeks after Kennedy was elected president, one of his aides, Walt Rostow, informed a Soviet diplomat what conditions would have to be met before Kennedy would agree to a meeting with Khrushchev: The premier would have to release the RB–47 fliers, agree to a test ban accord, and come to the meeting "wearing his shoes."

Not long after Khrushchev left New York, the editors of *Esquire* magazine asked novelist Saul Bellow to speculate on "why the Soviet premier used his shoe to make his point." Bellow interrupted work on his novel *Herzog* to analyze the dictator in an essay entitled "Literary Notes on Khrushchev."

"It's hard to know whether the Khrushchev we saw banging with his shoe at the UN Assembly is the 'real' Khrushchev," Bellow wrote. "But one of the privileges of power seems to be the privilege of direct emotional self-expression. . . . Masked in smiles and peasant charm, or in anger, the Russian premier releases his deepest feelings and if we are not shaken by them it is because we are not in close touch with reality."

Western politicians strive for dignity and seek to avoid unpleasant confrontations, Bellow wrote, and that is precisely why Khrushchev enjoyed shocking them with explosions of unrestrained emotion. "Perhaps Khrushchev feels himself, or attempts to reach himself, in these outbursts. And perhaps it is when the entire world is watching him soar and he is touching the limits of control that he feels most alive."

But Khrushchev's outbursts were not merely tantrums: "This, friends, is art," he wrote. The premier displayed his scorn for the West by playing both "villain and buffoon" in a "brutal and angry comedy." The banging of the shoe, the singing of the Internationale, the feisty press conference on the balcony—all these were, Bellow believed, the work of "a comic artist in a show written and directed by himself."

Bellow, a future Nobel laureate, identified Khrushchev as a comic actor in the theater of the absurd. But it took the mad geniuses at *Mad* magazine to actually cast Khrushchev as the lead in a cold war musical comedy.

By the early 1960s, *Mad* had outgrown its comic book origins to become America's leading satire magazine, and it transformed Khrushchev's antics at the United Nations into a parody of the popular musical *West Side Story*. Using Mort Drucker's brilliant caricatures of Khrushchev, Castro, Macmillan, and other leaders, *Mad* created "East Side Story," a nine-page tale of rival cold war street gangs eager to rumble at the United Nations.

In the opening scene, Khrushchev and his Commie cronies, Castro, Gromyko, and Tito, dance across the U.N. plaza while the premier leads them in song:

When you're a Red,
You're a Red all the way
From your first Party purge
To your last power play!
When you're a Red
You've got agents galore;

You give prizes for peace
While they stir up a war!

After that showstopper, Khrushchev's gang confronts its rivals, led by Macmillan, de Gaulle, and Adlai Stevenson, who had become the American U.N. ambassador.

"Why don't you come off it, Nikita?" Stevenson taunts.

"I'll tell you why," Khrushchev replies, and he sings his explanation to the tune of *West Side Story*'s "I Feel Pretty," while he dances through the fountain at the U.N. and emerges, dripping wet and clutching his famous shoe.

I feel vicious,
Oh so vicious,
I feel vicious, malicious, and low!
How delicious,
Just to know that I am hated so!

82. WHY DON'T YOU DROP BY AND SEE ME SOMETIME?

Nine months later, in the summer of 1961, with Eisenhower retired and Kennedy in the White House, Nikita Khrushchev invited John J. McCloy to his dacha on the Black Sea.

They'd met before, at Averell Harriman's cocktail party in New York during Khrushchev's first trip to America, and McCloy, then chairman of Chase Manhattan Bank, tried to convince Khrushchev that capitalists did not control America or its foreign policy. Now McCloy was serving as President Kennedy's envoy to a disarmament conference in Moscow, which undercut his argument a bit. The Moscow talks did not go well, with McCloy engaged in fruitless semantic hairsplitting with Khrushchev's disarmament negotiator, Valerian A. Zorin.

"For a week, the two men argued over language, mechanically reading prepared speeches to each other," wrote Kai Bird, McCloy's biographer. "Zorin continued to insist on the phrase 'general and complete disarmament' while McCloy held to his own formulation of 'total and universal disarmament.' The Russian translations of the two phrases were actually identical, so the argument seemed rather nonsensical."

When McCloy traveled from Moscow to Khrushchev's dacha, he found the premier in a playful mood. Khrushchev challenged McCloy to a game of tennis and invited him to swim in his pool. He even lent the capitalist one of his gargantuan black boxer-style bathing suits, and they posed for pictures bobbing around in the pool.

Later the two men sat down for a serious talk. They discussed disarmament and Berlin and President Kennedy. When the subject of nuclear war came up, as it inevitably did when Khrushchev met Americans, the premier bragged that his scientists were about to test a powerful new hundred-megaton bomb. At one point, Khrushchev brought up Dwight Eisenhower. The premier praised Ike's genius as a general—his masterful leadership of the Normandy invasion and his decision to allow the Red Army the honor of liberating Berlin in 1945. After extolling Eisenhower, Khrushchev said he regretted that the U–2 incident had scuttled plans for Ike's trip to Russia and he suggested that perhaps the former president could visit sometime soon. He was certain, he told McCloy, that Eisenhower would be received warmly.

"He seemed to be personally very much interested in having such a visit take place," McCloy later recalled.

When he returned to the United States, McCloy dutifully relayed Khrushchev's message to Eisenhower.

"Maybe you won't believe it," Ike told his son John that day as they drove home from a golf course, "but this fellow Khrushchev has had the temerity to hint that he would like to reinstate the invitation to go to Moscow."

The unexpected invitation left Eisenhower flabbergasted. Khrushchev had ruined the Paris summit with a tirade against him, denounced him as "stinky" at a press conference, then called him a liar and threatened to start a nuclear war in a speech at the United Nations. It was astounding that Khrushchev should invite Ike to drop by for a friendly visit.

"Of course, I'd never do it," Eisenhower told his son, "but why Khrushchev would bring up such a thing sort of beats me."

Eisenhower sat there for a long pensive moment, pondering the baffling news. Ike was still mystified by the puzzling, unpredictable, funny, nasty, prickly, charming, insecure, obnoxious, frustrating man he had accidentally invited to America two long, long years earlier.

EPILOGUE: "LIFE IS A COSMIC JOKE"

In October 1962, I was a fifth grader at St. Boniface School in Sea Cliff, New York, and the world was on the brink of nuclear annihilation.

"Boys and girls, your attention please," said Sister Superior's voice coming from the brown, boxy speaker above the blackboard. "I am in my office listening to the news on the radio. As some of you may know, the Russians have put nuclear missiles in Communist Cuba. President Kennedy has sent our navy to blockade Cuba. Now, Russian ships are heading toward our ships. If they do not stop, we will shoot at them, which might cause a nuclear war that could lead to the end of the world as prophesied in the Bible."

The end of the world? That certainly caught our attention. Since kindergarten we'd practiced for nuclear war by crouching in the hallway in the duck-and-cover position. But nobody, not even the dumbest kids, actually believed that would save us from an atomic bomb.

"Boys and girls," Sister Superior continued, "we may not have enough time to walk from our classrooms to the church, so let us now kneel beside our desks and say a rosary."

Not enough time to get to the church? It was only a few blocks away. Obviously this was serious. We knelt and prayed. The hard wood floor hurt my bony knees but I ignored the pain and prayed like I'd never prayed before.

I knew nothing about geopolitics. I didn't know that the United States had tried to overthrow Castro by organizing the Bay of Pigs invasion. I didn't know that Khrushchev had secretly sent dozens of nuclear missiles to Cuba to defend it against another attack, and to counter the American missiles in Turkey. I didn't know that U–2 flights had discovered the missiles. Or that the Soviets had shot down a U–2 over Cuba. Or that the Soviet ambassador had informed Robert Kennedy that Soviet ships would refuse to stop at the American blockade. Or that, for the first time in history, America's military was on DEFCON–2, a status just short of all-out war, and planes loaded with atomic bombs were circling in the air, awaiting orders to hit targets in Cuba and the Soviet Union. All I knew was that Khrushchev, the nutty Russian who banged his shoe at the United Nations, seemed crazy enough to blow up the world.

In Moscow, the man who'd banged his shoe at the U.N. convened a meeting of his advisers. "In order to save the world," he told them, "we must retreat."

The Soviet ships heading toward Cuba stopped before they reached the American blockade. Confrontation was avoided while Khrushchev and Kennedy cut a deal: Khrushchev agreed to remove all nuclear weapons from Cuba; Kennedy publicly pledged never to invade Cuba and secretly promised to remove American missiles from Turkey.

And the world did not end.

In Havana, Castro was enraged that Khrushchev had backed down. "No balls," he said.

In Washington, Kennedy crowed about his victory over Khrushchev. "I cut off his balls," he told friends.

In Moscow, Khrushchev told the Supreme Soviet that he had saved the world from "a crisis that threatened general thermonuclear war."

Many of Khrushchev's colleagues disagreed, viewing the outcome as a national humiliation. The premier had powerful enemies in high places— old Stalinists, generals angry at his cuts in the military budget, party hacks irked at his efforts to curtail their privileges. His enemies had tried to oust him in 1957 and failed, but his handling of the missile crisis gave them more ammunition. So did the failure of his agricultural policies, which led to food shortages. And so did his behavior, which had become increasingly irascible and unpredictable.

Quietly, carefully, his underlings plotted against him. On October 12, 1964, Leonid Brezhnev, the number two man in the Kremlin, called Khrushchev at his dacha and summoned him to a meeting. When the premier arrived, Brezhnev and the other members of the Presidium denounced him, enumerating his sins: He was arrogant, incompetent, megalomaniacal. They said he'd abandoned the teachings of Lenin, instituted his own cult of personality, botched the Cuban missile showdown, and acted like a fool at the U.N. Brezhnev also noted that Khrushchev had once compared the members of the Central Committee to "dogs peeing against curbstones."

"Your behavior is incomprehensible," Brezhnev said, and he suggested that Khrushchev "voluntarily" retire.

Too exhausted and depressed to resist, Khrushchev agreed. "I'll do what's best for the Party," he said, with tears in his eyes.

To Khrushchev, the fact that he could be fired was a perverse proof of his success. "Could anyone have dreamed of telling Stalin that he didn't suit us anymore and suggesting he retire?" he asked his friend Mikoyan that night. "Not even a wet spot would have remained where we had been standing. Now everything is different. The fear is gone and we can talk as equals. That's my contribution."

He was right. The men who overthrew Khrushchev did not kill him or send him to the gulag. Instead, they gave him a pension and a dacha outside Moscow. But his name and face immediately disappeared from the media and his old comrades stopped visiting. At seventy, the former premier became a nonperson. He sank into a depression that lasted for months. When a school principal asked one of Khrushchev's grandsons what the old man was doing in his retirement, the boy answered, "Grandfather cries."

His wife and children encouraged him to take up hobbies. He tried fishing but found it boring: "You sit there feeling like an absolute idiot! You can even hear the fish laughing at you underwater." He dabbled in photography, took long walks, and planted a garden, raising potatoes, pumpkins, and, of course, corn. He read *Pravda* and scoffed at its absurd propaganda: "This is just garbage. Who will believe it?"

He built bonfires and stared into them, brooding about the past. He was obsessed with Stalin's crimes and his own complicity in them. A visitor once asked Khrushchev what he regretted. "Most of all the blood," the old man answered. "My arms are up to the elbows in blood. That is the most terrible thing that lies in my soul."

In 1966, his family gave him a tape recorder and he began dictating his memoirs. Finally he'd found a hobby that engaged his restless mind. He talked to the tape recorder for hours. At first he concentrated on his obsession—the horrors of the Stalin years—but soon he began jumping from topic to topic as the story of his extraordinary life poured out of him in a stream of consciousness. Over the next three years, he recorded 800,000 words. His son Sergei and a typist friend began transcribing the tapes into a manuscript that grew to 3,500 pages.

The KGB knew what he was doing, having bugged his house and assigned "guards" to watch him. In 1967, he was summoned to the Kremlin and three of his old protégés ordered him to stop writing his memoir and surrender the manuscript.

"I refuse to obey you," he replied. The order was unconstitutional, he told them, and so were the KGB bugs. "You stuck listening devices all over the dacha—even in the bathroom. You spend the people's money to eavesdrop on my farts."

In 1970, the KGB demanded that Sergei hand over the manuscript. He complied, knowing that a copy had already been smuggled to the West. In December 1970, the first volume of *Khrushchev Remembers* was published in the United States and serialized in *Life* magazine. Soon it became a best-seller in a dozen countries but not in Russia, where it went unpublished until the 1990s. Reviewers warned that the book was sometimes inaccurate, evasive, and self-serving but praised it as a salty, compelling, and important look at the secret inner world of the Kremlin.

"The book transfixed me; it seized me by the lapels, forced me rudely into my chair and held me there fascinated until its tale was done," wrote the *New York Times* reviewer, Christopher Lehmann-Haupt. "What makes

Khrushchev Remembers irresistible to read is the pungency and immediacy of Khrushchev's personality."

In early September 1971, Khrushchev suffered a heart attack and was driven to a hospital. A few days later, on September 11, he died. The old Bolshevik was seventy-seven.

Not one of his old comrades attended his funeral. He was buried without fanfare in a cemetery surrounded by soldiers of the Red Army, who were there not to honor their former commander in chief but to keep mourners away. The man who'd led the Soviet Union for a decade was still a nonperson and would remain one until the late 1980s, when Premier Mikhail Gorbachev, who thought himself a Khrushchev-style reformer, resurrected his memory.

Pravda reported Khrushchev's passing in a one-sentence notice, but American papers were far more generous. The *New York Times* published a half dozen articles, including an analysis by veteran Moscow correspondent Harry Schwartz, entitled "We Know Now That He Was a Giant Among Men." Khrushchev was a demagogue who brought the world to the brink of nuclear war during the Cuban missile crisis, Schwartz wrote, but he had transformed the Soviet Union: "He let in fresh air and fresh ideas, producing changes which time already has shown are irreversible and fundamental."

"He was an authentic person, not a tyrant, not a zealot, not an automaton, not a clerk," a *Washington Post* editorial noted. "He was in a peculiar sense a great man."

Khrushchev's death gave the reporters who'd covered the "surreal extravaganza" of his 1959 trip a chance to recycle some of their fondest memories. "No world statesman would have felt such utter disappointment at not going to Disneyland that great tears formed in the corner of his eyes," Harrison Salisbury wrote in the *Times*. "Nor is it likely that any other world statesman would have publicly threatened Jovian retaliation of missiles if Henry Cabot Lodge did not manage to treat him with a bit more politeness."

In the *Post*, Chalmers Roberts recounted the story of Khrushchev's tantrums in Los Angeles and his clowning on the train to San Francisco. "He was a master of theatrics, turning rage or laughter or charm on or off at will and always to a purpose." But the trip was more than merely theatrical: "The American visit of Nikita Khrushchev was one of the most profoundly important trips ever taken by a leading statesman. Khrushchev would never admit it but the sight of America altered his view of this country and its power and potential."

If the 1959 trip taught Khrushchev something about America, it also taught America something about Khrushchev. The hated enemy was a man not a monster—a man who could be funny, charming, nasty, and frightening, sometimes simultaneously.

Another effect of Khrushchev's visits was more subtle. The surreal spectacle of a dictator armed with nuclear weapons banging his shoe or throwing a tantrum about Disneyland contributed to an immeasurable but palpable feeling that the world had gone mad, that some angry fool might soon annihilate humanity in the most absurd manner. This feeling was manifested in the black humor of the early 1960s—Joseph Heller's 1961 comic novel *Catch–22*, Kurt Vonnegut's 1963 end-of-the-world novel *Cat's Cradle*, and Stanley Kubrick's 1964 cinematic comedy of nuclear apocalypse, *Dr. Strangelove*.

In fact, Kubrick swiped one of Khrushchev's jokes for *Strangelove*. In 1960, the premier amused the Supreme Soviet with his comic recitation of the contents of Francis Gary Powers's survival pack—7,500 rubles, two dozen gold coins, seven women's rings—then added, "Perhaps the pilot was to have flown even higher—to Mars—and intended to seduce Martian ladies." In *Strangelove*, Slim Pickens, playing an American airman flying off to bomb Russia, recites the contents of *his* survival pack: "one hundred dollars in rubles, one hundred dollars in gold, five packs of chewin' gum, one issue of prophylactics, three pairs of nylon stockings." Then he adds, "Shoot, a guy could have a pretty good weekend in Vegas with all that stuff!"

On the day Khrushchev died, the president of the United States was the man he'd called "that son of a bitch Richard Nixon." The two men had much in common. Like Khrushchev, Nixon made a diplomatic trip that amazed the world—traveling to China to meet Mao Zedong in 1972. Like Khrushchev, Nixon was driven from office by lower-ranking politicians appalled by his misbehavior. Like Khrushchev, Nixon eased the psychic pain of forced retirement by writing a series of memoirs. In one book, *Leaders*, he described Khrushchev as driven by "a pervasive sense of insecurity," a statement that was as true of Nixon as it was of Khrushchev.

None of the other Americans Khrushchev encountered in his travels rose so high or fell so far as Nixon. But life tossed many of them in unexpected directions, as life tends to do.

Henry Cabot Lodge became President Kennedy's ambassador to South Vietnam in 1963, and he helped to plan the coup that overthrew the country's corrupt president, Ngo Dinh Diem, a few months later. During the coup, Diem called Lodge to plead for help. Lodge told him to call back if he feared for his safety. The next morning Diem was dead. But the generals who took his place proved no better at waging war against Communist guerrillas. In his final press conference before leaving Vietnam in 1967, Lodge ventured a prediction about the enemy: "They cannot win and we cannot be pushed out." He was wrong on both counts.

Roswell Garst, Khrushchev's corn guru and one of the great talkers of his time, contracted cancer of the vocal cords in 1962 and lost the ability to speak. A year later, he bought an artificial voice machine that enabled him to talk again, albeit in a mechanical monotone, and he kept up a stream of chatter, much of it about corn, until he died in 1977.

Los Angeles mayor Norris Poulson lost his bid for reelection in 1961 but the main issue wasn't Khrushchev, it was trash. Poulson had established a trash collection system that required two cans, one for rubbish and one for recyclables. His opponent, Sam Yorty, declared that it was outrageous that housewives had to sort their garbage, and he promised to let them throw it all into one can. Yorty won.

Francis Gary Powers was released from a Soviet prison in 1962, exchanged for a Soviet spy imprisoned in the United States. A few months after his return, Powers divorced his wife, Barbara, who got her revenge by writing *Spy Wife*, the tell-all memoir featuring a lurid sex scene in Lubyanka prison. Powers later remarried and settled in Los Angeles, where he became a helicopter pilot for KNBC-TV, covering traffic jams and car chases. In 1977, he was killed when his traffic helicopter crashed in a Little League baseball field in Encino.

In 1985, at the age of eighty-six, Ezra Taft Benson, the agriculture secretary who handed Khrushchev a turkey at the Beltsville farm, became the thirteenth "president, prophet, seer and revelator" of the Mormon Church. He held that position until his death in 1994, although he had long since lost his ability to walk, talk, feed himself, dress himself, or recognize close relatives—a condition that caused a grandson to publicly compare him to the geriatric leaders of the Soviet Union.

Marilyn Monroe, who dazzled the premier in Hollywood, died of an overdose of sleeping pills in 1962.

Dorothy Kilgallen, who mocked Nina Khrushchev's couture, died of an overdose of sleeping pills in 1965.

Ronald Reagan, the actor who refused to attend the Hollywood luncheon for Khrushchev, was elected president and invited Premier Mikhail Gorbachev to visit the United States. "I would like to take the Soviet leaders up in a helicopter over Los Angeles," Reagan said, inadvertently echoing Eisenhower. "I would point to all the small houses with swimming pools and I would say, 'Those are the workers' houses!'"

Shirley MacLaine, who danced the can-can for Khrushchev, won an Oscar in 1983 for her role in *Terms of Endearment*. She also wrote several memoirs, chronicling not only her current life but her many past lives, during which she'd been a harem dancer, a monk, a Moorish maiden, a Brazilian involved in voodoo, an American revolutionary, and Charlemagne's lover.

"These days, I'm laughing a lot," MacLaine told an interviewer in 1985.

"Do you know why?" the interviewer asked.

"Sure, I know why," MacLaine replied. "Life is a cosmic joke."

MacLaine's *Can-Can* costar, Frank Sinatra, continued recording hit songs, one of which turned out to have an unexpected effect on the history of the cold war. Titled "My Way," it was a brassy ode to pugnacious individuality, and it became Sinatra's signature song, famous all over the world. In October 1989, when Poland and Hungary began inching away from the Communist bloc, a reporter asked Soviet press secretary Gennadi Gerasimov if Gorbachev would invoke the Brezhnev doctrine—the 1968 declaration that the Soviets would use military force to defend Communism—and invade Poland or Hungary.

"You know the Frank Sinatra song, 'My Way'?" Gerasimov replied. "Hungary and Poland are doing it their way. We now have the Sinatra doctrine."

News that the Sinatra doctrine had replaced the Brezhnev doctrine emboldened dissidents throughout the Soviet empire. By the end of 1989, Communist governments had collapsed across Eastern Europe and gleeful Germans sledge-hammered the Berlin Wall into souvenir-sized chunks.

The Soviet republics of Lithuania, Latvia, and Estonia also opted to go their own way, and in 1991, the Soviet Union collapsed into fifteen separate countries.

On Christmas Day 1991, Gorbachev called President George H. W. Bush to wish him a Merry Christmas. Then he reached for a pen to sign the document that would officially end the existence of the nation known as the Union of Soviet Socialist Republics. As it happened, Gorbachev's pen was out of ink, so he borrowed one from the CNN crew that was covering the event. That pen worked. The Soviet Union was dead. It was seventy-four years old.

Sixteen years later, in 2007, as if to underscore the triumph of capitalism, Gorbachev appeared in advertisements for Louis Vuitton luggage. The ads showed the former Soviet premier sitting in the back of a limo with his Louis Vuitton bag, gazing out the window at what was left of the Berlin Wall.

On his trip across the United States in 1959, Nikita Khrushchev repeatedly informed Americans that their grandchildren would live under Communism. As it turned out, *his* grandchildren lived under capitalism, some in Russia, some in the United States. In 1991, Khrushchev's son Sergei moved to Providence, Rhode Island, to become a visiting scholar at Brown University's Thomas Watson Institute for International Studies, which had been founded by the man who hosted Nikita Khrushchev in the IBM cafeteria in 1959. While Sergei was in Providence, the Soviet Union died. Suddenly he was a man without a country and he remained at Brown, teaching and writing. In 1999, Sergei and his wife became American citizens. A few days later, an interviewer asked Sergei what he liked about America.

"I like Home Depot," he said.

"Why?"

"Because you can buy everything," he said. "You can go there and get anything that you can imagine."

I met Sergei in 2006, when he appeared at a symposium on the cold war at the National Archives, looking very much like his father. Also on the panel that day was Susan Eisenhower, who had met Nikita Khrushchev on her grandfather's farm in Gettysburg in 1959. An international business consultant, she noted with amusement that Sergei was an American citizen living in Rhode Island while she was married to a Russian and dividing her time between Washington and Moscow.

After the symposium, I interviewed Sergei and he invited me to come to Providence to watch his home movies of the 1959 trip. I arrived a few days after Christmas, carrying a plate of my wife's Christmas cookies. He picked me up at the airport, carrying two salami-and-cheese sandwiches, and we drove to his office at Brown. On the walls hung a dozen magazine covers bearing his father's picture. On the desk sat a coffee mug bearing an American flag. He turned on his home movie, which had been transferred to a DVD, and we watched it while eating the sandwiches and cookies. The movie showed the sights Sergei found interesting in America in 1959, the things he never saw back home—tollbooths, highway inter-changes, motorcycle cops, neon signs and endless billboards.

"We never experienced anything like this—it was all new for us," he said. "It was very similar to when Christopher Columbus arrived in the New World."

After living in the United States for more than fifteen years, Sergei noted with some chagrin that his fellow Americans tend to remember only one thing about his famous father: He banged his shoe at the United Nations.

Khrushchev's biographer, William Taubman, has noticed the same phenomenon. "Ask many Westerners, and even quite a few Russians, about the man who succeeded Stalin and then denounced him, who ruled the Soviet Union for a decade and brought the world to the nuclear brink in Cuba," Taubman wrote, "and what they remember most is the shoe."

As Shirley MacLaine said, "Life is a cosmic joke."

The phrase "Khrushchev banging his shoe" conjures up such a vivid mental image that many Americans believe they watched the event on tel-evision. Actually, no video camera caught the moment and the only pho-tograph of the incident shows the shoe sitting on Khrushchev's desk after he stopped pounding it. But people are convinced they saw the whole thing on TV.

"In each of my lectures, they ask about the shoe," Sergei told me. "I say, 'Please raise your hand if you saw it,' and many people raise their hands. They really think they saw it."

Khrushchev's shoe has become an icon of the cold war, a symbol not only of one man's bad temper, but of the bizarre madness of the first era in history when humans—flawed, angry, irrational humans—possessed the power to incinerate civilization.

"A shoe pounding the table was the distinctive sound of the 'cold' war, as much as the report of a gun was the sound of a 'hot' war," Nina L.

Khrushcheva, the premier's granddaughter, wrote in an essay in 2000. Khrushcheva, the daughter of Khrushchev's daughter Yulia, earned a Ph.D. in comparative literature at Princeton in 1998. Two years later, she wrote a semiotic analysis of Khrushchev's shoe, concluding that it has endured because it sums up the spirit of the age. "The best anecdote is always the one that reflects the morality and character of certain times. The shoe incident became a potent symbol of the cold war, probably the only war in which fear and humor peacefully coexisted."

Now Khrushchev's shoe has become part of pop culture. It inspired a million-dollar question on the TV quiz show *Who Wants to Be a Millionaire?* as well as a book on public speaking—*Khrushchev's Shoe: And Other Ways to Captivate an Audience of 1 to 1,000.* Ironically, a bogus version of the shoe-banging story found its way into a best-selling how-to book for aspiring capitalists, Mark McCormack's *What They Don't Teach You at Harvard Business School.* "Anger and other strong emotions can be effective negotiating tools, but only as a calculated act," McCormack wrote. "I read somewhere that a photo of Nikita Khrushchev's historic shoe-pounding incident at the United Nations revealed that he was still wearing both his shoes. A third 'for pounding only' shoe? That's calculation."

Of course, no such picture exists and there was no third shoe, but legends are more powerful than mere facts.

As legends go, the various versions of the shoe-banging story are fairly benign. It could have been worse. In 1982, the prestigious literary magazine *Paris Review* published a shocking account of Khrushchev's 1959 trip to America. Entitled "Ike and Nina," it was written by a professor who identified himself by the pseudonym "Paderewski" and claimed he'd served as a White House aide during the visit.

"My sole interest in coming forward at this late date," he wrote, "is to provide succeeding generations with a keener insight into the events of those tumultuous times."

After that innocuous beginning, Paderewski unleashed his bombshell: He had helped to facilitate a dangerous liaison between Dwight Eisenhower and Nina Khrushchev—an illicit affair consummated in the back of a limousine as Paderewski drove the lovers around the streets of Washington.

Khrushchev learned of the affair later, in Los Angeles, Paderewsi wrote. That's why the premier erupted in his famous temper tantrums and why he was so nasty at Camp David, and why he canceled Ike's visit to Moscow.

Paderewski's incredible tale explained many of the previously inexplicable events of the cold war. Suddenly the strange story of Khrushchev's behavior in America almost made sense.

Alas, none of it was true. Paderewski did not exist, and "Ike and Nina" was a fraud, a fake, a prank—a cheeky satirical short story by novelist T. Coraghessan Boyle.

Nikita Khrushchev's trips to the United States were bizarre, of course, but they weren't quite *that* bizarre.

ACKNOWLEDGMENTS

Many kind and generous people helped in the creation of this book and I'd like to thank them here.

Mary McGrory, Chalmers Roberts, Daniel Schorr, Murray Kempton, Ben Bradlee, Alexander Akalovsky, Susan Eisenhower, John Jay Daly, and Sergei Khrushchev took the time to share their recollections of the Khrushchev trips with me.

Miriam Kleiman guided me through the intricacies of the National Archives. Timothy Naftali of the Nixon Library uncovered old documents and e-mailed them to me. The folks at the Library of Congress periodicals room dug out countless old newspapers for me, and cheerfully fixed cranky microfilm machines. Charles "Stu" Kennedy, the founding genius of the Foreign Affairs Oral History Collection, steered me to interviews with diplomats who dealt with Khrushchev. My mother-in-law, Beatrice Oehl, provided generous hospitality during my research trips to New York. Jerry O'Brien, a barber/scholar, shared his many books on Marilyn Monroe and J. Edgar Hoover with me. Jerry is the proud owner of Hoover's back brace, which hangs on the wall of his barbershop, the Yankee Clipper in Rockville, Maryland, along with a gallery of photos of Marilyn.

My agent, Scott Mendel, took this bizarre book idea to the right editor, Clive Priddle of PublicAffairs, who immediately got it and signed on for the ride. Niki Papadopoulos, an unusually enthusiastic and energetic editor, located my worse prose and demanded that I do something about it, which made the book both shorter and better. Melissa Raymond oversaw the production of the book. Copy editor Chrisona Schmidt sharpened the manuscript, and Megan Holobowicz created the index.

My neighbor Dennis Ruggeri built the desk on which I wrote the book. My friends Todd Ruby, Peter Coras, and Susie and George Spangler rode to the rescue on those many scary occasions when my computer and I weren't getting along. George Ramick shot my picture, never an easy task. And my daughters, Caitlin and Emily, encouraged me and kept me laughing.

I was lucky and privileged to spend twenty-two years writing for one of the world's greatest newspapers, the *Washington Post*, and I'd like to thank Ben Bradlee for hiring me. I'd also like to thank the many *Post* people who taught me about writing and about the world—Len Downie, Jay Lovinger, Steve Petranek, Henry Allen, Jeanne McManus, Walt Harrington, David Finkel, Peter Perl, Deborah Heard, Paul Richard, Steve Coll, Lynn Medford, Steve Reiss, Linton Weeks, John Cotter, Bill O'Brian, Bob Thompson, David Von Drehle, David Broder, Eddy Palanzo, John McDonnell, Gene Robinson, Joel Garreau, Michael Powell, Ann Gerhart, Hank Stuever, Gene Weingarten, Tom Frail, Laura Stepp, Al Kamen, Steve Hunter, Rose Jacobius, Michael Williamson, Neely Tucker, Tom Shroder, and lots of other people that I'll kick myself for forgetting to mention.

Most of all I'd like to thank my wife Kathy Oehl, who, as always, encouraged me, read rough drafts, offered smart criticism, and listened patiently as her obsessed husband rambled on endlessly about Khrushchev's trip—an absurd ordeal she never could have imagined thirty years ago, when she courageously uttered that frightening phrase, "I do."

NOTES ON SOURCES

Despite its many bizarre aspects, *K Blows Top* is a true story. All the events, facts, and quotes are accurate—or as accurate as possible fifty years after the events described. I have tried to tell this story in an accessible and popular style without embellishing or fictionalizing anything. (Why bother? The truth was stranger than anything I could concoct.) I'm not an academic and I haven't attempted to write a "scholarly" or "definitive" book, so I don't feel the need to footnote every fact. But I do believe that the curious reader is entitled to a documentation of my sources.

As I mentioned in the prologue, I photocopied hundreds of newspaper clippings on Khrushchev's 1959 trip in the files of Time-Life library. Later I pored through the microfilms of the *Washington Post, Washington Star, New York Times, New York Daily News, New York Journal-American, Los Angeles Times, San Francisco Chronicle, Des Moines Register,* and *Pittsburgh Post-Gazette,* all of which provided great anecdotes and delicious details. So did the coverage in *Time, Newsweek,* and *Life* magazines. Quotes from foreign newspapers, including Soviet papers, were taken from American newspapers and magazines.

Adding immeasurably to those journalistic accounts of the trips were the memoirs of those who participated in or witnessed the events:

Wiley T. Buchanan, *Red Carpet at the White House* (Dutton, 1964).
Dwight Eisenhower, *Waging Peace* (Doubleday, 1965).
John S. D. Eisenhower, *Strictly Personal* (Doubleday, 1974).
William R. Hearst et al., *Ask Me Anything* (McGraw-Hill, 1960).

Sergei Khrushchev, *Khrushchev on Khrushchev* (Little, Brown, 1990); *Nikita Khrushchev and the Creation of a Superpower* (Pennsylvania State University Press, 2000).

Henry Cabot Lodge, *The Storm Has Many Eyes* (Norton, 1973).

Robert Murphy, *Diplomat Among Warriors* (Doubleday, 1964).

Richard Nixon, *Six Crises* (Doubleday, 1962); *Leaders* (Warner Books, 1982).

Barbara Powers, *Spy Wife* (Pyramid, 1965).

Chalmers Roberts, *First Rough Draft* (Praeger, 1973).

Victor G. Reuther, *The Brothers Reuther* (Houghton Mifflin, 1976).

William Safire, *Before the Fall* (Doubleday, 1975).

Harrison E. Salisbury, *A Journey for Our Times* (Harper & Row, 1983).

Arkady Shevchenko, *Breaking with Moscow* (Knopf, 1985).

Thomas J. Watson Jr., *Father, Son & Co.* (Bantam, 1990).

Of course, I also used Nikita Khrushchev's memoir, dictated into a tape recorder during his retirement and published in different versions over the years. *Khrushchev Remembers,* translated by Strobe Talbott, was published by Little, Brown in two volumes: *Khrushchev Remembers* (1970) and *Khrushchev Remembers: The Last Testament* (1974), which contains K's memories of his two trips to America and Nixon's trip to Moscow. Decades later, Sergei Khrushchev edited George Shriver's three-volume translation of the premier's memories, entitled *Memoirs of Nikita Khrushchev.* Volume 3 of the series—*Statesman* (2007)—contains the material on Khrushchev's trips to the United States. In general, Talbott's translation is earthier and saltier while Shriver's translation contains a lot of material omitted from Talbott's books. I quoted from both versions.

A shelf full of other books aided my research. *Face to Face with America,* an account of the trip written by twelve Soviet journalists and published by the Soviet government, provided insights into the visitors' views of the events. Michael R. Beschloss's *Mayday: Eisenhower, Khrushchev, and the U–2 Affair* (Harper & Row, 1986) contains excellent accounts of the U–2 crisis and the 1959 Khrushchev visit. William Taubman's Pulitzer Prize–winning biography, *Khrushchev: The Man and His Era* (Norton, 2003), is a brilliant portrait of a complicated man. *Khrushchev's Cold War* by Aleksandr Fursenko and Timothy Naftali (Norton, 2006) provides additional insights into Khrushchev's foreign policy and tipped me off about the irradiation of Nixon's bedroom in Moscow. Several books provided valuable information and insights into the cold war era, most notably *Postwar* by Tony Judt (Penguin, 2005), *The Fifties* by David Halberstam (Villard, 1993), *Reds: McCarthyism in Twentieth Century America* by Ted Morgan (Random House, 2003), *The Day After World War III* by Edward Zuckerman (Avon, 1987), and *The Cold War: A New History* by John Lewis Gaddis (Penguin, 2005), which is the source of Gaddis's description of Khrushchev's 1959 tour as a "surreal extravaganza." Another valuable—and immensely entertaining—source of information on what might be termed cold war culture is the excellent Web site www.conelrad.com.

Biographies of the other characters in this story were helpful: *Nixon: The Education of a Politician* by Stephen E. Ambrose (Touchstone 1987); *Eisenhower: The President* (Simon & Schuster, 1984), also by Stephen E. Ambrose; *Roswell Garst* by Harold Lee (Iowa State University Press, 1984); and *Henry Cabot Lodge* by William J. Miller (Heineman, 1967), which was the source of the bizarre traveling salesman joke Khrushchev told Lodge on the train to New York. *Legend: The Life and Death of Marilyn Monroe* by Fred Lawrence Guiles (Stein & Day, 1984) revealed the delightful details about Marilyn's elaborate cosmetic and sartorial preparations for her meeting with the premier.

Except for a few words of English ("okay" was his favorite), Nikita Khrushchev spoke entirely in Russian during his trips. Inevitably his words were translated differently by different people, including the official Soviet and American translators and various reporters. Thus there were slight differences in Khrushchev's quotes as printed in different sources. In 1960, Crosscurrents Press published the official Soviet translations of Khrushchev's major speeches and press conferences during his two trips to the United States in two books—*Khrushchev in America* and *Khrushchev in New York*. These translations are valuable but flawed, omitting or toning down some of the premier's zestier utterances. Fortunately, several of the reporters covering the trips, most notably Harrison Salisbury of the *New York Times* and Thomas P. Whitney of the *Washington Post*, spoke fluent Russian and provided their own translations, day by day. I studied all available translations of each quote and used those that seemed appropriate.

The State Department's official compendium of its historical documents, *Foreign Relations of the United States*, volume 10, *1958 to 1960*, provided many of the memos and accounts of meetings that I quoted, including several of the daily cables sent by Lodge and his translator, Alex Akalovsky, during the 1959 trip. Several of those cables were not included in *Foreign Relations* but are now declassified and available in the State Department files (record group 033.6111) at the National Archives in College Park, Maryland. Those files also contain numerous press clippings, as well as letters to the State Department from politicians, diplomats, and private citizens, including the scores of people and organizations that wrote to invite Khrushchev to visit them.

Perhaps the most amusing part of my research was watching hours of TV coverage of the Khrushchev trips at the Paley Center for Media in New York, which possesses the entirety of the Nixon-Khrushchev debate in Moscow as well as KTLA-TV's hilarious coverage of Khrushchev watching the can-can in Hollywood.

Unfortunately, many of the participants in these events died long before I began my research, but I did manage to interview Chalmers Roberts, Murray Kempton, Mary McGrory, Daniel Schorr, Alexander Akalovsky, John Jay Daly, Susan Eisenhower, and, of course, Sergei Khrushchev. I'm indebted to all of them for their time and their insights. I also used the interviews with Vladimir Toumanoff and Richard Townsend Davies that were conducted by the Foreign Affairs Oral History Collection of the Association for Diplomatic Studies. They are available on the Library of Congress Web site.

Well, that long list of sources ought to satisfy most readers. But if you are a more curious (or skeptical) person and want to know exactly where I got a specific quote or fact, you can email me at kblowstop@gmail.com. You can write, for instance, Hey, Mr. Hot-Shot Historian, how the hell do you know exactly what Edward G. Robinson and Judy Garland were saying at their table during the Khrushchev luncheon in Hollywood? And I will report back that Philip K. Scheuer, the motion picture editor of the *Los Angeles Times,* was sitting at Table 18 with them and recorded their utterances in a story called "Stars Shine in Sunshine for Visitor," which the *Times* published the next day, September 20, 1959.

As the great American humorist Dave Barry likes to say, "I'm not making this up."

INDEX

George Ramick

Peter Carlson is a former reporter and feature writer for the *Washington Post*, where he wrote the weekly column "The Magazine Reader." Before coming to the *Post* in 1986, he was a reporter for the *Boston Herald-American*, where he wrote about local politicians and minor league ballplayers; and then he was a senior writer for *People* magazine, where he profiled celebrities ranging from cartoonist R. Crumb to actress Whoopi Goldberg. He is the author of *Roughneck: The Life and Times of Big Bill Haywood* (W. W. Norton, 1983) and a coauthor—with Hunter S. Thompson and George Plimpton, among others—of *The Gospel According to ESPN*, a coffee-table book on American sports heroes. He lives in Rockville, Maryland.

CPSIA information can be obtained
at www.ICGtesting.com
Printed in the USA
LVHW09s1137270818
588254LV00001B/61/P